Scaling Migrant Worker Rights

Scaling Migrant Worker Rights

How Advocates Collaborate and Contest State Power

Xóchitl Bada and Shannon Gleeson

UNIVERSITY OF CALIFORNIA PRESS

University of California Press
Oakland, California

Suggested citation: Bada, X., and Gleeson, S. *Scaling Migrant Worker Rights: How Advocates Collaborate and Contest State Power*. Oakland: University of California Press, 2023. DOI: https://doi.org/10.1525/luminos.138

Cataloging-in-Publication Data is on file at the Library of Congress.

ISBN 978-0-520-38445-3 (pbk. : alk. paper)
ISBN 978-0-520-38446-0 (ebook)

28   27   26   25   24   23
10   9   8   7   6   5   4   3   2   1

CONTENTS

LIST OF ILLUSTRATIONS

FIGURES

TABLES

This book is the culmination of over a decade of research with Mexican immigrant workers and the legions of civil society groups who advocate on their behalf. We first and foremost thank Jonathan Fox for bringing us together to realize this joint interest when he introduced us during a conference on Latino immigrant civic engagement at the Woodrow Wilson International Center for Scholars in the summer of 2010. Jonathan's pioneering work on accountability politics in Mexico and immigrant civil society was formative to us both, as was his dedication to mentoring us as junior scholars.

We came together to understand the role of the Mexican consulate in labor standards enforcement after participating in the workshop "Mexico and Its Diaspora in the United States: Past and Present Emigration Policies," convened by Ale Délano during the 30th Latin American Studies Association Annual Conference in San Francisco in 2012. After a transformative conversation that continued after all workshop participants were long gone, we left the room with the goal of launching the first national survey to assess the Mexican consular network's role in the Labor Rights Week that had long intrigued us both.

Over two hundred interviews across the United States and Mexico were completed with the help of many amazing graduate students, undergraduates, and colleagues, including Manlio Correa, Tania Cruz Salazar, Rubén Espinoza, Jackie Estrada, Nick Ghezavat, Vanesa Guridy, Claudia López, Gloria Marvic, Patricia Nicolás Flores, David Rocha Romero, Heidy Sarabia, and Guillermo Yrizar-Barbosa.

We also thank our research assistants at Cornell (Hannah Cho, Clady Corona, Amy Saz, Albaro Tutasig, and Zakiya Williams Wells) and the University of Illinois-Chicago (UIC) (Michaela Byrd, Jackie Estrada, Nick Ghezavat, Vanessa

Guridy, Debbie Patiño, Ashwini Reddy, and Agnieszka Wieczorek) for their many hours transcribing and coding interviews, managing bibliographies, and conducting many other aspects of the research. Florio Arguillas at Cornell University provided expert research training and software support with Atlas.ti.

Early analysis of book themes were workshopped during annual meetings of the American Sociological Association, the Law and Society Association, the Latin American Studies Association, and the United Association for Labor Education, as well as other convenings hosted by generous colleagues at the University of Colorado Law School, Texas A&M Law School, Rutgers University, the Ruhr-Universität Bochum, the Universidad Nacional Autónoma de México, Queen's University, Berlin's Institute for Advanced Study, El Colegio de la Frontera Norte, and Bielefeld University.

Generous funding has been provided by each of our home institutions, including, at UIC, the College of Liberal Arts and Sciences (LAS), the Institute for Research on Race and Public Policy, the Chancellor's Undergraduate Research Award, and the LAS Undergraduate Research Initiative; the University of California–Santa Cruz Committee on Research; UC MEXUS-CONACYT (University of California Institute for Mexico and the United States–Consejo Nacional de Ciencia y Tecnología); and, at Cornell, the Cornell Institute for the Social Sciences, the Mario Einaudi Center for International Studies, the Qualitative and Interpretive Research Institute, and the Center for Social Sciences. Open Access was funded through Cornell's Hull Fund and a grant from the American Sociological Association's Fund for the Advancement of the Discipline.

The Wissenschaftskolleg zu Berlin (WIKO) provided invaluable support to Xóchitl during her academic fellowship, which she spent writing and navigating the first few months of the pandemic. At the WIKO, we received important feedback on our book proposal from Nicolas Dodier, Bénédicte Zimmermann, and Norbert Cyrus in the winter of 2019 during one of the last business trips that Shannon made prior to the pandemic.

With support from the Cornell University ILR School Pierce Memorial Fund, we hosted a workshop in 2016 where many of our generous colleagues provided feedback on our previous edited volume *Accountability across Borders* (University of Texas Press, 2019), which provided much of the intellectual stimulus for this monograph.

With support from the National Science Foundation and the Law and Society Association International Research Collaborative, we also hosted two roundtables in 2017 and 2019, "Enforcing Rights across Borders: The Case of Mexican Migrants," and "The Future of Immigrant and Worker Rights after NAFTA." These convenings offered invaluable feedback from colleagues and advocates from across North America.

We give immense gratitude to our colleagues at Cornell University, the University of California–Santa Cruz, UIC, and the University of Houston for all their support and feedback throughout the development of this manuscript. Special thanks go to Adam Goodman, Alejandro Madrid, and Pamela Anne Quiroz.

Our incredible support staff at Cornell (Claire Concepcion) and UIC (Bruce Tyler) spent hours shepherding us through the university bureaucracies.

Four anonymous reviewers provided valuable feedback to the manuscript at different stages.

The maps in chapter 1 were created by award-winning cartographer Mike Boruta. Yoselinda Mendoza assisted with tabulations for the population maps.

Matt Seidel and Elisabeth Magnus provided vital editing throughout the many versions of the manuscript. We thank Lisa Rivero for compiling the index. All errors are our own.

The cover art was photographed with the help of Claudio Ugalde.

University of California Press staff Maura Roessner, Madison Wetzell, Cindy Fulton, and Teresa Iafolla, as well as Paige MacKay helped shepherd the book to publication.

Earlier analyses of this research can be found in our previous publications in the *Journal of Ethnic and Migration Studies*, the *International Journal of Comparative Labour Law and Industrial Relations*, and the *Labor Studies Journal*, and in the volumes *Diaspora Organizations in International Affairs* (Global Institutions Series, Routledge), *Activismos transnacionales desde México* (Instituto de Investigaciones Dr. José María Luis Mora), the Labor Employment Relations Association Research Volume Series, and chapter 5 of Shannon's 2009 book *Conflicting Commitments: The Politics of Enforcing Immigrant Worker Rights in San Jose and Houston* (Cornell University Press). With thanks also to our coauthor, friend, and colleague Els de Graauw.

AEU	arrangement establishing understanding
ANEC	Asociación Nacional de Empresas Comercializadoras de Productores del Campo / National Association of Marketing Companies of Rural Producers
CCIME	Consejo Consultivo del IME / Advisory Board of the IME
CDM	Centro de los Derechos del Migrante / Migrant Rights Center
CIAM	Centro de Información y Asistencia a Mexicanos / Center for Assistance and Information to Mexicans
CIBAC	Carpeta Informativa Básica Consular / Basic Consular Information Binder
CMW	UN International Convention on the Protection of the Rights of All Migrant Workers and Members of Their Families
COMPA	Colectivo Migraciones para las Américas / Migration Collective for the Americas
CORPS	Community Outreach and Resource Planning Specialists
DACA	Deferred Action for Childhood Arrivals
DGPME	Dirección General de Protección a Mexicanos en el Exterior / General Directorate for the Protection of Mexicans Abroad
DOL	Department of Labor
EEOC	Equal Employment Opportunity Commission
EMPLEO	Employment, Education and Outreach
FAT	Frente Auténtico del Trabajo / Authentic Workers' Front
ICE	Immigration and Customs Enforcement
ILO	International Labour Organization
IME	Instituto de los Mexicanos en el Exterior / Institute of Mexicans Abroad

INAI	Instituto Nacional de Transparencia, Acceso a la Información y Protección de Datos Personales / National Institute of Transparency, Information Access and Private Data Protection
INILAB	Regional Initiative on Labor Mobility
LOA	letter of agreement
MOU	memorandum of understanding
NAALC	North American Agreement on Labor Cooperation
NAFTA	North American Free Trade Agreement
NLRB	National Labor Relations Board
OSHA	Occupational Safety and Health Administration
PALE	Programa de Asistencia Jurídica a Personas Mexicanas a través de Asesorías Legales Externas en los Estados Unidos de América / Legal Assistance Program to Mexicans by Attorneys in the United States
PCME	Programa para las Comunidades Mexicanas en el Extranjero / Program for Mexican Communities Abroad
PRECADEM	Prevención, Capacitación y Defensa del Migrante
PRI	Partido Revolucionario Institucional / Institutional Revolutionary Party
ProDESC	Proyecto de Derechos Económicos, Sociales y Culturales / Economic, Social, and Cultural Rights Project
RMALC	Red Mexicana de Acción Frente al Libre Comercio / Mexican Action Network Confronting Free Trade
SEIU	Service Employees International Union
SEM	Servicio Exterior Mexicano / Diplomatic Civil Service
SHCP	Secretaría de Hacienda y Crédito Público / Finance Ministry
SITRAJOR	Sindicato Independiente de Trabajadores de La Jornada / Independent Trade Union of Workers of "La Jornada"
SRE	Secretaría de Relaciones Exteriores / Ministry of Foreign Affairs
STPS	Secretaría del Trabajo y Previsión Social / Ministry of Labor
TPS	Temporary Protected Status
UE	United Electrical, Radio and Machine Workers of America
UFCW	United Food and Commercial Workers International Union
WHO	World Health Organization

1

Introduction

Constructing Portable Rights for Migrant Workers

As international migration continues to rise, sending states[1] have increasingly created policies and programs to engage their diasporas, in some cases even offering a plethora of services and acting as the legal champions of their erstwhile residents. In fact, countries are actively using their engagement with diasporas as a tool for nation building (Délano Alonso and Mylonas 2019). Citing sovereignty constraints, many nation-states engage in immigration governance directly and unilaterally rather than adopting a coalitional approach. There are, however, some exceptions. In December 2018, more than 150 United Nations member states approved the Global Compact for Migration, the first internationally negotiated statement of objectives for migration governance. This compact attempts to balance migrant rights and the principle of national sovereignty (Newland, McAuliff, and Bauloz 2020). Chief among its objectives is safe, orderly, and regular migration. Member states also pledged to facilitate the fair and ethical recruitment of migrant workers and to ensure safe and decent working conditions according to the basic principles of the International Labour Organization (ILO). While neither the Global Compact's nor the ILO's principles are legally binding in practice, the growing collection of multilateral "soft laws" around the governance of migrant workers (Serna de la Garza 2019) nonetheless sends a clear message: migration policy must involve both sending and receiving states (i.e., origin and destination countries) cooperating bilaterally and multilaterally to address the needs of diaspora populations.

Excellent comparative work has been done on the institutions and governance of global diasporas across various countries (Collyer 2013; Gamlen 2014). In this volume, we focus on the Mexican government as perhaps the clearest example of a country with a growing interest in the rights of its diaspora, the second largest in the world. Mexico has increasingly directed resources to its more than eleven

1

million nationals living in Canada and the United States, notably by extending expatriate voting to facilitate the de jure political rights of Mexicans living abroad (Délano 2011; Délano Alonso 2018). Yet as Délano Alonso (2018) also documents, Mexico's diaspora policies have extended to other arenas of social rights as well, including health, education, financial literacy, and finally labor rights—this book's focus. Mexico is not alone in this shift (Lafleur 2012; Pedroza et al. 2016), as many other countries have also moved to further engage their diaspora via expanding voting and social protection rights.[2] Indeed, Mexico's relatively active consular structure has been replicated throughout Latin America (Délano Alonso 2018).

While Mexican emigrants have enjoyed renewed political power in their country of origin, they face a litany of challenges in their destination contexts. Voting and full citizenship rights are vital to the well-being of Mexican emigrants, though an array of other rights and forms of social protection are equally important. There are promising signs, as the sending state has moved away from simply enabling a pool of exportable emigrant labor to also working to uphold the rights of these workers. However, we still know little about *how* sending states are being held accountable for the everyday lives of their diaspora. Here we argue that migrant civil society on both sides of the border has been a vital force driving the Mexican state's relatively prolabor policy shifts.

While past research has chronicled various aspects of migrant life such as voting, workplace experiences, and remittance behavior (Duquette-Rury 2019; Gleeson 2012, 2016; Leal, Lee, and McCann 2012; Medina Vidal 2018; Apostolidis 2010), this focus tends to obscure the important role that civil society and other meso-level institutions play in helping migrants access rights and resources in their local communities. Supranational governing bodies have called on origin and sending states to ensure that migrant workers can access basic social security and services, though national enforcement instruments lack the ability to actually implement the rights encoded within the domestic laws of the receiving state. Instead, meso-level institutions (such as unions, legal aid groups, social service organizations, and other migrant advocates) must hold the governments of immigrant destinations accountable. *Scaling Migrant Rights* is an account of these on-the-ground transnational efforts to defend the rights of migrant workers.

The Mexican diaspora in the United States is diverse in all respects, but in this book we focus on those precarious migrants laboring in low-wage agricultural, restaurant, construction, and cleaning jobs, as well as those occupying a whole host of service-sector positions in the gig economy. Of these workers, of whom close to five million are Mexican immigrants, many are undocumented (Passel and Cohn 2019). With few exceptions, undocumented workers in the United States are afforded the same basic labor protections as their documented counterparts, but overburdened and underresourced agencies at the federal, state, and local levels often fail to uphold the laws on the books. Immigrant workers' struggle for rights is compounded by language and cultural barriers, along with a well-founded distrust of both Mexican and US governments. These challenges can frustrate the efforts of labor regulation, a largely claims-driven system that relies almost entirely on vulnerable workers' willingness or ability to come forward and submit a complaint to the appropriate labor regulator for wage theft or any other violation. The COVID-19 pandemic has only exacerbated these challenges, rendering this enforcement system aspirational at best.

Across the United States, local civil society groups have led outreach efforts to disseminate worker education materials and ensure that basic workplace protections are enforced for migrant workers. These protections cover not only lawful permanent residents and naturalized citizens but also the nearly 5 percent of the US civilian workforce that are estimated to be undocumented; the many migrants in liminal statuses such as DACA (Deferred Action for Childhood Arrivals) and TPS (Temporary Protected Status) (Passel and Cohn 2018); and the tens of thousands of temporary agricultural guest workers in the country (Beltran 2018).

Immigrant workers—especially those in low-wage and unregulated workplaces—are particularly vulnerable to wage theft, occupational safety and health hazards, racial discrimination, and sexual harassment (Bernhardt, Spiller, and Polson 2013; Bernhardt, Spiller, and Theodore 2013). Consequently, local worker advocates have pressed for more proactive enforcement models and have leveraged community organizations to strengthen existing enforcement efforts (Fine and Gordon 2010). Co-enforcement frameworks have proliferated, as neither regulators nor advocates alone can ensure employer compliance. These cooperative models seek to bring government enforcers, workers, and businesses to the table with the understanding that—despite the limitations of such cooperative efforts—an exclusively individualist claims-driven approach has proven unworkable. A range of meso-level civic groups have also taken part in these efforts, including traditional labor unions, worker centers, legal aid groups, and other immigrant advocates, each with its own relationship to immigrant workers, US regulators, and the Mexican state. To be sure, sending states benefit enormously from the economic engine of migrant labor and have been called upon by advocates to play a stronger role in the enforcement of labor standards. Transnational advocates, too, have worked across borders. Many argue that sending states have a responsibility to protect the rights of their emigrating citizens as forcefully as they would the rights of those citizens who stay behind. For example, early twentieth-century transnational labor activists such as the Flores Magón brothers and Vicente Lombardo Toledano attempted to build international working-class solidarity and a cooperative relationship with organized labor unions across the United States (Álvarez 1995). In contrast, some staunch activists, most famously the Zapatista revolutionary movements of the mid-1990s, have argued against devoting resources to the needs of emigrants, viewing them as essentially defectors from national struggles. However, today the overwhelming consensus of activists is that immigrant rights should be championed across borders (Héctor 2017; Fox 2001). To realize a functional system of portable worker rights, however, requires both a grander vision of universal justice and a sharp focus on improving the bureaucratic minutiae of local labor enforcement. This tension is at the heart of increased efforts to improve Mexico's accountability to its emigrant workers through large-scale social movement organizing and everyday claims processing. This book explores these parallel efforts to reform migrant labor rights enforcement.

THEORETICAL FRAMEWORK

Migrant Labor Rights Enforcement and the Role of Tripartism

On March 25, 1911, the Triangle Shirtwaist Factory burned to the ground in New York City, killing 154 garment workers and precipitating the growth of the modern system of workplace regulation in the United States. One would think that more than a century after the implementation of such regulations, workplace fatalities would be a thing of the past. However, while significant progress has been made, work is now more deadly than war. According to Guy Ryder, the general director of the ILO, workplace fatalities account for approximately 2.3 million deaths per year (ILO 2014). These workplace risks persist despite the enactment of countless new worker protections because the labor standards enforcement regime is broken. Enforcement agencies are underfunded, understaffed, and often the target of political machinations. In the United States, it would take sixty-six years for investigators of the Occupational Safety and Health Administration (OSHA) to inspect each workplace under its jurisdiction just once, assuming 2012 staffing levels (Piore and Schrank 2018).

Foreign-born workers, especially the undocumented (Hall and Greenman 2014), are particularly vulnerable to workplace hazards and other violations (Loh and Richardson 2004), in large part because of their concentration in key offending industries (Bernhardt, Spiller, and Theodore 2013).[3] Existing immigration scholarship has tended to focus on the rights afforded to legal migrants through international instruments and through relevant federal, state, and local statutes and enforcement agencies. Less attention, though, has been paid to the mechanisms in place that actually help workers realize these rights. Through the lens of Mexican immigrant workers, this book takes a closer look at the relationship between governing bodies and migrant civil society organizations in the fight to access migrant labor rights.

In this examination of government and civil society interactions, we unpack the role of the state, across various scales and statutes, and consider the enforcement capacity of domestic agencies, which together form a "jurisdictional patchwork" (Varsanyi et al. 2012). Within this context, we center the sending state, as it operates on both sides of the border to ensure the rights of its emigrants and to oversee the returns on its export labor. Both sending and receiving states have become targets of accountability efforts led by civil society groups. Our analysis takes seriously the impact of these civil society groups in working with—and targeting—state agencies tasked with ensuring migrant worker rights. Some of these groups work domestically with migrant workers, while others operate transnationally to demand a more portable rights regime, often through a human rights frame that poses particular challenges and opportunities for forging coalitions and staging successful campaigns (Keck and Sikkink 1998). Using the case of Mexico and the United States, we assess the feasibility of advocating for the portability of worker rights across borders and the key role that the sending state and transnational civil society can play in such struggles.

We begin by considering the rights afforded to migrant workers in the United States. In general, most federal, state, and local labor laws grant all workers basic protections—like the right to a minimum wage, overtime pay, and a safe and healthy workplace. US courts have affirmed that even undocumented workers have standing as employees and are eligible to bring claims against their employers. Antiretaliation measures prevent employers from threatening, intimidating, or in any other way taking actions against any workers attempting to mobilize their rights under the law (Gleeson 2016). Yet despite these protections, a steady "race to the bottom" in terms of labor rights has disproportionately affected immigrant workers and foiled the realization of these statutory aims. Post-Fordist labor enforcement models are poorly equipped to deal with the realities of fissured labor markets in which the large assembly plant is no longer the norm. In the current gloves-off economy of fragmented and flexible work arrangements, workers fall outside the legal definitions of covered employees, and subcontracting helps employers evade their responsibilities to these workers (Bernhardt et al. 2008; Weil 2014).

Underfunded agencies often work in jurisdictional silos and thus are reliant on legal specialists rather than a generalist staff who can work across issue areas and coordinate with sister agencies to tailor their outreach to specific vulnerable populations like immigrants. In the United States, "street-level bureaucrats" (Lipsky 1980) typically follow an "economies of scale" model where inspectors focus on a small subset of violations that afflict a wide swath of workers (Piore and Schrank 2018). This model relies heavily on individual claims, which has benefits and drawbacks. On the one hand, a claims-based system provides an equal opportunity structure for all those seeking redress and limits the biases harbored by inspectors, who may devalue the claims of certain laborers (e.g., temporary or migrant workers). On the other hand, this "fire alarm" approach to claims making has heavy time, opportunity, and financial costs for workers, who must navigate a highly technical claims process and rely on expensive, and often unattainable, legal counsel (Gleeson 2016). Worker advocates play an important role in bridging these jurisdictional gaps and holding regulatory agencies accountable.

The tripartite protection model seeks to address some of these challenges by relying on coordination between state regulatory agencies and worker organizations to jointly enforce labor standards (Amengual and Fine 2017).[4] These alliances often operate in conjunction with migrant and worker civil society, which have better access to sectors that are difficult for government inspectors to penetrate (Fine and Gordon 2010).[5] In this book, we highlight an additional partner in the model: the sending state, which often operates via a global network of consular offices whose charge is to advocate on behalf of its emigrants across a range of issues, including health care, education, family law, immigration protections, and indeed labor rights. We draw specifically on the example of Mexico and its consular network across the United States, which, despite its many shortcomings, is arguably the most widespread and influential of any Latin American country. In the next section, we consider the legal framework for governing migrant worker rights.

The International Framework for Migrant Worker Rights

Over the past two decades, US immigration policy (particularly toward its southern border and Latin American migrants) has seen the rise of two opposing forces. On the one hand, the United States has ramped up immigrant surveillance and deportation efforts, often in conjunction with state and local authorities. There have also been attempts, even during Democratic administrations (which have claimed to be less xenophobic and to champion immigrant rights), to curtail the rights of immigrants in the workplace and beyond (Macías-Rojas 2018). On the other hand, a growing number of localities have declared themselves "sanctuary" or "welcoming" cities, pushed back on enforcement efforts, and extended additional rights even to undocumented workers (such as protections against wage theft, the right to organize farmworkers, and COVID-19 pandemic relief). Meanwhile, civil society watchdogs have advocated on behalf of those low-wage migrant workers most vulnerable to exploitation and have pressed state actors to guarantee their rights. Similarly, global governance bodies have leveraged instruments to extend migrant rights. For example, the UN International Convention on the Protection of the Rights of All Migrant Workers and Members of Their Families (CMW)—while nonbinding and currently pending ratification by 130 countries—has influenced regional processes such as the labor side accords of the North American Free Trade Agreement (NAFTA), leading to the development and dissemination of best practices concerning migrant labor rights in trade negotiations.

Within this framework, sending states play a unique role in migrant worker advocacy. In 2003, the Inter-American Court of Human Rights, in response to a request by Mexico, issued a landmark advisory opinion on the juridical condition and rights of undocumented migrants. The court ruled, inter alia, that the legal status of migrant workers can never constitute a justification for depriving them of enjoying and exercising their human rights, including those related to work. The court also ruled that upon procuring employment, migrants acquire rights by virtue of being workers and that these rights should be recognized and guaranteed independently of their legal status (Cholewinski 2008). While an advisory opinion is mostly hortatory, the request issued by the Mexican government signaled a clear shift in its interest and investment in the well-being of its diaspora.

While some argue that international laws are merely symbolic instruments, especially in the United States, they do help determine minimum principles and parameters for regulating global problems that transcend national borders. These ideals alone, however, cannot enact social change without accompanying resources or enforcement mechanisms. For example, the World Health Organization lacks both the financial and political heft to singularly manage an actual epidemic, let alone a full-blown pandemic (Global Preparedness Monitoring Board 2019). Similarly, international labor law offers limited protections to migrants working in the United States (authorized and unauthorized) but does not prescribe national enforcement paradigms for labor regulation. There are still further examples of arguably symbolic instruments. The ILO's Migrant Workers (Supplementary Provisions) Convention 143 (1975) sets basic minimum protections, and building upon that and ILO Migration and Employment Convention 47 (1949), the CMW includes protections for both documented and undocumented migrants. More recently, in the declaration of the High-Level Dialogue on Migration and Development of 2013, member states collectively vowed to protect the rights of migrants irrespective of their legal status (Berg 2016). However, all these declarations are nonbinding and lack effective oversight mechanisms. True to form, the United States has not ratified the CMW, and in 2017 it ended its participation in the UN Global Compact for Migration, citing sovereignty concerns.

That said, these international instruments provide a form of "soft law" that can be a useful tool for advocates as they work to hold host and sending states accountable for the labor conditions of migrant workers (Compa 2017). While civil society organizations have over the past two decades succeeded in raising their profile, many countries have not ratified them, largely because of stalled economic growth, increased xenophobia, and a growing disdain for global governance structures. In truth, many national laws (in theory) already cover the rights stipulated in these international agreements. Yet many other laws directly undermine these rights (Ruhs 2013). Even before the spate of punitive US immigrant legislation passed in the mid-1990s, immigration law scholar Arthur Helton (1991) warned that the CMW would entail significant changes to US labor, immigration, and civil rights laws, thus raising serious doubts about the likelihood of its ratification.

This book offers a glimpse into how a now two-decades-old set of evolving labor rights agreements between Mexico and the United States has been implemented on the ground in both countries. We argue that this cooperation should not be seen as an organic flowering of goodwill; rather, it has been the result of (ongoing and often adversarial) civil society advocacy. Our research complements extant analyses across diverse destination contexts, including Laurie Berg's (2016) case study on the vulnerability of temporary migrant workers in Australia; Leah Vosko's (2019) extensive work on the challenges of collective bargaining in the

Mexico-Canada temporary migrant work program; Ines Wagner's (2018) study of the challenges facing migrant workers in the European Union; and Luis Enrique González Araiza's (2018) analysis of Mexico's mostly failed attempts to prevent labor trafficking. Through a multisited set of interviews and archival analysis, we affirm the ultimately local nature of all enforcement efforts, documenting the varying ways that binational agreements are implemented across the United States and the many roles played by the Mexican state at home and abroad.

Holding the Sending State Accountable on Migrant Worker Rights

Mexico shares almost two thousand miles of a porous border with the United States, a geopolitical reality that keeps Mexico often beholden to US interests when it comes to border control. Thus, although Mexico has attempted to craft a more humane border control policy, this goal has proven elusive, and during bilateral trade negotiations much of the discussion usually focuses on Mexico's willingness to institute containment and deterrence mechanisms to discourage the northward exodus of Central Americans. Mexican politicians have long used the CMW (which Mexico has ratified but the United States has not) to push for better treatment of Mexican workers in the United States. They have done so, however, without granting similar rights to migrant workers living in or transiting through Mexico. Transnational advocates also argue that the Mexican government enjoys the economic benefit of labor exports while failing to guarantee its citizens at home the right to "dignified and socially useful employment" (as stated in Article 123 of Mexico's constitution).[6] In other words, Mexico has in effect deprived its citizens of the right to find decent work, and thus to remain, in Mexico. While the CMW has fueled Mexico's attempt to promote migrant rights in the United States (Díaz Prieto and Kuhner 2009), Mexico's reputation has been marred by its own poor record of human rights and labor abuses against Central Americans and other migrants in transit.[7]

In this book, we describe the Mexican government's shift from a *limited* to an *active* engagement with its diaspora (Délano 2009) as it navigates the tricky terrain of being both a sending and a transit state with its own uneven labor rights track record. We home in on the different instantiations of the US-Mexico accords on labor cooperation, which vary across US cities and have led to locally defined, transnationally coproduced enforcement practices. We demonstrate that cross-sectorial alliances are responsible for building a migrant rights movement and institutionalizing migrant protections. We focus especially on efforts to develop and implement the binational accord between Mexico's Secretaría de Relaciones Exteriores / Ministry of Foreign Affairs (SRE) and the US Department of Labor (DOL) in 2008, interrogating the diverse perspectives of bureaucrats and advocates who have participated in these initiatives over the last fifteen years. We argue that these tripartite models of co-enforcement are promising but not panaceas, working better in some communities than in others.

This volume expands on our earlier work (Bada and Gleeson 2019), which presented a general overview on the best practices and pitfalls of enforcing employment, health, and educational immigrant rights across borders in Canada, Mexico, and the United States. Rather than adopting the dominant framework in immigration studies that centers immigrant integration to the host country, our focus here is on Mexico, the sending state, and its engagement with migrant civil society. Pioneering scholars of this approach have (in our view) rightly abandoned methodological nationalism (i.e., concentrating on immigrant communities within the sole context of their host countries) to document the sending-state policies driving migrants to invest back home and to explain the ways in which that state manages the economic and political demands of its nationals living abroad (Byrnes 2003; Duquette-Rury 2019; Iskander 2010; Félix 2019; Bada 2014). We build on Alexandra Délano Alonso's foundational work on the evolution of the Mexican government's policies from a limited to an active engagement with its thirty million nationals living in the United States, as well as her more recent work on how Mexico's newest model of consular advocacy has facilitated the incorporation of Mexican immigrants into US institutions (Délano 2011; Délano Alonso 2018). Moreover, we highlight a range of advocacy strategies that often (but not always) involve civil society and the Mexican government working together. These range from the consular network facilitating the minutiae of everyday worker claims making (chapter 3) to migrant civil society's demand for broader accountability across a variety of social issues (chapter 4) to high-profile, grasstops litigation across borders (chapter 5).

While our previous work discussed the dynamics of local labor agencies tasked with enforcing immigrant worker rights (Gleeson 2014, 2016), here we privilege the perspectives of domestic and transnational nonprofits in brokering binational enforcement initiatives. We also highlight the importance of consular initiatives on labor advocacy and the extent to which advocates have engaged with the consular network. To do so, we document the genesis and evolution of the annual Labor Rights Week, a nationwide consular partnership between the US DOL and Mexico's SRE that began in 2007 as a pilot with a few consular offices and has now been institutionalized across all Mexican consulates in the United States. The legal backbone of this federal initiative comprises more than sixty bilateral memoranda of understanding that have been periodically signed between various local US labor standards enforcement agencies and Mexico's government over the last fifteen years. We also draw on examples of iconic transnational struggles, such as the decades-long campaigns to strengthen labor rights for temporary H-2 immigrant workers via the symbolic power of a nonbinding trade policy framework under the North American Agreement on Labor Cooperation (NAALC) (Brooks and Fox 2002b; Hertel 2006; Kay 2011; Kay and Evans 2018). Finally, in examining bottom-up processes, we reveal how top-down attempts to build solidarity have also reproduced cross-border power imbalances.

Beyond outlining the aspirational proclamations of governments, this book reveals the key role that advocacy organizations play in pressuring government bureaucracies to defend migrant rights in theory and in practice. Adopting a multiscalar approach, we detail the varied strategies pursued by transnational civil society organizations across a range of social arenas. We talk to an array of actors, including Mexican diplomats, US labor agency officials, and a host of civil society groups such as legal service providers, worker advocates, and other migrant-serving nonprofits. In doing so, we identify the particular challenges facing migrants who inhabit a transnational existence: away from their homeland, and often liminally tied to their host society, they have precarious rights on both sides of the border. Our study follows in the bottom-up analytical tradition of other works focused on Europe and Latin America (García Agustín and Jørgensen 2016; Margheritis 2016) by not only considering the impact of elite actors but also viewing migrants as political actors in their own right. We look at advocacy on both sides of the border but see transnational alliances as opportunities for solidarity that can either be fruitful (though never tension-free) or entrench divisions.

MEXICAN MIGRANTS IN THE UNITED STATES

Demographic Profile

The Mexican consular network in the United States, as described in greater detail in chapter 2, has fifty-two offices. The uneven distribution of offices across the country reflects a story about Mexican immigrant demography in the United States. Mexico's diplomatic presence in the United States has widely varying capacity and priorities: some states or even certain metropolitan regions are home to multiple consular offices, while other offices cover several states where the immigrant density is lower (figure 1).

In terms of demographics, all told, in 2019 there were approximately 10.9 million Mexican-born individuals living in the United States, a 7 percent decline over the decade prior (Israel and Batalova 2020). Mexicans constitute the largest national-origin plurality of immigrants in the United States, at about a quarter of the foreign born in 2018 (Budiman et al. 2020). Nationally, Mexican-origin individuals are by far the largest national-origin subgroup of Latinos in the United States (Noe-Bustamante and Flores 2019), making up nearly two-thirds of the total. The immigrant populations with the largest proportion of Mexican nationals are concentrated in the Southwest, and especially in the states and cities along the border (figure 2). These are the areas with the densest concentration of consular offices. However, Mexicans are a very small (though growing) part of the Latino population in the South and along the Eastern Seaboard (figure 3).

The local contexts of immigration policy differ widely, and each region has a unique industrial profile in which Mexican immigrant workers are embedded. Labor regulations also vary most significantly from state to state. Some cities have created their own protections and policies, and co-enforcement models with

FIGURE 1. Mexican consulates in the United States. Source: Authors' compilation, based on the consulate's directory published by Mexico's Secretaría de Relaciones Exteriores / Ministry of Foreign Affairs (SRE n.d.-b). This map includes all offices that existed at some point during our period of fieldwork. The consulate in Anchorage no longer operates.

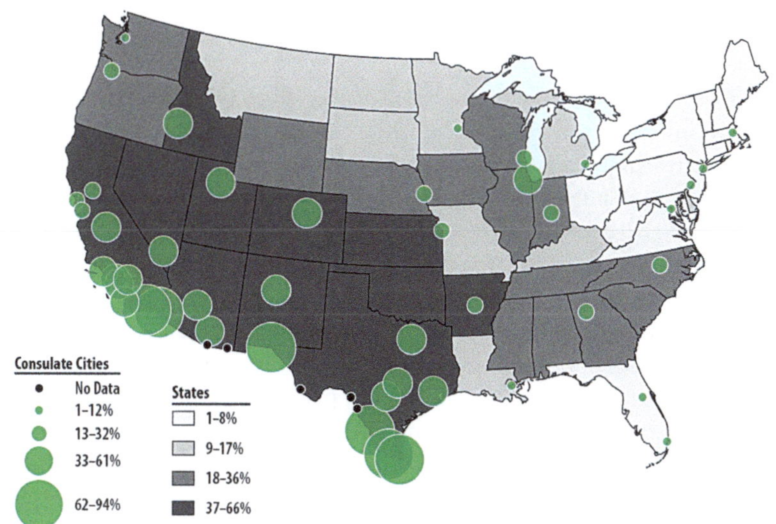

FIGURE 2. Percentage of foreign-born population that is Mexican born. Source: All maps in this series are compiled using estimates from the five-year sample of the American Community Survey 2014–2018 (US Census Bureau 2019). We include in the foreign-born sample anyone who is born outside of the United States (which we define to include all US possessions) (IPUMS USA n.d.-a).

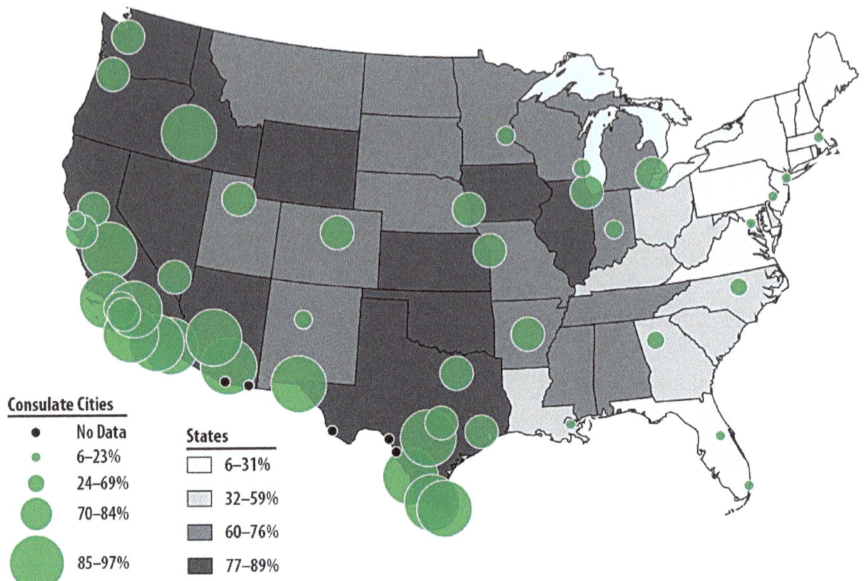

FIGURE 3. Percentage of Latino population identifying as Mexican. Source: The American Community Survey queries all individuals regarding their "Hispanic status" using the question "Is Person X of Hispanic, Latino, or Spanish origin?" Here we classify as "Latino" all those who affirm YES, including the categories "Mexican, Mexican Am., Chicano," "Puerto Rican," "Cuban," or "another Hispanic, Latino, or Spanish origin" (IPUMS USA n.d.-c). We classify as Mexican those who select the "Mexican, Mexican Am., Chicano" subcategory of Hispanic and those who were born in Mexico.

civil society are more likely to emerge in urban areas (Fine and Gordon 2010; de Graauw 2016; Gleeson 2016). Meanwhile rural and suburban communities—which are increasingly migrant destinations—are typically far removed from consular resources, lack public transportation options, and face a dearth of both labor regulation and civil society resources (de Graauw, Gleeson, and Bloemraad 2013; de Graauw and Gleeson 2020). The unauthorized immigrant workforce is particularly disadvantaged by these obstacles.

The 10.5 million unauthorized immigrants in the United States constitute about a quarter of the US immigrant population. Forty-seven percent of these unauthorized immigrants are from Mexico, and 43 percent of all Mexican immigrants are unauthorized (Gonzalez-Barrera and Krogstad 2019; Passel and Cohn 2019). Notably, the US's unauthorized population has changed substantially in the last decade, with a 28 percent decrease in undocumented Mexicans since 2010 (CMS 2021). Again, the characteristics of Mexican migrants differ across place. Proportionally, the noncitizen population of Mexicans is currently highest in "new destinations" where Mexican immigrants have relatively recently arrived (figure 4). These places are also more likely to have more restrictive immigration policies that

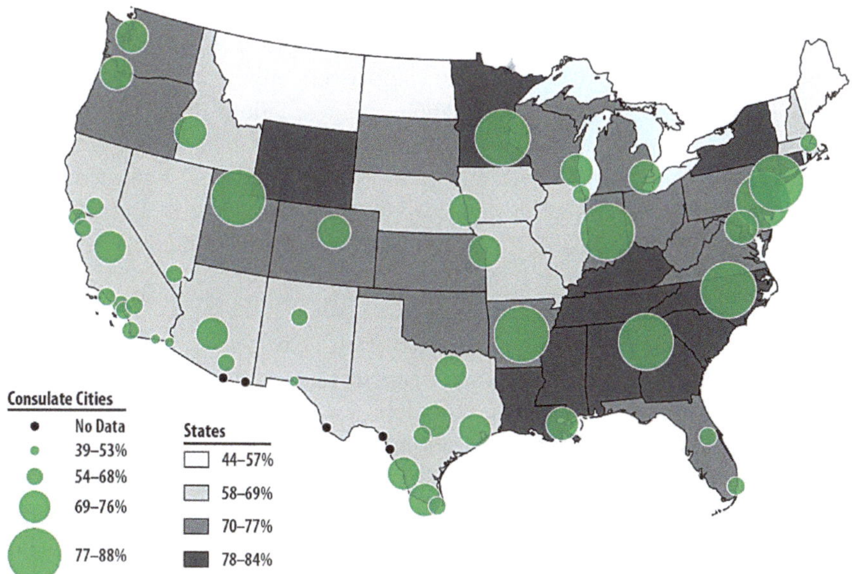

FIGURE 4. Percentage of Mexican immigrant population that is noncitizen. Source: The American Community Survey queries citizenship status of all foreign-born persons. We classify noncitizens as those who identified as such, namely, those who were not born in the United States, were not born abroad of American parents, or were not naturalized citizens (IPUMS USA n.d.-b).

make migrant worker organizing even more challenging (Wong 2012; Pham and Van 2014).

Mexican Labor Precarity

Though the oldest and most established of Latino immigrant groups, Mexican migrants are also among the most precarious. Many Mexican migrants are recently arrived, have low levels of human capital, and have limited English proficiency. In general, low-wage migrant workers experience precarious employment and struggle to gain access to basic labor protections. A number of factors have made this precarity all but a foregone conclusion: a race to the bottom for cheap labor, a steep drop-off in unionization, and increasingly defunded labor agencies, which often lack the political will to enforce the laws on the books (Bernhardt et al. 2008; Gutelius and Theodore 2019). Many industries such as hospitality, caregiving, warehouse work, agriculture, and construction sectors across the United States and other developed economies are dependent on low-wage, precarious migrant labor (Ruhs 2013).

For the majority of Mexican low-wage immigrant workers, access to decently paid and adequately protected work is elusive. While Mexican immigrants have a 70 percent labor force participation rate, 33 percent earn salaries that are lower than half of the national median, and 58 percent lack access to basic social protections like health care and a pension. In comparison, only 36 percent of US native workers are in similarly precarious employment situations (Canales Cerón and Rojas Wiesner 2018). Low-wage Mexican workers toil in dangerous industries with scant regulation, and Mexican migrant workers are the most affected by fatal occupational injuries among foreign-born workers. Between 2011 and 2018, 4,453 foreign-born workers died in the workplace, 65 percent of whom were Mexican (BLS-DOL 2019).

Fifty percent of the Mexican immigrant labor force have low-wage jobs, mostly working as day laborers in construction or in personal services such as domestic work, food preparation, cleaning services, and other service occupations. Apart from the low wages, these jobs are characterized by unpredictable scheduling and low rates of unionization. Immigrant workers fill 38 percent of the US structural employment deficit (Canales Cerón and Rojas Wiesner 2018), reflecting both a degradation of the jobs listed above and the increasing recruitment of exploitable immigrant labor (Milkman 2020).

In this labor environment, wage theft is one of the most common forms of workplace abuse.[8] As such, it has become one of the most tangible targets of co-enforcement efforts, spurring partnerships between the sending state and domestic labor regulation agencies, including cities that have developed their own regulatory frameworks.[9] The most vulnerable workers are the most targeted: foreign-born workers are 1.5 times more likely than their US-born counterparts to suffer a minimum-wage violation. According to the labor intake database published by Mexico's SRE, between 2010 and 2018, 4,539 Mexican victims of wage theft requested help to recover their US-earned wages inside Mexican consular offices across the United States. These efforts are the subject of our analyses. In addition to workplace abuse, highly criminalized immigration employment systems continue to foil labor regulation efforts the world over (Berg 2016; González Araiza 2018; Kip 2017; Vosko 2019; Wagner 2018). This is especially true for the 4.6 percent of the foreign-born workforce in the United States who are unauthorized. In a statistic that demonstrates the permanent nature of undocumented work, Mexican unauthorized workers now average fifteen years of continuous residence in the United States (Passel and Cohn 2019), and they are usually confined to precarious labor markets and occupations with weak—and sometimes nonexistent—enforcement mechanisms.

While the number of Mexican immigrants living in the United States without authorization has declined, three-quarters of immigrants deported by the Department of Homeland Security every year are Mexican nationals. In a national environment that insists on criminalizing Mexican low-wage workers (Goodman 2020; Macías-Rojas 2016), it is imperative to assess the mechanisms that advocates and bureaucracies have implemented to facilitate (or hinder) claims making in labor rights enforcement.

It is within this context that Mexico has begun to rethink how it addresses the rights of its highly precarious emigrants living and working in the United States, as well as those who ultimately return and attempt to reintegrate into Mexican society.

RESEARCH STRATEGY

The analysis presented in this book draws on surveys and interviews with relevant stakeholders from both civil society and government bureaucracies who have been instrumental in establishing transnational practices of labor co-enforcement for Mexican migrant workers. These include staff from various labor enforcement agencies, Mexican diplomats, labor union and worker center organizers, legal aid organizations, and immigrant grassroots associations. We focus on the local and transnational challenges across multiple levels of governance and the importance of migrant civil society in holding government actors accountable.

In the fall of 2012, we conducted a survey of fifty-two Mexican consular offices to assess their cooperation with US labor standard enforcement agencies and to gather information on Labor Rights Week, the most important co-enforcement program established by bilateral agreements between the United States and Mexico. We asked survey respondents to outline the extent of the outreach and resources provided to workers as well as the nature of consular collaborations with other labor standards enforcement agencies and community organizations. We then conducted twenty-five in-depth interviews with embassy and legal affairs staff at consular offices who had pioneered Labor Rights Week. On the basis of the survey results and the consular interviews, we created an organizational database of local civil society actors who had collaborated with the Mexican consular offices to implement the Labor Rights Week or who were part of broader advocacy referral networks.

The second stage of data collection took place between 2013 and 2015, when we interviewed Mexican diplomats, government agency staff, and nonprofit organization leaders across fifteen consular jurisdictions. We spoke with representatives of organizations in regions that spanned the political gamut (see figure 5): Atlanta, Austin, Chicago, Fresno, Houston, Los Angeles, Miami, Nashville, New York, Omaha, Orlando, Phoenix, Raleigh, Sacramento, Salt Lake City, San Diego, San Francisco/Oakland, San Jose, Tucson, and Washington, D.C.[10] Additionally, during 2016–17, we interviewed staff from transnational labor advocacy nonprofits operating in Juxtlahuaca, San Luis Potosí, Piedras Negras, and Mexico City. Altogether, we draw on 206 interviews with labor standards government bureaucracies, diplomats, worker centers, labor unions, and other migrant-serving nonprofits operating across the United States and Mexico.

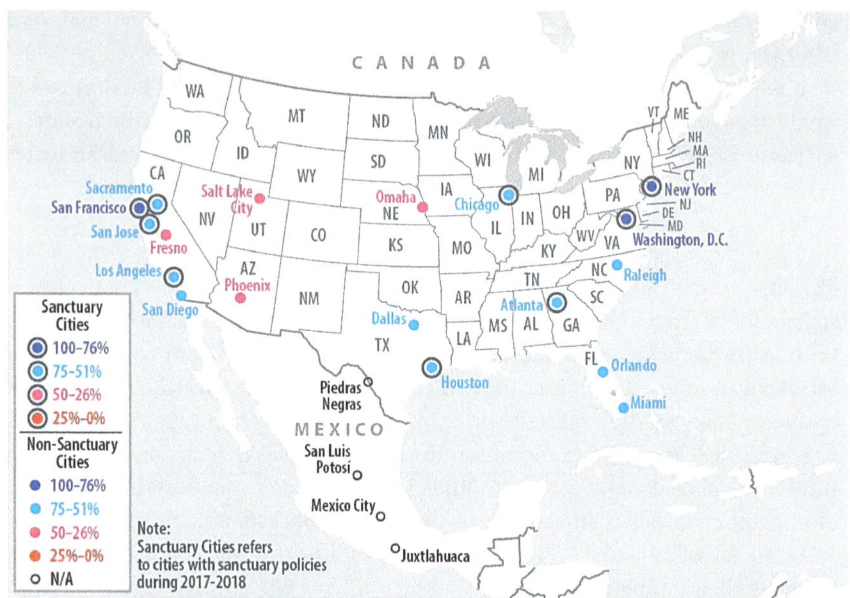

FIGURE 5. 2016 presidential election: Democratic percentage of vote for cities included in project. Source: Presidential election voting data are drawn from *Politico* (2016). Data identifying sanctuary cities—which we define as jurisdictions that have enacted policies to curb local officials' involvement in the enforcement of federal immigration law—are drawn from Ballotpedia (n.d.).

We also relied on participant observation at selected events and field sites in order to examine the co-enforcement challenges encountered by the sending state. For instance, we attended *charlas* (talks) held in consular offices and across the broader community, as well as resource fairs where various community partners distributed informational material. To complement our data collection efforts, we organized two action research panels with labor activists to discuss migrant rights enforcement across borders at the annual Law and Society Association conferences in Mexico City and Washington, D.C., in the spring of 2017 and 2019. In October of 2017, we participated in a Trinational Labor Gathering discussing labor responses to the renegotiation of NAFTA in Chicago.

Finally, we requested statistical and budget information on consular outreach programs from Mexico's Instituto Nacional de Transparencia, Acceso a la Información y Protección de Datos Personales / National Institute of Transparency, Information Access, and Private Data Protection and reviewed key institutional documents going back to the original 2002 ministerial negotiations between the DOL and the SRE; more than sixty memoranda of understanding established between the DOL and various consulates; one hundred local media announcements about Labor Rights Week; correspondence between stakeholders while implementing Labor Rights Week; and local press releases from government agencies that developed collaborative relationships with immigrant worker advocates.

ROAD MAP FOR THE BOOK

Our story of transnational labor co-enforcement practices in the United States unfolds across six chapters. Chapter 2 offers a road map for understanding the Mexican consular network as an advocacy institution. We describe the genesis and evolution of consular efforts to enforce the workplace rights of immigrant workers in the United States and introduce Labor Rights Week, a significant program that coordinates efforts among local consular offices, federal and state labor standards enforcement agencies, and other immigrant worker advocates. We trace how the consular network expanded its territorial notions of citizenship and became the premier support system for the most vulnerable of migrant workers. We examine the current role of the Mexican consular network in co-enforcement efforts with the US DOL (and sister agencies), detailing how these efforts have been institutionalized through a web of consular bureaucracies. We argue that consular representatives depend on this international cooperation because, while they are endowed with unique resources and legitimacy, their efforts to defend the rights of immigrant workers are constrained by the US enforcement bureaucratic apparatus and by budgetary issues.

Chapter 3 analyzes the local implementation of binational agreements between the US DOL and Mexico's SRE in cooperation with local civil society organizations, in particular labor unions and legal services providers. We find that consular partnerships are highly variable, depending on the given jurisdiction and the characteristics of the local immigrant community. We consider the motivations and goals for participating in co-enforcement efforts with the consulates, finding that collaboration with the Mexican government, among other benefits, can fortify claims making, the engine of labor regulation in the United States. We also find that while the Mexican consulates can wield substantial influence, help civil society organizations access the formal halls of power, and act as a linguistic and cultural resource for migrant communities, they are cautious and reluctant advocates. Moreover, their constantly shifting staff further hampers advocacy efforts. We therefore conclude that tripartite enforcement is more challenging than the recurring memoranda of understanding suggest and that scaling up and sustaining these partnerships is difficult at best.

Chapter 4 examines the diverse relationships that emerge beyond the well-defined realms of labor co-enforcement by exploring the wide array of immigrant rights organizations that are seeking to expand the scope of sending-state accountability. We find that immigrant rights organizations have slowly gained more negotiating power with diplomatic bureaucracies over migrant labor rights. We situate migrant labor rights within the broader context of Mexico's historical state-society relations, noting how this history has shaped the wide-ranging demands that migrant groups have placed on the sending state, including, but also expanding far beyond, the issue of labor co-enforcement. Finally, we chronicle the many frustrations advocates have expressed about consular institutions and examine how advocates balance the collaborative potential of the consular network with the necessity of holding consulates and the sending state accountable.

In chapter 5, we shift our analytical approach to track the emergence of a "portable rights" frame to defend migrant workers. We map the conditions and challenges shaping organizations' ability to mobilize NAFTA's labor side accord protecting migrant worker rights, including funding limitations, mission foci, and the extent of civil society infrastructure. Focusing on the cross-border actions of twenty-two migrant rights advocacy institutions, we examine how organizations decide whom to defend (such as H-2 workers and undocumented Central Americans in transit), which policies to target (domestic, bilateral, or international), and which models of service provision to deploy on the ground. Considering Mexico as both a sender and a host of vulnerable migrant workers, we survey the field of transnational advocacy that defends migrants across both of Mexico's borders.

Our concluding chapter assesses the impact of efforts to increase sending-state accountability for migrant worker rights. While the sovereignty of the state remains unchallenged in immigration policy making, the state has certainly become less autonomous as unfettered globalization accelerates and multiple actors push for universalizing labor rights. Because of the enormous challenges that labor advocacy organizations face in defending the most precarious migrant workers, their impact has often been downplayed by social movement scholars. Indeed, we offer a sobering account of the nonbinding agreements that have proven to be minimally effective in ameliorating conditions on the ground. However, over the years, the influence of advocacy organizations has been undeniable. Despite the challenges of erecting a robust co-enforcement regime, the tripartite state-society labor relations we document here provide some optimism regarding advocates' strategies and give us hope for the future of transnational labor alliances and coalitions in North America.

The Mexican Consular Network as an Advocacy Institution

There is a limited but growing literature in the field of international relations regarding how sending states engage with their diasporas on demands for social protection. The programs offered by Mexico's consular network are situated within a larger set of policies aiming to respond to the social vulnerabilities faced by its nonresident citizens. Most sending states in Europe and Latin America have developed some infrastructure on this front, ranging between *descriptive* (mainly a consular network presence offering basic services) and *substantive* (providing rights and services that address social welfare needs of nonresident nationals) (Lafleur and Vintila 2020; Pedroza et al. 2016). Several Western European countries with robust welfare systems have the capacity to offer substantive diaspora infrastructure to their nonresident citizens living abroad by providing or facilitating access to concrete welfare services for nonresident nationals, thanks to bilateral agreements with host countries. For example, French citizens living abroad enjoy extensive health care services and contributory pensions offered by France's extensive consular network. In contrast, Latin American countries are less likely to offer substantive social protections to nonresident nationals working abroad. Part of the challenge is a matter of scale. While the French government is able to extend social services to a diaspora that represents less than 3 percent of the French population, the Mexican government is expected to offer services to the estimated 10 percent of its population who are emigrants, 97 percent of whom reside in the United States (Li Ng 2022).

In the late 1990s, the Mexican consular network expanded its offices throughout the United States and increased its volume of services related to documentation and civil, labor, and legal rights, as well as financial education, basic health services, literacy, and cultural programming. Perhaps it is not a coincidence that these changes followed an increase in the Bank of Mexico's annual estimate of family remittances. Once the state was presented with data about the scale and impact of their contributions to millions of Mexican households, migrant workers could collectively start making stronger claims on it by demanding more consular services.[1] Remittances from Mexican immigrants reached $20 billion in 2005 and $26 billion in 2007. This revenue was exceeded only by oil exports and was generally on par with the level of foreign investment, placing Mexico at the top of remittance-sending countries worldwide. In the recessionary year of 2008, annual remittances from Mexican immigrants surpassed foreign investment ($25 billion vs. 23 billion) (Mendoza González and Valdivia López 2016). Since 2014, remittances sent by Mexican immigrants have continued to grow steadily, reaching $51 billion in 2021, with 95 percent of the total amount coming from the United States (Li Ng 2022). While Mexican consular services are decidedly not capable of expanding social welfare protections to all nonresidents living abroad, the Mexican government has a clear vested interest in addressing the basic needs of migrant workers in the United States, as their economic contributions represent an increasingly large share of the GDP (3.8 percent in 2020) and offer an escape valve from poverty to the 5 percent of Mexican households who depend on family remittances (Associated Press 2022).

Mexican emigrants living in the United States do not have access to special retirement programming; the Mexican government does not have any pension or social security agreement with the United States. Mexicans working abroad without health insurance cannot access Mexico's public universal health care system except through the Seguro Popular, a public health insurance offering minimal health care services to the families left behind using an annual sliding fee scale. Thus the bureaucratic diasporic infrastructure for most Mexican workers in the United States is limited to basic consular services aimed at informing low-wage workers how to access services in their local destination. They may be directed, for example, to health services offered by federally qualified health centers to undocumented workers, food pantries and literacy services offered through partnerships with local NGOs, and legal consultants for advice regarding workplace complaints.

To deliver on *both* descriptive and substantive services, the Mexican consular network and its representatives must navigate the legal mandates and cultural norms of at least four jurisdictions: the supranational instruments of international law, the national mandates of the Mexican government (and whatever political party is in power), the eternally polarized partisan politics of the United States (or of other host countries), and the subfederal (state and municipal) governments where the physical consular office is located. These mandates affect not only the parameters of diplomatic engagement but also the rights of migrant workers more specifically. In this chapter, we describe how each of these arenas shapes the ability to implement the Mexican government's aspirational promise to advocate for Mexican immigrants working in the United States. In the pages that follow, we provide the legal and institutional context for how street-level bureaucrats (at both

US labor agencies and the Mexican consulate) are implementing their mandate to address immigrant worker precarity. We assess the practical impact that these bilateral investments may have in the long run, beyond their symbolic importance for bilateral cooperation.

In this analysis, we use Lipsky's (1980) concept of street-level bureaucrats, understood as frontline governmental staff workers who directly administer and enforce labor and employment law in the United States or who offer direct social services in the Mexican consular network. These bureaucrats typically work for perpetually underfunded and overburdened organizations. We aim to understand how frontline staff prioritize their goals because of limited time and resources due to the chronic underfunding of services to meet the needs of precarious migrant workers. In the next section, we outline the framework for labor standards enforcement in the United States. We highlight the need for a co-enforcement model that engages relevant domestic civil society organizations as well as for the cross-border approach that has been embraced—to varying degrees—by diaspora bureaucracies.

LABOR STANDARDS ENFORCEMENT
IN THE UNITED STATES: CHALLENGES
AND OPPORTUNITIES FOR CONSULAR ADVOCACY

Several volumes have chronicled the specifics of US labor regulation and the many endemic challenges of a system in which employer compliance is elusive and companies race to the bottom in terms of labor rights in a globalizing capitalist world (e.g., Bernhardt, Milkman, and Theodore 2009; Parks 2014; Gleeson 2016). These dynamics have rendered migrant workers among the most vulnerable, leading both labor advocates and enforcement agencies to seek ways to promote their rights. It is in this context, and following immense grassroots pressure to hold both governments accountable for the workplace conditions of migrant workers, that a bilateral partnership has emerged between Mexico and the United States.

Workers and their advocates must navigate a multijurisdictional regulatory apparatus that both offers and frustrates opportunities for collaboration. While different statutory arenas often process their own claims entirely separately (e.g., wage and hour violations at the Department of Labor [DOL], sexual harassment claims at the Equal Employment Opportunity Commission [EEOC], or unfair labor practices at the National Labor Relations Board [NLRB]), consulates are in theory able to bridge these bureaucratic divisions in order to provide holistic assistance to workers, who are often considering filing a multitude of claims.

Another challenge is that despite increasing efforts to invest in strategic enforcement (Piore and Schrank 2018), the vast majority of labor compliance is still claims driven. This approach disadvantages the most vulnerable, especially undocumented workers, who may be especially wary of approaching government regulators and who have higher exposure to occupational health risks than their documented counterparts (Rocha Romero, Medina Sánchez, and Orraca Romano, 2022). For all these reasons (detailed further below), there is ample opportunity for local consulates to act as critical intermediary institutions.

Siloed Issue Arenas

The US labor standards enforcement system is a collection of agencies charged with enforcing a variety of disparate statutes. Employment relations and workers' rights have been dispersed across a complicated menu of regulations. Take, for example, the minimum-wage and overtime rules. These federal rules are set by the DOL's Wage and Hour Division, which enforces the Fair Labor Standards Act, a law that also guarantees meal and rest breaks. A separate unit within the DOL— the Occupational Safety and Health Administration (OSHA)—enforces training and hazard prevention requirements, often in conjunction with state OSHA agencies. These regulations are separate from the workers' compensation system, which relies on private insurance schemes, each regulated by the nation's fifty state boards. Other civil rights protections—against harassment, retaliation, or other discrimination on the basis of race, color, national origin, gender, disability, religion, or genetic information—fall to the EEOC and the dozens of partner state and local Fair Employment Practice Agencies across the country. Finally, the rights of the small percentage of unionized workers engaged in collective bargaining activities are overseen by the twenty-six regional offices of the NLRB.

Unlike Mexico's more consolidated approach, the siloed nature of workers' rights in the United States complicates workers' and Mexican diplomats' ability to quickly identify the appropriate advocate in the event of a violation. Mexico's model of labor inspection employs dedicated health and safety inspectors as well as generalists capable of addressing wages and hours, working conditions, child labor, and other areas of the labor code in a single visit, as opposed to the highly specialized nature of US labor inspectors (Piore and Schrank 2018). These differences in labor enforcement mechanisms make it necessary for consular bureaucrats to undergo specialized trainings offered by US labor standard agencies to become proficient in the alphabet soup of labor enforcement silos. The challenges are multiplied for immigrant workers, who may have limited English proficiency or may lack experience interacting with US bureaucracies. While some agencies have informally developed joint task forces or engaged in collaborative outreach efforts, there is no statutory requirement for cross-filing claims across agencies. And even when there is coordination, each statute may have distinct employee and firm coverage, statutes of limitations, and claims processes. Within this context, worker advocates become critical intermediaries for helping claimants navigate the patchwork of laws and offices. Consulates can also play a key intermediary role and are especially needed in places with a thin network of worker advocates serving Spanish-speaking immigrant workers. In some cities, as we detail in the next chapter, consulates have been critical for coordinating the cross-filing of claims. To this end, in 2004, Mexico's Secretaría de Relaciones Exteriores / Ministry of Foreign Affairs (SRE) and the US DOL signed a Joint Declaration to advance immigrant worker rights, setting the stage for other sister agencies to follow suit.

Overlapping Jurisdictions

Labor standards enforcement in the United States is complicated not only by the ways it is split up by issue among various federal agencies but by the ways state and local governments have increasingly taken the initiative to address labor standards themselves (Galvin 2016; Fine et al. 2020). This shift can be attributed in part to the intransigence of the US Congress, which has neglected to raise the minimum requirements of key protections. For example, the minimum wage, which requires congressional approval, has remained stagnant for more than a decade. Labor standards at the federal level make exceptions for certain precarious workers such as domestic caregivers or farmworkers, categories that several states have now chosen to include in their basic protections. Meanwhile, many states and localities have stepped in to provide stronger standards and enforcement mechanisms (Goldman 2018). As a result, workers pursuing restitution, particularly those living in big cities, are faced with a plethora of overlapping jurisdictions and options for legal mobilization. This array is both a blessing and a curse, and can be especially confusing for workers who need translators and cannot afford a lawyer to help them navigate the bureaucratic labyrinth.

Within this context, there is ample opportunity for consulates to collaborate with government agencies and civil society groups that advocate on behalf of immigrant workers. Generally, federal memoranda of understanding (MOUs) can set the tone at the local level. As described in chapter 3, MOUs are frequently replicated in local jurisdictions in the form of letters of agreement (LOAs), which are signed by the local agency lead (e.g., district director or regional administrator for the local DOL's Wage and Hour Division Office). While the template for federal bilaterally negotiated MOU agreements with the DOL, EEOC, and NLRB dates back to the Joint Declaration signed between the DOL and the Ministry of Foreign Affairs in 2004, certain local offices of these federal agencies were coordinating with Mexico's consular network across the United States long before their national agencies signed onto the federal MOU, thanks to collaborative relationships between street-level diplomatic bureaucrats across Mexico's consular network and local labor standards enforcement agents (Gleeson and Bada 2019). However, because of the explicitly diplomatic mission of Mexico's consular network, federal agencies are their sole official counterparts, the only body with whom they are able to sign formal MOUs.

While these memoranda are arguably only symbolic agreements that do not necessarily determine the actual extent of consular collaboration on the ground, our interviews with key stakeholders reveal that the jurisdictional mismatch between federal and local initiatives has implications for generating sustained political will and commitment from consular leadership to advance workers' rights.[2] More mundanely, the consular-federal relationship steepens the learning curve for new consular staff, who must familiarize themselves with both local and national regulations and players. In places like San Francisco—where the California Labor Commission enforces a more robust set of policies than does the federal DOL's Wage and Hour Division and where the city/county Office of Labor Standards Enforcement enforces one of the highest minimum wages in the country (twice that of the national standard)—the relationships between local consulates and their federal counterparts are practically inconsequential.

Finally, this federated approach to labor standards enforcement also heightens the importance of proactive local consular initiatives. Top-down national outreach strategies like the annual Semana de Derechos Laborales / Labor Rights Week are critical to coordinating the entire consular network around promoting workers' rights as a key part of consular protection. However, without consular leadership that is attuned to the realities facing the local immigrant workforce (be they agricultural workers in Salinas, meatpackers outside of Chicago, or restaurant workers in Houston), a uniform approach to workers' rights advocacy is bound to fail. Local co-enforcement efforts—usually instigated by civil society actors—have emerged precisely from the on-the-ground experiences of these workers, and thus local consulates must learn to carefully navigate and not co-opt these movements.

Claims-Driven Worker Regulation

The defining aspect of the labor standards enforcement regime in the United States is that it is fueled almost entirely by worker-generated claims. Though many of these agencies have proactive outreach and education initiatives (including the DOL's Community Outreach and Resource Planning Specialists program) (Wage and Hour Division 2021), a bottom-up "fire alarm" approach to labor investigation predominates and disadvantages the most vulnerable of workers, especially those who may be undocumented (McCubbins and Schwartz 1984; Griffith 2012; Alexander and Prasad 2014). This approach is problematic for compliance efficacy, given that it necessarily directs regulators to focus on those willing workers most capable of filing complaints by themselves. It is also problematic for marginalized workers (Garcia 2012), who must surmount a long list of challenges in order to ascend the dispute pyramid and file a formal claim (Felstiner, Abel, and Sarat 1980; Gleeson 2016). Owing to these barriers, the claims-driven approach heightens the importance of institutional intermediaries, a role that civil society organizations and other legal advocates have long played.

Consulates are particularly well equipped to broker workers' claims given their ability to wield state power in communications with employers or to coordinate with US agencies as diplomatic counterparts. In contrast to the siloed nature of the claims-making bureaucracy, some consulates even serve as case managers for workers struggling to navigate disparate agencies. Language and cultural connections, as well as the (limited) community trust they have established, grant consular officials a huge advantage over US agencies. But more practically, consular officials can be granted unique access to overworked and underresourced US labor agency staff, who may otherwise keep worker advocates at arm's length or view them as adversarial. In some rare cases, consulates may also provide their citizens with legal referrals and even pay for outside representation. Usually, though, consulates at the very least act as a central referral node for the various community partners able to provide additional assistance and organizing support.

However, the availability of third parties who can educate workers about their rights and shepherd their claims through the system depends on a number of factors. Only immigrant workers in central cities tend to have access to pro bono legal advocates willing to take their cases. In the absence of these pro bono lawyers, few workers possess the resources to hire an attorney for this work, and lawyers will typically offer a contingency plan only for certain rare, high-reward cases. Given this context, a consular office enjoys certain advantages over other organizations in performing this brokering role. For example, consulates are particularly well positioned not only because they can provide workers with information and (potentially) legal advice in their native language but also because they can take on cases regardless of a worker's immigration status. While worker centers and other legal advocates serving immigrant workers have proliferated across the country (Fine and Gordon 2010; Fine 2011), many legal aid organizations are prohibited from taking cases for undocumented workers (Compa 2017, 232; Guild and Figueroa 2018, 161), and these organizations are often inaccessible in many suburban and rural areas. Moreover, when workers are captured in a raid at the workplace, many immigrant advocacy organizations do not have the direct and immediate access to detention centers that consular officials have when citizens of their country face difficulties in a foreign state (according to Article 36 of the Vienna Convention on Consular Relations).[3] Consequently, good relationships between advocates and consular staff are necessary to establish smooth triage and communication channels to prevent the potential deportations of workers. The perennial challenge, however, is the disconnect between the scale of the need and consular capacity.

Immigration Enforcement Considerations

Perhaps the most consequential aspect of claims making for consular advocacy is the particular vulnerability of undocumented immigrants, who make up 43 percent of the Mexican immigrant population in the United States (Gonzalez-Barrera and Krogstad 2019). As other scholars have explained in more detail (Griffith 2011), undocumented workers or those with other precarious statuses face a complicated labor protection framework. Protections in the United States are by and large available to workers without regard to their immigration status, but, with several exceptions, remedies are often severely limited for claims involving back pay or reinstatement (arguably rendering relevant protections meaningless in the aftermath of ubiquitous employer retaliation).[4] Furthermore, immigration enforcement in the United States has long relied on the workplace as a site of enforcement, be it through large-scale raids (common in the George W. Bush era), workplace Social Security number audits (which proliferated during Barack Obama's presidency and could be thought of as "silent raids"), or both (as with the all-in enforcement strategy of the Donald Trump administration) (Griffith and Gleeson 2019).

While there do (still) exist long-standing MOUs between the DOL and the Department of Homeland Security (US DOL 2011; National Employment Law Project 2016), these are viewed as privileging the directives of immigration enforcement and have proven largely ineffective in protecting the rights of undocumented workers. In other words, there is no functional "firewall" between the information gathered by labor agencies and immigration enforcement officials (including Immigration and Customs Enforcement [ICE]). In fact, examples abound of workers who lodged claims against an abusive employer then being swept up in an ICE raid (e.g., Rosenberg and Cooke 2019), with labor advocates able to do little to slow their removal or advance their claims (Landon 2008). While some protections do empower undocumented workers to file a claim against their employer, such as applying for a U or T visa (designed for victims of crime and trafficking), these legal options have many requirements and place claimants on a long waiting list; moreover, efforts to broaden these protections have been unsuccessful (Constante 2018).

The entanglements between worker protections and immigration enforcement place consulates in a complicated situation. Despite the many institutional motivations to remain independent from immigration enforcement (Gleeson 2014), some state agencies have capitulated and shared information with federal immigration enforcement agencies (Thomsen 2018). More practically, many federal buildings (where both immigration and labor agency offices are often located), may prove inaccessible for workers who lack the proper documentation to get through security or simply do not want to risk being in proximity to ICE offices. As a result, despite the Mexican government's sordid history of exposing vulnerable immigrant workers to possible deportation in the United States and interfering with the unionization efforts of Mexican farmworkers (Goodman 2020; González 1999), its consulates have become one of the few official federal government allies to whom an undocumented worker can safely turn. However, consulates' trademark "noninterventionist" stance, while helpful diplomatically, severely limits their ability to fully mobilize their power and resources on behalf of their most vulnerable emigrants seeking labor protection. This neutrality—or, as some would call it, indifference—not only enhances the cynicism of an already disaffected diaspora but can also create huge rifts with civil society advocates.

It can be difficult for Mexican diplomats to negotiate better working conditions for migrants without alienating Mexico's largest commercial partner, the United States. For example, Mexican ambassador Medina Mora often defended migrant rights and offered support for a comprehensive immigration reform when speaking to connationals. Yet the ambassador noted the challenge of this dual obligation in an address to community leaders at the Chicago consulate during the Obama administration:

> The Mexican consuls and the ambassador have to be very careful. They can't appear publicly as an advocate. I don't shy away when I need to say something, but I have to say it in a way that supports the desired outcome without blocking it. So, it is not by showing high levels of militancy that we will win. We need to search the best way to be vocal instead. We have to ask ourselves, where can we be more efficient? I assure you that we are not shy, but we try to be very smart in approaching this delicate subject.[5]

Civil society advocates are not satisfied with these explanations, however, frequently decrying what they see as the refusal of consular and embassy officials to make bold moves toward comprehensive immigration reform.

MEXICO'S HISTORY OF MIGRANT
WORKER ENGAGEMENT

The Supranational Legal Framework for Migrant Worker Protection

According to embassy staff, the principal legal function of the SRE and its consular network across the globe is to protect the rights of Mexicans living abroad. The Mexican Secretaría del Trabajo y Previsión Social / Ministry of Labor (STPS) also has an important role to play both within Mexico and in countries where there are bilateral labor export programs. Yet there are relatively few temporary foreign workers in the United States, which limits the STPS's reach there. Since the end of the Bracero Programs (1942–64), which issued temporary work permits to millions of Mexicans to ease US labor shortages after the Second World War, temporary labor programs available to Mexican migrants through the STPS have been small in scale, with annual quotas of less than half a million temporary work visas allocated to Mexicans each year to work legally in the United States. The STPS manages an even smaller (but proportionally more significant) program, the Mexico-Canada Seasonal Agricultural Workers Program, which was inaugurated in 1974 and still operates. In 2022, twenty-six thousand farmworkers participated in this program (STPS 2022).

While the STPS regulates basic protections for temporary workers in Canada (STPS 2019), Mexico's labor law does not include any special enforcement mechanism governing labor disputes for Mexican workers posted abroad. The STPS does have a Federal Attorney's Office for Labor Protection / Procuraduría Federal de la Defensa del Trabajo, though this agency focuses on worker-driven claims and has neither the capacity nor the jurisdiction to intervene in labor disputes in the United States, except in cases of international labor recruitment (as discussed in chapter 5).

The STPS has therefore played a largely consultative role, while the SRE—as the major actor with the legal responsibility of protecting Mexicans living abroad—was the key bilateral US counterpart in the MOUs that were signed in 2004 between the two countries. Bilateral agreements such as the MOUs between the SRE and the US DOL helped to solidify the notion that consulates have a duty to aid their citizens. These MOUs stemmed from a number of bilateral instruments, including the North American Agreement on Labor Cooperation (NAALC), which was signed in 1993 alongside the hallmark North American Free Trade Agreement (NAFTA). The NAALC established a National Administrative Office in each party country (Canada, Mexico, and the United States), whose job is to review complaints, coordinate tripartite activities, and provide information to the public (ILAB 2005) As shown in table 1, bilateral collaborations on issues related to trade, worker rights, and health care have increased in the region since the mid-1990s.

In practice, these consular obligations have manifested perhaps most visibly around law enforcement, with consuls intervening in the event that a citizen is jailed without counsel. The Vienna Convention on Consular Relations requires "consular notification" upon arrest and the right for consulates to access their detained foreign nationals (US Department of State 2018). The Mexican SRE describes this function as a core aspect of their presence abroad, vital to ensuring that their emigrants are afforded their rights in a timely and consistent manner (SRE 2016). Though officials in various detention facilities may reach out directly to consular staff, in practice this communication relies on detained individuals invoking these rights themselves. Moreover, while detention centers routinely have the rights posted, the volume of immigration enforcement activity (even in "immigrant-friendly" jurisdictions) far outweighs the capacity of consular per-sonnel to *actually* respond in a timely manner, thus rendering them an ineffective resource in all but the most extraordinary cases.

Consular officials are similarly obliged to intervene in the case of nonpayment of child support or alimony, especially when the child or spouse or both have remained in Mexico. In these cases, consular officials often have direct agreements with local law enforcement to, for example, carry out judicial orders for partners and children back in Mexico. Yet these local arrangements are rarely replicated with consular offi-cials to enforce labor protections. In fact, many consular leaders explained that their diplomatic post limited the formal arrangements they could create with subfed-eral governments.[6] As labor standards enforcement increasingly becomes a subject for states and municipalities (Fine and Round 2021), though, these arrangements are almost certain to be made with local community partners, at least informally.

TABLE 1 Time line of key events in bilateral collaboration (1994–2017)

Date	Key Event
1994	The North American Free Trade Agreement (NAFTA) is enacted.
1994	The North American Agreement on Labor Cooperation (NAALC) establishes the Commission for Labor Cooperation and country-level National Administrative Offices (NAOs).
2001–9	Elaine Chao's term as US DOL (Department of Labor) secretary.
2001	Houston's Justice and Equality in the Workplace Program is created (to be modeled in Dallas in 2003).
2001	Binational Health Week is established in seven California counties.
2002	The Instituto de los Mexicanos en el Exterior (IME) is created, and the first cohort of the Consejo Consultivo del Instituto de los Mexicanos en el Exterior (CCIME) is appointed/elected.
2002	The OSHA (Occupational Safety and Health Administration) Alliance Program is created with various community partners, including the Mexican consulate, along with the Centers for Disease Control's National Institute for Occupational Safety and Health (NIOSH).
2002	*Hoffman Plastic Compounds, Inc. v. National Labor Relations Board*—a landmark US Supreme Court decision.
2002	Mexico's federal Tres por Uno program is expanded to all Mexican states.
2003	The Employment Education and Outreach Alliance (EMPLEO) partnership is launched in Las Vegas, then expanded to Los Angeles.
2003	The Washington, D.C.–based Farmworker Justice Fund, Inc., files the first petition with the Mexican NAO in conjunction with the Central Independiente de Obreros Agrícolas y Campesinos, an agricultural worker organization based in Mexico City.
2003	Immigrant Workers Freedom Ride.
2004	President Fox inaugurates Seguro Popular, which includes access for returned migrants from Mexico and offers health care services to Mexico-based families of migrant workers living in the US who wish to pay the corresponding family contributions.
2004	A joint declaration is signed between the DOL and the Mexican Secretaría de Relaciones Exteriores. This leads to the creation of memoranda of understanding (or letters of agreement) between national agencies and the consulates, followed by arrangements establishing understanding (AEUs) implementing these agreements at the local level.
2005	The Northwest Workers' Justice Project of Oregon, the Andrade Law Office of Boise, Idaho, and the Brennan Center for Justice in New York submit a new petition to the Mexican NAO in conjunction with six NGOs in Mexico and four in the US.
2006	Historic immigration protests take place across the US in response to the controversial 2005 Sensenbrenner Bill.
2006	El Salvador and Guatemala join Binational Health Week.
2007	Colombia, Honduras, Ecuador, Bolivia, and Peru join Binational Health Week.

(Contd.)

Date	Key Event
2007	Chicago's first Ventanilla Laboral is established.
2008	The first memorandum of understanding is signed to establish a framework for the Semana de Derechos Laborales.
2008	The fifty-fifth *jornada informativa* of the IME: Líderes Sindicales is celebrated in Mexico City, May 11–14.
2008	The Consular Partnership Program is created at the US DOL, facilitated by the Bureau of International Labor Affairs (ILAB).
2009–13	Hilda Solis's term as DOL secretary.
2009	The LABORAL call center is established with the US DOL, the New York State DOL, and the Catholic Migration Office of the Roman Catholic Diocese of Brooklyn.
2010	Ambassador Arturo Sarukhán and DOL secretary Hilda Solis re-sign the joint declaration.
2010	SB 1070—Support Our Law Enforcement and Safe Neighborhoods Act—is passed in Arizona.
2010	The Centro de Información y Asistencia a Mexicanos (CIAM) is established (in part to respond to SB 1070 concerns).
2011	The Centro de los Derechos del Migrante introduces a new petition on behalf of three migrant returnees, supported by a binational coalition of fourteen organizations.
2011	The entire consular network is now participating in the Semana, along with ten other members of the Latin American consular corps (Brazil, Chile, Colombia, Costa Rica, Dominican Republic, El Salvador, Guatemala, Honduras, Nicaragua, and Peru).
2013	The Secretaría del Trabajo y Previsión Social establishes a labor attaché office in Washington, D.C., to address public petitions under the NAALC.
2013–17	Tom Perez's term as DOL secretary.
2014	The Tres Amigos Cumbre is held in Toluca to outline trade goals between the US, Canada, and Mexico (February 9).
2014	Ambassador Medina Mora and DOL secretary Perez re-sign the joint declaration.
2014	Ministerial consultations are held following the NAALC.
2014	Predeparture workshops are held in Mexico (for H-2 guest workers) in eleven sending states (Estado de México, Guanajuato, Hidalgo, Jalisco, Michoacán, Oaxaca, Querétaro, San Luis Potosí, Sinaloa, Veracruz, and Zacatecas).
2014	Argentina, Bolivia, Guatemala, Uruguay, and the Philippines are now collaborating with the Semana de Derechos Laborales.
2014	The CCIME comes to an end.
2014	Mexico offers temporary, ninety-day access to health care, funded by Seguro Popular, to undocumented migrants entering by Campeche, Chiapas, Quintana Roo, and Tabasco.
2017	Colombia expands Binational Health Week from the US and Canada to Colombian consulates in Mexico, Venezuela, Ecuador, Chile, Argentina, Uruguay, Costa Rica, Panama, Brazil, France, Spain, and Belgium.
2020	The Tres por Uno Program comes to an end.

While many other volumes have delved deeply into the global governance instruments protecting migrant workers, here we choose to highlight several that are relevant to how the Mexican-US relationship operates. According to legal scholar José María Serna de la Garza (2019), these instruments are neutral structures that reflect massive power imbalances on the international stage. Especially for the United States, global governance is typically not legally binding and has minimal consequences. However, this is not necessarily the case for the Estados Unidos Mexicanos. Mexico has signed far more mechanisms for migrant rights than has the United States, which, along with many other migrant-receiving countries in Western Europe and Australia, has not signed the Convention on the Protection of the Rights of All Migrant Workers and Members of Their Families (Ruhs 2013). As of August 2021, only fifty-five countries—many of them primarily countries of origin such as Mexico, Philippines, and Morocco—have ratified the convention. This deference to international standards arguably provides Mexico with a modicum of moral leverage against the hegemonic power of the United States. But it also reflects a major paradox of geopolitical power: while Mexico purports to defend the rights of its emigrant population in the United States, half of whom are undocumented, and elsewhere, it also deports a stunning majority of Central American migrants at its own southern border without due process (Feldmann Pietsch, Bada, and Durand Arp-Niesse 2020; Rojas Wiesner 2022).

In his work, Serna de la Garza (2019) magnificently details the various instruments and institutions that have established standards of immigrant rights, the three most significant of them being UN General Assembly resolutions and UN Secretary General reports, the Inter-American System for the Protection of Human Rights and Migrant Worker Rights, and the NAALC. He argues that viewed cynically, these nonbinding "soft laws" open the door for "empty promises" from politicians (56). By contrast, Lance Compa (2001), a renowned international labor law lawyer and scholar, contends that while these instruments may be symbolic, they are still useful, providing advocates a framework for leaning on employers and other leaders to recognize, and do something to protect, migrant worker rights.

In previous accounts (Bada and Gleeson 2019), we have detailed the significance of these international instruments for transnational advocacy networks, which we also revisit in chapter 5. It is clear that UN conventions and bilateral accords have created openings for groups like labor unions, worker centers, and migrant advocates operating on both sides of the border to bring their concerns before supranational bodies. But unlike the traditional "boomerang effect" model introduced by Keck and Sikkink (1998), we find evidence for a two-way dynamic whereby advocating on behalf of migrants in or bound to the United States can also aid advocacy efforts for workers who remain in or return to Mexico.[7] By pressuring the Mexican government to be accountable to its diaspora, advocates have exposed its hypocritical failure to uplift the conditions of workers within its own national territory. This irony is not lost on advocates: the very degradation of workers at home is one of the key drivers of out-migration, or as Sassen (2014) and Golash-Boza (2015) call it, their neoliberal *expulsion.*

These same instruments have been leveraged by the Mexican labor movement, which has also used the labor regulation infrastructure of free trade governance to hold the Mexican government to account for violations of collective bargaining rights (Graubart 2010). These struggles have exposed state-allied *charro* unions and have aligned the demands of Mexican workers who have remained with those of migrant workers abroad.[8] Such transnational solidarity was clearly evident in the high-profile campaigns waged by Campbell's Soup farmworkers in the early 1980s and North Carolina cucumber pickers in the early 2000s, both of which garnered solidarity from Mexican labor movements.

Mexico's Labor Regimes

Over the last century, Mexico has made significant progress toward a fairer labor regime inspired by the ideals of the 1910 Mexican Revolution. Article 123 of Mexico's 1917 Constitution established expansive protections for workers, including the ability to organize unions, conduct strikes, and bargain collectively. After the initial triumph of these revolution-era laws, it was elite liberal reformers, and not the peasantry, who legislated labor law regulations in the 1930s and granted enormous power to the state to enforce worker protection (Bensusán 2000).

In the 1930s, governments across the world had to cope with the Great Depression and devise policies to benefit struggling workers. In Sweden, for example, the victorious Labor Party brought about the modern welfare state. Germany and Italy produced pro-worker programs during the fascist era, and Franklin Roosevelt created Social Security and signed the National Labor Relations Act. Many of those moves secured the political loyalties of the labor movement, and Mexico was no exception (Hathaway 2000). Few independent unions flourished prior to the 1970s, though, as the Mexican state used clientelism, political patronage, and corporatism to exercise absolute control over organized labor, requiring unions to be official members of the ruling Partido Revolucionario Institucional / Institutional Revolutionary Party (PRI). Every member of the Confederación de Trabajadores de México (Confederation of Mexican Workers), the largest confederation of labor unions, was automatically enrolled in the PRI, and the party and the unions formed a natural alliance that allowed political elites to control resources (Roberts 2014).

Over time, multiple reforms to Article 123 mandated minimum wages, overtime pay, minimum health and safety standards, seniority, bonuses, paid vacations, rest days, housing subsidies, an eight-hour workday, participation in profit sharing, equal pay for equal work, and protections against sex discrimination and child labor (La Botz 1992). With regard to enforcement and protection, federal labor law established the Board of Conciliation and Arbitration, a tripartite mechanism operating at federal and state levels in Mexico. The federal government had a privileged role in deciding labor management and intraunion conflicts, as well as discretionary authority to interpret constitutional labor protections through its control of the tripartite labor boards and tribunals, which still maintain tight control over wages and strikes (Bensusán 2000; Bensusán and Cook 2003). In managing labor disputes, the government representative on the arbitration board could cast the tie-breaking, controlling vote. Moreover, very few cases went to trial after mediation provided by these government-controlled arbitration boards, which, it could be argued, reduced the possibility of widespread labor reforms. While dissident labor groups periodically threatened the hegemony of the Confederación de Trabajadores de México (as explained in chapter 5), the purchasing power of the working class plummeted after Mexico's tripartite mechanism began exerting unmitigated market-based control over wage levels during the 1980s and 1990s.

In the 1980s, Mexico entered the General Agreement on Tariffs and Trade in order to compete in the global economy by attracting international investment with low-priced natural resources and low-priced labor. Throughout that decade, Mexican workers had lost purchasing power because of a strict austerity policy designed by international banking institutions to reduce the country's debt burden. Subsequent neoliberal administrations secured Mexico's place in the global economy and paved the way to negotiate NAFTA. There were minimal revolts by peasants and industrial workers because the authoritarian regime quickly squashed the Zapatista Army for National Liberation in January 1994 (right after NAFTA was enacted) and disrupted multiple worker strikes demanding union democratization. By and large, NAFTA created an exodus of Mexican workers, who left low-wage rural work in search of jobs in maquiladoras in northern Mexico or crossed the border without documents to find low-wage jobs in the United States (Massey, Durand, and Malone 2002).

In terms of labor regulation, trade agreements signed between Latin American and Caribbean countries with the United States have had largely positive effects, leading to an average increase of 20 percent in inspectors and a 60 percent increase in actual inspections from 2009 to 2012 (Dewan and Ronconi 2018). NAFTA, however, did not produce the same measurable labor regulation impacts in Mexico and the United States, as the NAALC failed to incorporate core International Labour Organization (ILO) labor rights in the original agreement (Russo 2011), despite being designed to facilitate a broad international framework of labor rights protection within free trade agreements (Perez-Lopez 1996). However, NAFTA did bring about a few positive developments in the parallel labor agreements. The system of public petitions established by the NAALC increased cooperation between independent labor unions such as the Frente Auténtico del Trabajo / Authentic Workers' Front, their Canadian and US counterparts, and transnational immigrant advocacy organizations by allowing union leaders in the three countries to submit strategic petitions on behalf of industrial workers and migrant farmworkers.

By 2018, almost twenty-five years after NAFTA went into effect, the Mexican Senate recognized the ILO convention on collective bargaining by unanimously ratifying ILO Convention Number 98, which guarantees workers the right to organize, as well as the right to voluntary and authentic collective bargaining in Mexico (Gacek 2019). The ratification of this convention is expected to invalidate much of the protection provided to state-allied *charro* unions. It is the culmination of dozens of petitions accumulated in the National Administrative Offices of the United States, Mexico, and Canada denouncing protection contracts in Mexico,[9] labor violations of temporary migrant workers, and abuses in international recruitment practices, among other labor issues.

Such human rights frames based on international jurisdictions are increasingly significant in transnational labor advocacy (Gest, Kysel, and Wong 2019). However, domestic laws (in both origin and destination states) still remain the most relevant vehicles for securing rights, especially in the United States. By taking steps to eliminate the protection contracts regime and allow free and democratic elections in Mexican labor unions, Mexico, experts agree, is currently well aligned with an international human rights framework and should proceed to enact necessary enabling legislation, regulation, and judicial action. And having ratified both ILO Conventions 87 (1950) and 98 (2018), Mexico is now required by international law to ensure a genuinely democratic labor relations system.

Since the Great Recession hit low-wage workers in the United States in 2007, many migrants returned voluntarily to Mexico or were deported, pressuring the Mexican government to offer relocation assistance and access to employment opportunities to workers who returned home. More recently, the pandemic has pushed Mexico to function as a reluctant buffer zone to slow down or deter the surge of migrants from Central America, the Caribbean, and Venezuela. This position presents enormous challenges for Mexico in offering asylum protection to vulnerable migrants fleeing violence, poverty, and climate change and in continuing to advocate for the rights of Mexican workers living in the United States.

How Migrant Work Became a Central Focus for Mexico

Mexico's investment in immigrant workers' rights is rooted in several traditions, according to embassy staff we interviewed in Washington, D.C.[10] First and foremost, Mexico has long played a central role in interviewing and selecting the guest workers to travel abroad. In Canada, this process requires engaging national leaders, as well as provincial governments and employer groups. However, this formal role in labor brokerage is largely absent in the United States, where there are relatively few guest workers. In 2016, the United States hosted 438,190 H-2A (seasonal agricultural), H-2B (nonagricultural), and J-1 (exchange visitor) guest workers (Costa 2017). During fiscal year 2018, 93 percent of H-2A workers admitted to the United States hailed from Mexico. Compared to the approximately five million Mexican undocumented citizens who now average fifteen years of continuous residence in the United States (Passel and Cohn 2019), temporary legal workers are a comparatively small population in need of consular protection.

In Canada, labor unions and other advocates have been some of the most vocal critics of the temporary foreign worker program and key stakeholders in the co-enforcement of immigrant workers' rights (Dias-Abey 2018; Preibisch and Encalada Grez 2010). Traditionally in these Canadian consular jurisdictions, there is a staff member dedicated exclusively to guest worker issues who intervenes during disputes. However, as Leah Vosko (2016, 2018) has shown, the Mexican consular network in Canada has not necessarily been an unwavering advocate for immigrant workers, and the same has been true historically in the United States, particularly during the Bracero Programs (1942–64), which brought in guest workers from Mexico during the Second World War (García y Griego 1988). In terms of consular support, Tanya Basok and documentary filmmaker Min Sook Lee have shown how the Mexican consulate intervened on behalf of tomato pickers in Canada, whose government has mostly privileged continuing the labor agreement at the expense of improving the labor rights of low-wage, largely unprotected Mexican tomato pickers (Basok 2000, 1999; M. Lee 2003). Historically, the Mexican federal government has been largely ineffective in protecting the rights of its citizens in migration programs in Mexico and Canada, and abuses have been legion. The Mexican government has even been sued alongside the US government for its failure to accurately account for millions of dollars withheld by authorities from braceros' paychecks and, in theory, sent to Mexican banks to be distributed to the workers once they returned home. As explained in chapter 5, recovering these lost funds has been a unifying force among transnational advocates as they demand bilateral frameworks to defend worker rights.

In an important shift for Mexican labor relations with its northern neighbors, an STPS labor attaché was moved from Ottawa to Washington, DC, in 2013 to help address public petitions under the NAALC. This realignment strengthened the SRE's agenda on Mexican migrant labor issues and responded to changing demographic realities and resource constraints, as well as the edicts laid out under the 2004 and 2008 ministerial agreements, which identified labor issues as a clear priority for bilateral cooperation with the United States.[11] Embassy staff we interviewed about this move indicated that the transferred STPS could one day play a larger role in implementing the binational labor rights MOUs.[12] By and large, however, the STPS's role seems to be limited mostly to addressing petitions filed against the labor side accords.

According to the staff of the SRE's Dirección General de Protección a Mexicanos en el Exterior / General Directorate for the Protection of Mexicans Abroad (DGPME), Mexico's role in brokering worker claims is critical given immigrant workers' fear of losing their job or provoking employer retaliation against their family members in response to filing claims: "Part of our efforts go towards empowering our citizens, so that they know their rights, and can then be motivated to mobilize them," one staff member said.[13] Such efforts face difficulties, because along with immigrant fears are practical hurdles: not having a car, driver's license, or other method of transportation to attend a consular event, much less the spare time.

One way consular staff address this reluctance and overcome these barriers is by conducting outreach throughout the year and by taking advantage of "captive audiences" gathered for educational programming (including the Plazas Comunitarias), which are more likely to take place in community settings far from the actual consular office. The goal is that these community collaborators (in conjunction also with the Instituto de los Mexicanos en el Exterior / Institute of Mexicans Abroad [IME]) become the "eyes and ears" of consulates, learning about cases of workplace abuse that consular officials might not otherwise encounter directly.[14]

Consular networks also reach out to the community through ethnic media, such as Univision, as well as local Spanish-language radio. As one official noted: "Our consulate in Boise, which covers some of our most remote communities in the jurisdiction, offers a good example of the significance of outreach networks. There may not even be Spanish-language radio, or it is stock Univision programming that doesn't permit local content. . . . In those places, the work of community events, in churches, community centers, and other organizations, is key."[15]

Furthermore, the consul general and the heads of the Departamento de Protección y Asistencia Consular / Department of Legal Protection and Consular Assistance, the Departamento de Asuntos Comunitarios / Department of Community Affairs, and even the Departamento de Documentación / Department of Documentation may join to advertise the range of resources available through local consulates. As a staff member from the IME in Mexico City explained: "One of the messages that we've asked our staff, and especially those in the Department of Protection, [to promote] is that regardless of immigration status, people should be confident in approaching the consulate to get help in their case and to promote their rights."[16]

INSTITUTIONALIZING THE JOINT COMMITMENT
OF MEXICO AND THE UNITED STATES
TO MIGRANT WORKER RIGHTS

Historical accounts have confirmed how consulates have shaped the lives of migrant workers as long as the border has existed between the United States and Mexico (Balderrama 1982; García y Griego 1988; Weise 2015). Consular involvement has often occurred without formal issue-specific agreements between the two countries and almost always has included interfacing with local civil society. Yet Mexico's recently heightened role in labor standards enforcement rests especially on a series of formal agreements struck over the last twenty years.

2002 to 2014: Instituto de los Mexicanos en el Exterior

The IME and the Consejo Consultivo.   The election of Mexican president Salinas de Gortari in 1988, widely seen as fraudulent, sparked a long series of demonstrations across Mexican consulates in the United States. Salinas immediately set out to address this migrant discontent in an attempt to legitimize his presidency among members of the organized diaspora who had sided with Cárdenas Solórzano, the iconic opposition candidate. In 1989, his administration instituted the Programa Paisano, which was housed in the Secretaría de Gobernación / Ministry of the Interior. To increase communication with Mexican migrant civil society, Salinas sought to reform and expand Mexico's consular network by gradually adding new consulates, upgrading personnel, expanding roles for the consuls, and requiring them to increase engagement with migrants, Mexican Americans, other Latinos, and a broad range of US leaders and organizations. To accomplish these reforms, in 1990 foreign minister Fernando Solana created the Programa para las Comunidades Mexicanas en el Extranjero / Program for the Mexican Communities Abroad (PCME) within the SRE. This program operated in the United States through the consular network (Ayón 2010).

The PCME staff conducted outreach across existing hometown clubs in the United States, with the ultimate objective that these clubs might eventually organize into state federations. The network of hometown associations grew in the 1990s and became more vocal in demanding restitution of their members' political rights and increased funding for community development programs in communities of origin (Bada 2014). During this period, Mexican leaders increasingly called for the right to vote from abroad and for direct congressional representation from abroad for migrants. After coming to power in 2000, President Vicente Fox promised migrants that he would restructure the government's relationship with migrants by creating a Presidential Office for Mexicans Abroad. This presidential office gave Fox a direct channel to the diaspora, but it was abolished in mid-2002. Its collapse, however, paved the way for the IME, created in late 2002, which was housed in the SRE (Ross Pineda and Mora 2003).

One major component of the IME's work was a program of professional and leadership networking known as *jornadas informativas*. Here the IME staff identified a particular sector of mainly Mexican immigrant professionals or community leaders in the United States and devised a two- to three-day program of activities for them in Mexico City (Ayón 2010). However, the IME's most significant innovation was the formation of a large advisory council made up of migrants representing Mexico's forty-five US consular jurisdictions at that time. The body came to be known as the Consejo Consultivo / Advisory Board of the IME, or the CCIME. The IME had an executive director frequently selected from the consular corps, and it absorbed all the functions and personnel of the PCME.[17] The CCIME called for one hundred *consejeros* to be chosen for three-year terms by migrant communities in a selection process initiated by consulates, with several seats reserved for *consejeros* appointed by professional merit. Depending on consular jurisdiction and the level of organization of the migrant civil society, the mode of selection varied considerably from one location to another. In Los Angeles, the meetings convened by the Consulate General agreed to reserve the majority of that consular jurisdiction's seats for the presidents of hometown association federations. In Chicago, an open election with printed ballots was organized by immigrant organizations and activists at a public high school in Pilsen, a Mexican neighborhood, and in similar public locations in Chicago and its metropolitan area in subsequent elections (Bayes and Gonzalez 2011; Ayón 2010; Ross Pineda and Mora 2003). Elected *consejeros* consisted of leaders throughout Mexican immigrant civil society in the United States, including health advocates, social service providers, hometown association leaders, business owners, artistic directors, educators, journalists, civil rights advocates, sports league coordinators, local elected officials, union members, and philanthropists, among others (Godoy Padilla 2018).

In its first term, the CCIME was internally divided into six committees dedicated to different policy areas. These committees met twice yearly, issued policy recommendations to the Mexican government, and monitored the action taken in response. The second CCIME term (2006–8) was highly successful. It created a subcommittee on human and labor rights within the political affairs committee that included key *consejeros* who held organizing positions in labor unions in Canada and the United States, namely with United Food and Commercial Workers International Union (UFCW) and the Service Employees International Union (SEIU). This cohort was instrumental in inviting key figures of the labor movement such as Eliseo Medina (SEIU) and Esther López (UFCW) to serve as appointed members to the CCIME. In May of 2008 in Mexico City, this cohort leveraged the IME's fifty-fifth *jornada informativa,* devoted to the topic "State of Labor in Mexico," to raise awareness about labor rights abuses in Mexico and the United States. It provided a forum for US and Mexican union leaders to brainstorm how best to institutionalize Labor Rights Week in the United States. Subsequently, CCIME secured the commitment and support of the SEIU and UFCW to partner with several consulates in implementing Labor Rights Week pilot programs across fifteen consulates.[18] This cohort had observed the successful implementation of a binational health week and sought to host a similar event focused on labor issues. Ultimately, the CCIME structure lasted for only four three-year terms (2002–14) before being dissolved by the IME.

The IME's Impact on Semana/Labor Outreach.   While accounts vary as to the extent of the IME's influence in initiating the Semana, many sources confirmed that CCIME-connected labor leaders in particular were crucial to the coordinated effort. However, IME *consejeros* represented all walks of life. Many were business leaders and represented their own interests, which were frequently at odds with those of a minority of labor leaders. This naturally led to some organizational tensions. For example, after the dissolution of the CCIME, pioneering labor leaders who participated in creating Labor Rights Week confirmed that the SRE was no longer interested in allowing unions to take ownership of the Semana and expand their geographical outreach.[19]

Nonetheless, the IME still cultivated union participation. In May 2008, it held its fifty-fifth *jornada informativa* focused on union leaders with three key objectives: (1) to develop a strategy for collaborating with US union leaders to inform Mexican immigrant workers about their rights, (2) to foster a better understanding of the organizing dynamics in both countries, and (3) to forge networks between Mexican and US union leaders to improve Mexico's international cooperation. Key themes included "Unions and Labor Rights in Mexico," "Consular Protection and Initiatives to Protect Immigrant Worker Rights," "Free Trade in the US, Mexico and Canada," and others related to remittances and financial access (SRE 2008).[20]

The 2004 Joint Declaration and the 2008 Memoranda of Understanding

The SRE's role in regulating immigrant workers' rights was inaugurated in 2004 with an MOU signed by US labor secretary Elaine Chao and Mexican minister of foreign affairs Ernesto Derbez. It established cooperative models between the US DOL Wage and Hour Division, OSHA, and the Mexican consular network via two separate LOAs. This landmark accord emerged during an era when President Vicente Fox had doubled down on outreach to civil society via the consular network.

The 2004 formal bilateral agreements were also the culmination of efforts already under way in regions such as Houston, Dallas, Las Vegas, and Los Angeles, as well as in many other community organizations. OSHA had also been cooperating with national industry groups such as the Hispanic Contractors of America and the National Safety Council (US DOL 2004). The discussions around the MOUs took place alongside significant negotiations around border security (its buildup, militarization, and resulting deaths) and the humane repatriation of Mexican nationals (Storrs 2006). This agreement also increased the role of the DOL's Consular Partnership Program, which solidified migrant worker outreach cooperation (ILAB 2021).

The 2004 MOUs paved the way for establishing formal relationships between the staffs of the DOL, OSHA, and Mexico's consular network. However, the MOUs that established the Semana resulted less from interagency planning than from successful pilot programs supported by labor unions (SEIU and UFCW) and rolled out by consulates in California and Chicago in 2006 and 2007, immediately following the massive immigrant rights mobilizations organized by migrant civil society across the United States (Pallares and Flores González 2010; Voss and Bloemraad 2011). In 2008, the CCIME—with support from key *consejeros* representing labor union leadership (Eliseo Medina for the SEIU and Esther López for UFCW)—recommended to the SRE that the Labor Rights Weeks of Chicago and California be expanded. The Mexican embassy realized that it had sufficient strategic partnerships to make Labor Rights Week a success, and DOL leadership was also interested in expanding services to Mexican immigrants. The public engagement office of the DOL thus entered into frequent conversations with the Mexican embassy, and the 2008 (and subsequent) MOUs established a cooperative framework between the DOL and a greater number of consulates.

In addition to formalizing long-standing cooperation on the ground, these national agreements formed part of a larger diplomatic strategy. Behind the scenes, the US DOL's Bureau of International Labor Affairs and the Office of the Secretary were working on similar agreements with a dozen other Latin American countries and the Philippines.[21] Beyond the Bureau of International Labor Affairs, the Wage and Hour Division and OSHA played key roles in worker outreach and consular partnerships. In 2002, OSHA created its Alliance Program (OSHA n.d.), which worked closely with the National Institute of Occupational Safety and Health at the Centers for Disease Control, the consular network's Ventanilla de Salud / Health Access Window Program, and the Departamento de Asuntos Comunitarios. Of the 232 OSHA Alliance signatories, consular agreements (32) represent a significant portion, second only to trade associations (89) (OSHA 2021).

Consular relationships with local civil society and government agencies can be traced back to the 1990s in some jurisdictions, especially around the issues of wage theft and workplace safety. Yet this model did not gain formal buy-in from national authorities until the signing of a bilateral MOU in 2008, which established the framework for the Semana de Derechos Laborales / Labor Rights Week. Following the DOL's MOU, other labor agencies followed suit with their own formal agreements, including the EEOC, the NLRB, and, to a lesser extent, the Department of Justice's Office of Special Counsel for Immigration-Related Unfair Employment Practices (which focuses on national-origin discrimination). Each national agency head now signs a stock LOA with its consular counterpart, followed by two- or three-year local arrangements establishing understanding (*arreglos de entendimiento*, AEUs).[22]

As we describe further in chapter 3, signing ceremonies for these agency partnerships are highly publicized displays of renewed commitment between partner stakeholders. They are also a practical opportunity to come together and ensure continuity between constantly rotating consular staff. Further, the partnerships commit US agencies to providing a modicum of outreach to the local consulate. Together, these agencies come up with a theme, a logo, dates, and outreach material for the week's activities. Indeed, the uniformity of the local agreements is meant to serve as a general "floor," a baseline that will ensure a minimum commitment from consular and agency staff, who are very likely to have competing interests and priorities. The agreements also prevent the long bureaucratic delays that constantly amending a diplomatic accord between representatives of two countries would require.[23] Key leadership described these instruments as an "everyday strategic collaboration" helping to defend the rights of Mexican workers, regardless of their immigration status,[24] and they are consequential, especially in jurisdictions where preexisting relationships with enforcement agencies and labor advocates don't exist, or where there are insufficient resources to invest significantly in these goals.

Apart from these mechanisms, very few US labor agency staff do intra-agency work, and in some cases, consular officials themselves report being a key liaison between US agencies on the ground. Differing agency cultures (even between the Wage and Hour Division and OSHA, both at the DOL) can create confusion, as each set of regulators juggle varying inspection and claims processes and industry priorities. Indeed, coordination is not the default, and even domestic labor agencies can operate as a series of siloed departments. This complicated enforcement bureaucracy can be near impossible for immigrants to navigate alone, as workers try to parse which aspects of their workplace experiences are relevant to which agency (as described at the beginning of this chapter).

While state and local labor agencies have become increasingly important actors in the labyrinth of US labor regulation (Fine and Round 2021), formal labor agreements with consulates are far more difficult to establish given the unique bilateral relationship between diplomats and national leaders in their host country. Therefore, embassy officials repeatedly confirmed that LOAs followed a preapproved template, largely out of deference to national protocol and to ensure consistency.[25] Yet in many places LOAs were introduced long after coordination had become the norm, to address rampant wage theft and health/safety violations but also a broader set of issues specific to immigrant workers, such as protections under the Violence Against Women Act, concerns around human trafficking, and other immigrant integration goals. Moreover, hot-button issues such as organized crime in labor recruitment require bilateral cooperation to ensure prosecution, since foreign governments cannot mandate contractor practices in migrant-sending regions. All this demonstrates the ultimate importance of formalized bilateral agreements, difficult as they are to forge.

After a period of stagnation toward the end of the George W. Bush administration, the initial 2004 Chao-Derbez MOU was renewed and updated in May 2010 by Ambassador Arturo Sarukhán and longtime labor advocate and California political leader Hilda Solis when she began her appointment as secretary of labor during the first Obama administration (from 2009 to 2013).[26] It increased the number of participating consular offices to twenty-six, in conjunction with 291 community organizations. By 2011, the entire Mexican consular network had been commissioned to participate, along with ten other members of the Latin American consular corps (Brazil, Chile, Colombia, Costa Rica, the Dominican Republic, El Salvador, Guatemala, Honduras, Nicaragua, and Peru), and by 2014, Argentina, Bolivia, Guatemala, Uruguay, and the Philippines were collaborating as well.[27] These multinational agreements vary significantly depending on the location and capacity of other countries' consular offices and their respective demographic concentrations.

On the Mexican side, this coordination is in part spearheaded by Mexico's undersecretaries for Latin America and the Caribbean, as well as the undersecretary for North America. By many accounts, the annual MOUs stemming from the initial 2008 agreements are largely symbolic. However, the annual signing ceremonies that renew them mark the kickoff of Labor Rights Week and send an important signal that both countries are responsible for the well-being of Mexican immigrant workers.

As noted earlier, this formal partnership began in the early period of the Obama administration, an essential era for immigrant outreach at the DOL. By 2012, toward the end of President Obama's first term, DOL staff had hired additional inspectors, the vast majority of whom were bilingual.[28] An early administration goal to create an office of Migrant Workforce Partnerships (to address the challenge of coordinating the dozens of agency field offices) never came to fruition,[29] but several federal pilot projects for community engagement did emerge in key cities.[30]

In terms of the wider collaborative landscape, our review of consular partnerships found that as of 2020, only eight of the fifty-two consulates had MOUs with all four major federal labor standards enforcement agencies (the Wage and Hour Division, OSHA, the EEOC, and the NLRB). Fifteen consulates had three agency MOUs, eleven had two agency MOUs, and sixteen worked with only one. Out of the 115 collective agreements, the largest plurality (38) were with the Wage and Hour Division, 30 were with the EEOC, 29 with OSHA, and only 18 with the NLRB. This variation stems from the locations and capacities of regional US labor agency offices and the nearby consulate. As table 2 reveals, MOU renewals fluctuate every year and do not necessarily correlate with the number of legal cases consulates see or with how many agencies participate. All told, the MOUs significantly increased bilateral collaboration and improved the labor rights environment for Mexican workers. According to one key agency leader, consular partnership agencies compiled a series of high-visibility reports archiving these successes with Mexico and a number of other (mostly Latin American) countries: for example, collaborations between the consul general of Belize and the Wage and Hour Division in Los Angeles, and between the NLRB and the Philippines embassy in Washington, DC (ILAB 2014a, 2014b, 2014c, 2014d). But detailed updates eventually faded after congressional scrutiny highlighted concerns over potential undue influence from foreign governments.[31] Finally, aside from the national MOUs, local consulates also enter into formal agreements with local offices of federal labor standards enforcement agencies under embassy-approved stock language.

2014: Renewed MOU and National Administrative Office Responses to Petitions

In 2014, the Semana MOU was renewed. At the same time, the respective labor agencies in Mexico and the United States entered into a formal agreement

TABLE 2 Labor Rights Week outreach summary

	# Events	Pop. Served (#)	Legal Protection Identified Cases	Participating Agencies (Federal, State, Unions, Others)	Media Outreach (Interviews, PSAs, Special Programs, Etc.)	Central American and Other Countries' Participating Consulates	MOUs with Wage & Hour Division, OSHA, EEOC, NLRB
2009	199	18,788	829	255	137	N/A	N/A
2010	432	39,192	1,534	245	151	N/A	N/A
2011	809	35,745	1,462	625	432	10	11
2012	745	37,048	1,286	610	661	8	15
2013	793	60,284	719	698	326	13	49
2014	793	40,886	826	663	399	13	20
2015	840	59,490	1,045	852	464	16	62
2016	947	59,547	803	699	368	18	59
2017	741	72,156	797	649	338	18	19
2018	895	42,683	340	655	295	14	45

SOURCE: SRE (2019).

establishing a concrete outreach plan to address migrant workplace protections. This accord came on the heels of three public petitions (submitted in 2003, 2005, and 2011) by advocacy organizations demanding accountability under the NAALC mechanisms. From the perspective of embassy staff, these public petitions prompted a long-planned, coordinated bilateral outreach, though as chapter 5 expounds, one could also view Mexico's response as prompted exclusively by the decade-long transnational campaigns launched by grassroots advocates. Embassy staff explained that while the NAALC effectively covered the high-level bilateral economic policies and technical cooperation that shaped migrant work, the agreement had "stagnated" over time. Missing was the formalization of community-level mechanisms, fulfilled by the subsequent work plan, which officially included twenty-five workshops in the United States and eleven workshops (the first of their kind) in Mexico, some of them coinciding conveniently with Labor Rights Week.

In response to the "recommendations" offered by NGO petitions, predeparture workshops aimed at workers with H-2 temporary visas were eventually conducted in Mexico, as well as postdeparture ones in reception areas in the United States. The workshops were held between August of 2014 and February of 2015 and focused on "pre- and postdeparture" issues for H-2A and H-2B guest workers in the top eleven sending states (Estado de México, Guanajuato, Hidalgo, Jalisco, Michoacán, Oaxaca, Querétaro, San Luis Potosí, Sinaloa, Veracruz, and Zacatecas) and in twenty-nine high-impact areas identified by the US DOL across fourteen American states. This was the first time that Mexico had engaged in these predeparture workshops, which sought to inform migrants of their rights before they traveled north and which were run in conjunction with state governments and NGOs (such as Centro de los Derechos del Migrante and other petitioners), and at times even with the US embassy.

These "pilot phase" workshops in communities of origin were folded into the Semana rubric and operated with support from the STPS, which signed a separate joint declaration with the DOL, as well as from the SRE's General Directorate of Delegations and various NGOs. Key topics pertaining to guest workers, dubbed *actividades espejo* (mirror activities),[32] were also simultaneously folded into US consular activities. The theme for the 2015 Semana was "Yo tengo derechos en mi lugar de trabajo" (I have rights in the workplace), and all told, the week boasted more than eight hundred organized events across the fifty-office consular network, US labor agencies, and various unions and community organizations (SRE 2015).

With regard to actually managing the flow of Mexican workers, the STPS's Coordinación General del Servicio Nacional de Empleo, in coordination with the Mexican embassy, helps direct guest worker recruitment and contracting in the United States and Canada. However, only one staff member from the STPS is dedicated to fulfilling the mission's agency (i.e., protecting the rights of Mexican workers), and budgetary support from the SRE for outreach in the United States is limited largely to the mostly one-off events outlined in the Mexican work plan.

On the US governmental side, the DOL has conducted successful outreach activities in conjunction with the consular network in the United States. According to Mexican embassy staff, the activities coordinated through the Consular Partnership Program at the US DOL are uniquely ambitious in their magnitude and unrivaled by other countries, which typically relegate "labor issues" to their offices of commercial and economic affairs. These innovations are appropriate to the hegemonic presence of Mexico in the US immigration and consular structures, but it is unclear how far they take us on the path to securing workers' rights.

For example, the work plans under the labor side accords left a great deal of uncertainty about future initiatives. As one STPS official put it: "Both governments want to wrap up what is established by the declaration and work plan, publish results . . . and until then, it is hard to say for certain what comes next. But trust me, there is a lot of interest on both sides to continue this effort."[33] However, they stressed the need for continued attention to and advocacy for migrant labor rights, especially given the lack of any legal instrument that would compel new actions with the United States or with Canada's Seasonal Agricultural Workers Program. Mexican officials we spoke with indicated that long-term plans for permanent outreach remained uncertain, whether under the NAALC mandate or other ministerial priorities.

In effect, the partnership between Mexico and the United States can be characterized as a supply-side effort (reflecting the shifting positionality of the Mexican government vis-à-vis its emigrants). Yet it is also apparent that government accountability resulted from the demands of persistent migrant labor advocates on both sides of the border (which we discuss in more depth in chapter 5). For example, when a notorious visa fraud case unfolded in Mexico against Chambamex/ChambaMéxico—the largest of its kind on behalf of guest workers in the United States (EstanciaGyM 2014)—it was transnational groups such as the Centro de los Derechos del Migrante / Migrant Rights Center, the Global Workers Justice Alliance – Jornaleros SAFE project, the Instituto de Estudios y Divulgación sobre Migraciones / Institute for Studies and Disclosure on Migration, and the Proyecto de Derechos Económicos, Sociales y Culturales / Economic, Social, and Cultural Rights Project (ProDESC)[34] that pushed the Mexican government to conduct predeparture programs in Mexico to prepare departing guest workers and to advise them after they experienced abuses in the United States.[35] These organizational leaders have been described repeatedly as NGO collaborators, but (as discussed in more detail in chapter 5), our work shows that they are also claimants who seek to hold US agencies, employers who operate with impunity, and the Mexican government accountable.

Even in cities where advocates work closely with the Mexican consulate around immigrant advocacy, transnational labor solidarity efforts often target the local consulate as well (Shafer 2011). For an example of such transnational solidarity, consider the 2017 trinational conference on worker solidarity in action hosted in Chicago by the United Electrical, Radio and Machine Workers of America to discuss the organized labor response to NAFTA negotiations. There, union members representing the Sindicato Independiente de Trabajadores de La Jornada / Independent Trade Union of Workers of "La Jornada" (SITRAJOR), a Mexico City union, requested support from conference attendees to protest the decision made by a Mexico-based labor arbitration and conciliation board on the illegality of their summer strike over management's cutting of worker benefits by around 50 percent at the left-leaning Mexican newspaper. With support from UFCW, a small group of participants managed to secure a meeting with the Mexican consul to hand-deliver a letter with SITRAJOR's position while the rest of the conference participants organized a lively protest outside of the Mexican consulate in solidarity with SITRAJOR workers.[36] This action demonstrates the power of cross-border labor solidarity networks at both the national and transnational levels, garnering support from Mexican workers in Chicago and elsewhere for labor struggles in Mexico City by bringing attention to Mexico's labor violations to the public in the United States.

THE MEXICAN CONSULATE AS A KEY INSTITUTION FOR LABOR ADVOCACY

Who Are SRE and Consular Staff?

The consular network is mostly staffed by civil service officials (Servicio Exterior Mexicano, also known as SEM) who are selected and trained as diplomats through a rigorous process. The diplomatic corps includes various college-educated professionals such as scientists, engineers, economists, administrators, and international relations experts, among others. Its members represents different social classes but are mostly mestizos. They are not formally trained in the cultural sensitivities around precarious Mexican workers who have low levels of formal education and who often speak Spanish as a second language and identify as indigenous.

The consular network also includes non-SEM political appointees, who serve for specific terms and do not belong to the diplomatic civil service, and personnel usually hired from the community. However, these so-called local positions are sometimes staffed by people on loan from the central offices in Mexico City with special A-2 temporary labor visas. Consular personnel with A-2 visas and local personnel earn comparatively low wages and enjoy fewer benefits than the diplomatic corps, as a college degree is not always required to serve in various administrative positions.[37]

The diplomatic corps affiliated with the civil service has high turnover, with appointments lasting a maximum of six years at the same consular jurisdiction. The rotation of highly trained diplomatic staff makes it difficult to create long-term relationships with civil society organizations and local labor standards organizations.

The Consular Network, Its Functions and Resources

The Consular Partnership Program at the DOL (which includes the Wage and Hour Division and OSHA), has a formal staff dedicated to immigrant worker outreach and is coordinated through the DOL's Bureau of International Labor Affairs. In most places, this program primarily deals with the Mexican consulate, but in other hyperdiverse cities, partnerships with over a dozen other countries are involved as well.

The Mexican consular corps has grown over time and now includes fifty-seven offices in North America (SRE 2021b). These are located in traditional Mexican immigrant destinations such as Los Angeles, Houston, and Chicago but also in newer destinations in the South and Midwest. The consular network's primary function is processing documentation such as birth certificates, marriage certificates, passports, and the famed *matrícula consular* (consular ID), which has become increasingly important for those immigrants unable to access US-based documentation. While citizens may process a passport at any office, since 2001 *matrículas* can be requested only in the relevant jurisdiction. Consular staff rely on the information gathered from these transactions to track the size and profile of their local Mexican population, especially the undocumented, who principally rely on *matrículas* as a means to show proof of residence at banks, car dealerships, real estate offices, and so on.[38]

Consular offices vary widely in terms of the size of their physical space, their personnel, and the US jurisdictions with which they overlap. For example, the now-defunct consulate in Anchorage covers the entirety of the state of Alaska, while the consulate in Atlanta covers all of Georgia and Alabama, as well as seventy-four counties in Tennessee. By contrast, the states of Arizona and California are currently divided across several consular offices. As a result, consular advocates must help their citizens navigate a labyrinth of local laws, which are compiled in a classified master profile, the Carpeta Informativa Básica Consular (CIBAC; Basic Consular Information Binder), handed to each new consular leadership team. From the publicly available portions of the most recent CIBAC we were able to acquire (dated October 2012), the jurisdictional assignments can be thoroughly confusing and inconvenient. Office locations may also change, as was the case with the short-lived Alaska office, which opened in 2009 but then closed in 2015 because of budgetary constraints. The growing but relatively small Mexican population there must again rely on Seattle's office for support (Hillman 2015).

In addition to the fixed consular office, each jurisdiction deploys a mobile consulate, which is crucial for extending services beyond the cities in which consular staff are regularly located. This mobility is more consequential for some wide-ranging jurisdictions, such as the San Francisco office of the Mexican consulate, which also covers Hawaii. But the mobile consulate is also critical for those vulnerable populations for whom a trip to the local consulate office is unsafe (as is the case in regions riddled with border patrol checkpoints) or unfeasible because of costs and transportation constraints. Like the permanent office, mobile consulates issue key documents such as *matrículas consulares*, passports, voter identification cards, and birth/death/marriage certificates and conduct community outreach related to various health and social service efforts (Castañeda and Arango 2014; Dudley 2014). Mobile consulates rely on community organizations to host daylong outreach efforts and to get the word out to Mexican migrants in the area. Though they fill an important need, these outreach events (which typically occur no more than a few times a year in a given location) fall far short of the need in any given region.[39] Attendees must still reserve an appointment through the difficult-to-navigate MEXITEL system for consular appointments, and mobile consulates rely on the availability of Departamento de Documentación staff, who are in charge of verifying the authenticity of identification documents and of issuing passports and *matrículas*. While an office may also deploy a *consulado sobre ruedas* / consulate on wheels (which contracts out additional staff), this model is far more expensive and less common (SRE n.d.-c).

Over time, the budget for the SRE (and thus for consular offices and diplomacy in North America) has also decreased, first during the Calderón administration and then again under López Obrador, who emphasized national security as opposed to foreign relations. Yet it is also clear that the vast majority of these diplomatic funds are predictably concentrated in North America, despite the growing importance of Europe and Asia as receiving areas of Mexican migrants (Farfán Mares and Velázquez Flores 2012).

Aside from consular offices, the central SRE office in Mexico City staffs "delegations" throughout the interior of Mexico, which process passports and provide other key service functions in a devolution framework (SRE n.d.-d). These offices are also unevenly staffed, with the largest concentration of personnel in various sites across the country's capital cities as well as Monterrey, Nuevo León (at the border), and Guadalajara, Jalisco (also a major migrant-sending region). Central states with large populations of migrants in the United States, such as Michoacán and Guanajuato, have several satellite offices scattered throughout their regions to save their citizens unnecessary trips to the delegation to get a passport (a task that can be accomplished only in person, even for renewals). In states with a long tradition of transnational relations, migrant organizations have successfully advocated for more satellite offices. For example, the state of Michoacán has twelve satellite offices in addition to the central delegation in the capital city of Morelia.

Consular offices also vary substantially in their funding and personnel capacity. Allocations are based on revenues (typically from documentation requests), yet these resources are recouped by the central Secretaría de Hacienda y Crédito Público / Finance Ministry, then redistributed to individual offices—via a formula contested by many constituencies, who charge that it underfunds large jurisdictions with high demand. According to budget analysis by Farfán and Velázquez (2012), most of the allocations for the SRE are for salaries and operating expenses, and the authors characterize Mexico's approach as largely "incremental and discretionary," reflecting a strategy that is "reactive, improvised, and at times a low priority" (91). For instance, offices receive only 15 percent back from document fees,[40] and the cost of passports is typically US$165 for ten years (SRE 2021c); this seldom leaves offices with sufficient financial resources. Congressional leaders have long been lobbying for the Secretaría de Hacienda y Crédito Público to double this return (Comisión de Relaciones Exteriores 2021, 8). In 2020, in the shadow of the COVID-19 pandemic, the IME, the Departamento de Protección, and the Consular Services network suffered sizable budget cuts around 10–15 percent, though in a formal opinion issued to Congress a commission made clear the need to increase support for legal protection and body repatriation services despite the reigning austerity measures (Comisión de Relaciones Exteriores 2021, 7). Funding models also vary significantly within consular offices. For example, the famed Ventanilla de Salud, typically housed within the Department of Community Affairs, had a very modest budget under the Ministry of Health to cover coordination, support year-round activities, and put on the annual Binational Health Week event hosted by the consular network (SRE 2018). In the Departamento de Protección, however, no such resources are earmarked for labor protection. On the basis of public information requests to the Instituto Nacional de Transparencia, Acceso a la Información y Protección de Datos Personales / National Institute of Transparency, Information Access and Private Data Protection (SHCP 2021), as well as conversations with several embassy staff members, funding for the annual Semana / Labor Rights Week appears to be discretionary.[41] Again, our queries revealed no analogous specific appropriation for labor protection.

This is not to say that Mexico's commitment to helping workers mobilize their workplace protection is entirely symbolic. Indeed, as some officials argued, the allocation of Mexican government staff in Washington, DC, represents a financial commitment to realizing the assurances set forth in the 2004 and 2008 declarations. Furthermore, in 2017 the SRE began an initiative to increase services to Mexican migrants (Fortalecimiento para la Atención a Mexicanos en Estados Unidos). This one-time infusion of funds allocated a total of roughly $1.07 billion MX pesos by executive discretion to five key priority areas: (1) human resources (320 service contracts) (17 percent), (2) legal protection programs for Mexicans in the exterior (67 percent), (3) consular services (5 percent), (4) alimony and other family support ("Protección al Patrimonio") (5 percent), and (5) support for migrants via delegation offices (6 percent) (SRE n.d.-c). This largest allocation—for legal protection, administered by the DGPME—included resources for a referral hotline, outreach and representation, coordination with local authorities and community advocates, rapid response mechanisms, "Know Your Rights" workshops, help with collective demands, and prison visits. It is important to note, though, that labor protection is only one of several priorities for the consular network's Departamento de Protección (as we outline later in this chapter).

Despite these various supports, many popular and journalistic accounts have highlighted the frustration that the general public feels when seeking help from the underresourced and crowded consular offices (Avilés 2020), a situation only made worse by the COVID-19 pandemic (Conexión Migrante 2021; F. Martínez 2021). The vast majority of individuals approach the local consulate for vital records and travel documents, which must adhere to a strict and unforgiving set of rules subject to audit, much as the local DMV, county coroner, or Social Security office would. For decades, the Mexican government has sought to streamline the process for returnees attempting to prove their nationality (*presunción de nacionalidad*) (Gómez Arnaud 1990) while avoiding presumably fraudulent attempts by the rising number of Central Americans fleeing north (Suárez et al. 2017). Nonetheless, errors related to compound surnames and other misunderstandings abound.

Consular offices, especially in cities with large Mexican communities, almost always have a line winding around the building. The public must then pass through a gate manned by a (contracted) security guard into a waiting room before proceeding to an appointment with a frontline street bureaucrat who has little job security or power to exercise discretion. Even if the handling of a disagreement is passed up to a consul, the bureaucracy's rigidity and internal divisions can still stall a case depending on socioeconomic or nationalistic factors (Lomnitz 2001). Yet consulates are important lifelines for migrant communities, who could otherwise end up effectively stateless, without their country's recognition or access to documentation (CMS n.d.; UNHCR 2021). Consulates also have the ability to provide rapid-response documentation when US policies create openings, as they did during the 2012 and 2014 deferred-action programs (SRE 2021a).

Consular Labor Protection Services

The Mexican consulate's Departamento de Protección is the key entity for deploying labor rights resources and outreach (often in conjunction with the Departamento de Asuntos Comunitarios). Drawing on data from three consulates (El Paso, Raleigh, and San Francisco), Martínez-Schuldt, Hagan, and Weissman (2021) found that consulates help workers throughout the labor claims process, provide a wide range of services (from general information to legal referrals to in-house counsel), help broker interactions with various actors (including between migrants, with lawyers, and with other Mexican institutions), and can even be resources in the wake of an unsuccessful claim.

According to the 2013 *Guía de procedimientos de protección consular* (SRE 2013), the department encompasses a wide array of legal arenas, including human rights, immigration, criminal, administrative, civil, other special interest, and labor issues. Yet it is important to note that despite the binational agreements described above, there is no set budget for labor outreach. Rather, there are only norms for expenditures, laid out by case and expense type (SRE 2011c). For example, there is a maximum $1,000 allowance for contracted services (direct payments to a service provider), to be allocated if and only if a PALE resource (the Programa de Asistencia Jurídica a Personas Mexicanas a través de Asesorías Legales Externas en los Estados Unidos de América / Legal Assistance Program to Mexicans by Attorneys in the United States) has been pursued. (We discuss PALE further in the next section.) Any greater expenditure requires authorization from the DGPME. Criminal and immigration issues are overseen separately from civil and labor issues (SRE 2011a), and there is evidence that the consular network has shifted more of its resources toward penal cases after the interior enforcement program Secure Communities was reactivated during the Obama administration (Martínez-Schuldt 2020). This funding structure creates enormous pressures to stretch meager legal protection resources, as criminal cases can quickly consume the budget of any consulate because of the excessive cost of defense counsel in the US justice system.

Various mechanisms have been put in place over the years to facilitate consular legal advocacy. In some jurisdictions (including in California and Florida), the Programa de Asistencia Jurídica Telefónica Gratuita (JURIMEX) ran a 24/7 free hotline for legal advice. This program was eventually replaced by the network-wide Centro de Información y Asistencia a Mexicanos / Center for Assistance and Information to Mexicans (CIAM) hotline (SRE n.d.-a). The hotline was started in part in response to Arizona's infamous 2010 law, Senate Bill 1070, known as the "show me your papers law." Embassy staff emphasized that CIAM was available to anyone, and the hotline was an important resource during the "migration surge" of Central American migrants (among them unaccompanied minors.)[42] CIAM was envisioned as a more comprehensive resource than the locally based labor hotlines in places like Los Angeles (EMPLEO [Employment, Education and Outreach]), New York (LABORAL), and Houston (Justice and Equality in the Workplace). Most of these hotlines rely on volunteers to answer calls, often in conjunction with both consular and labor agency staff.

Today, CIAM runs a massive hotline out of Tucson offering global legal referrals of all sorts, including in Mexico. Public information requests reveal that the largest proportion of calls to CIAM originate in the United States (from 2013 to 2020, 1,186,543 out of 1,546,67) and that the largest proportion are information queries to the Departamento de Protección (593,847 out of 1,546,672).[43] Specifically within the category of labor cases, from 2010 to 2018, 37,021 calls came in, with the most frequent type of query involving what are known as "wage theft cases" (see table 3). In general, consular personnel are available to give general information (often in conjunction with community advocates), but as the *Guía de Procedimientos de Protección Consular* emphasizes, consular staff cannot represent workers in hearings or at trial.

In some cases, consular staff may contract with lawyers through the PALE program. From 2018 to 2021, PALE issued 310 total contracts. The number and types

TABLE 3 Labor cases intake at the Mexican consular network in the United States

	2010	2011	2012	2013	2014	2015	2016	2017	2018	Total
Labor discrimination	94	60	77	89	91	92	95	66	51	1,336
Workers' compensation	499	376	309	305	322	318	310	227	205	5,239
General info/ various	778	831	690	1,066	494	2,453	1,737	1,512	552	19,445
Wage theft	783	768	493	481	325	749	439	258	243	8,292
Labor rights violations	119	107	21	83	185	280	151	139	70	2,234
Labor trafficking	25	39	18	16	21	31	20	41	39	475
	2,298	2,181	1,608	2,040	1,438	3,923	2,752	2,243	1,160	37,021

SOURCE: SRE (2020).

of legal contracts (obtained through public records request) vary by city, and even within a state, patterns are not consistent. For example, Los Angeles saw the largest number of legal contracts (sixteen), seven of whose providers were classified as NGOs, while the border town of Eagle Pass, Texas, had only one contracted lawyer listed (based out of San Antonio, over two hours away) (SRE 2021d).

Each consulate's team of *abogados consultores* is a mix of pro bono volunteers and eligible paid contractors consulted when consular officials deem a case worthy of further investment and support. These services, however, are very limited, and not all affiliated attorneys are interested in taking cases that are either complex or difficult to win, or for which the demand for services is simply too widespread—as is the case with wage theft. Many of these cases thus go unprosecuted, and claimants have little recourse if the fundamental information for establishing a case is missing, as often occurs. As the Trump administration got under way and anti-immigrant public sentiment and state-sanctioned practices increased (CNN Español 2017; Cárdenas Suárez, Morayta, and Mabire 2019), President Peña Nieto responded to calls to add more resources to the Departamento de Protección. However, our review of these allocations concluded that they were extremely modest given the enormous need.

Consular Labor Outreach and Diplomatic Neutrality

The negotiations and agreements that have emerged over the last few decades are not the Mexican government's first foray into the migrant labor protection arena. Indeed, the eminent historian of the Bracero Program Gilbert González (1999) has revealed evidence of similar consular support of (government-sponsored) workers' unions. However, other scholars have documented government meddling that has undercut workers' rights, sometimes even resulting in their blacklisting (Vosko 2016). Therefore, the common refrain that we heard—that consulates are a neutral diplomatic entity that must follow the diplomatic protocol of nonintervention—is not entirely borne out by the historical record.

Some consular officials cited bylaws that prohibited them from commenting on US practices to avoid being construed as meddling in their host country's affairs. While a certain amount of commentary is allowed and does occur (González Gutiérrez 2019), diplomats must walk a fine line. In practice, this often means that voicing direct criticism, joining picket lines, and advocating labor strikes are prohibited. However, there are many examples where consular officials seem to tacitly support labor struggles, as when the consul general in California stressed the need to ensure that all building construction took place with union labor in order to maintain good relationships with Democratic leaders. Similarly, the Chicago consulate has allowed unions to use its space during organizing drives. Moreover, during the Trump administration, many consular officials and other diplomats went on record to criticize efforts to dismantle Deferred Action for Childhood

Arrivals (DACA) (Verel 2017), prolong family separation (Murray 2018), and build the border wall (Lara 2017).

At the local level, consular officials appeared to speak out more freely on issues, including capital punishment cases, which were often seen as human rights abuses in Mexico, where the death penalty does not exist (Navarro 2017). The politics of the southern border have increasingly become another sensitive topic for Mexico, especially as almost no Mexicans are granted asylum in the United States and Mexico has been increasingly roped into carrying out the US government's immigration directives through policies such as "Remain in Mexico," which have produced the sprawling camps for asylum seekers in untenable conditions in border cities such as Tijuana and Cd. Juárez (Kanno-Youngs 2020). This program was officially ended by President Biden in June of 2021, but a federal court compelled the Biden administration to restart the program in December of the same year while promising improved mechanisms to solve most asylum cases within six months (Human Rights Watch 2022). President López Obrador has defended the program, claiming that Mexico is now registering migrants to protect them and prevent migrant assassinations (López Obrador 2020). However, migrants continue to be frequent victims of crime while waiting in Mexico, regardless of being registered in the program. Moreover, Mexico has been roundly criticized for doing the US's dirty work by using heavy-handed tactics to "manage" northward migration from Central America (Correa-Cabrera 2020). This heated issue is complicated by the inconvenient fact that the greatest number of immigrants *in* Mexico are white Americans living in resort towns like Sayulita (M. Smith and Guarnizo 2009; Noriega and Gómez 2017). More than half (64.3 percent) of Mexico's foreign-born population were born in the United States, and almost a third arrived between 2015 and 2020. In Mexico, the number of Guatemalan, Salvadoran, and Honduran migrants represent less than 11 percent of the total foreign-born population. To be sure, Mexico still has an insignificant foreign-born population (1.2 million in 2020), less than 1 percent of the total population (Masferrer and Pedroza 2021).

The consular apparatus may espouse generally cautious diplomatic tendencies vis-à-vis Mexican-US bilateral affairs and other sensitive issues—opting instead to work toward feasible goals in a compartmentalized agenda (Ramírez García and Castillo 2012)—but at the local level, most consular officials strive to get their message out forcefully. As consular staff were quick to explain, all consular offices have a "community outreach mandate." In some cases, a consular official may reach out to a community organization, and in others, the community organization may seek out a relationship with consular staff. Local businesses with a significant Mexican clientele can also play a role in distributing worker education, though in some communities those local businesses have a track record of labor abuses (Mangaliman 2007).

And apart from the litany of centralized formal accords administered from the Mexican Embassy in Washington, there is a second track for consular collaboration.

Embassy staff recognize the importance of the rich history of *local* coordination, as in the pioneering office in Chicago (which benefits from a tight-knit base of labor unions that were key to consular coordination, such as UFCW), and those in Houston (which created the Justice and Employment in the Workplace Partnership), Los Angeles (which operates the EMPLEO hotline), and Sacramento (which collaborates with a university-based law clinic). Some of these relationships emerged "organically," without the centralized coordination of the SRE.

Furthermore, prior to the existence of the bilateral agreement, many local consular officials were already seeking out relationships with labor standards enforcement agencies, often brokered by community advocates working on behalf of immigrant workers. This was the case, for example, in the late 1990s in Mississippi, where a relatively recent flow of Mexican migrants were working in the fisheries. These immigrants relied on local churches and groups such as the Mississippi Immigrants Rights Alliance, which also worked hand in hand with the local consulate, OSHA, and the Wage and Hour Division.[44] Frontline federal inspectors played an important role in building these relationships, even if agency leadership turned over. In this context, the Semana was an attempt to join and brand these disparate efforts under a uniform protocol for cooperation with an annual theme.

LABOR RIGHTS WEEK

Origins of the Semana

Chicago was considered one of the pioneers, having carried out the first Semana in 2008. This event laid the foundation of the wider Semana, which was launched formally in 2009 with a pilot group of fifteen consular offices, under the direction of then secretary of labor (and former Los Angeles labor advocate) Hilda Solis. Embassy staff reported that in 2010, 291 organizations were registered as participants in the Semana. These included federal/federated groups such as the League of United Latin American Citizens (LULAC) and the National Council of La Raza (now UnidosUS), among others.

The first Semana was held around Labor Day as a way to highlight the various events that were already happening throughout the year. It was the first time the consular network coordinated these efforts around a central theme, based in large part on Chicago's model. The pilot cohort of Semana participants were selected on the basis of three criteria, according to embassy staff: (1) local consular capacity, (2) previous experience collaborating with key actors, and (3) the availability of resources and allies who could roll out the initiative. Once the various events were grouped under the Semana framework, the Mexican government coordinated outreach activities and a menu of collaborative strategies, such as talks hosted by mobile consulates, school-based workshops, or visits to local worker centers. Some locations also hosted film or theater presentations. However, as staff emphasized, each locality was free to follow "local norms" with "local allies."[45] More broadly, proactive consuls helped spread the program by instituting their unique models across offices, as did Joanna Navarrete, a former consul in Chicago who later moved to Boston and seeded similar collaborations.

In sum, the Semana de Derechos Laborales is a key civil society destination along the long arc bending toward greater US and Mexican accountability on immigrant workers' rights. Logistically, staging the event has required coordination between different units of the SRE, including the Consultoría Jurídica, the Dirección General de Comunicación Social, the Dirección General de Delegaciones, and the DGPME (and specifically the Dirección de Protección para Estados Unidos de América).[46] While the Mexican embassy in the United States and the US DOL signed a joint accord laying out general principles for the Semana, the Dirección de Protección para Estados Unidos de América coordinates a menu of on-the-ground activities and tracks attendance, caseload, participating agencies, press coverage, partner consulates, and local agreement renewals.

Initially a direct collaboration with the DOL, Labor Rights Week aimed to improve the Latino community's understanding of workplace rights and the resources available to them in the event they experienced a workplace violation. These goals built off the existing "preventative protection and follow-up" work that the Mexican government was already undertaking. In addition to circulating outreach material published by US regulatory agencies and advocates, the SRE produced guides outlining key themes such as workplace safety, wage and hour rules, guidelines governing guest work, discrimination protections, leave policies, and collective bargaining rights. These comprehensive guides also focus on the dynamics of "independent contractors"—many of whom are misclassified—and the rights of domestic workers (who are often excluded from key protections) (SRE and Consulado General de México en Chicago 2020).

Key Themes and Actors

Semana activities are centrally approved but are supported on the ground by local labor agencies and civil society collaborators. Nevertheless, national MOUs and local AEUs play an important role in the planning. Following the signing ceremony, the embassy circulates a memo to consular staff noting the importance of the week and providing a menu of events and workshops, as well as a list of "best practices" to make the week a success. One embassy official described the content of the memo matter-of-factly: "The Semana de Derechos Laborales is this week, this is the theme, these are the important uniform themes we want to communicate."[47] Then, in conjunction with local partners—and according to their respective capacities and priorities—"Each consulate plans a local program."[48] This centralized messaging ensures some continuity from place to place and from year to year. Starting in 2011 (the third year of the annual week), Semana themes covered specific topics such as women (2011) and education (2013); other themes have included the universality of worker rights, the importance of dignity, and the essential nature of labor protections, especially in the midst of the COVID pandemic (table 4).

TABLE 4 Yearly themes for the Semana de Derechos Laborales (2009–20)

Order	Year	Theme
1st	2009	(inaugural Semana de Derechos Laborales)
2nd	2010	(no theme)
3rd	2011	Women in the Workplace
4th	2012	Promoting Labor Rights Is Everyone's Responsibility
5th	2013	New Century Worker: Your Education and Work Count!
6th	2014	We All Have Workplace Rights
7th	2015	I Have Rights in the Workplace
8th	2016	Your Work Has Dignity! Know Your Rights
9th	2017	Know Your Rights at Work: The Well-Informed Worker
10th	2018	All Workers Have Rights
11th	2019	The Value of Your Work
12th	2020	Your Rights, Like You, Are Essential

SOURCE: Personal communication, Secretaría de Relaciones Exteriores, March 17, 2021.

Labor Rights Week activities are only a small part of the programming held throughout the year in many jurisdictions. Yet focusing on the frenzy of this week is useful, as it reveals the messaging and intentionality of consular efforts around labor advocacy. To this end, our research team assessed the last decade of consular labor rights outreach through a combination of mainstream and ethnic news media archives, social media searches (Facebook, Twitter), and advanced Google searches of Labor Rights Week events (including individual consulate websites, which in general are not frequently updated).

While the yearly themes set by the SRE are fairly generic, specific programming topics vary depending on the priorities of local civil society partners. Depending on capacity, Labor Rights Week outreach may focus specifically on a particular labor issue or more broadly on a menu of legal concerns. Information session topics have included DACA, U- and T-visas, the rights of H-2A and H-2B guest workers, wage theft, workplace safety and health, discrimination and sexual harassment protections, and even community leadership training. For one office, the focus may be on high rates of injury and fatalities on construction sites, for another, heat safety in agriculture. The Chicago consulate's Ventanilla Laboral / Labor Affairs Window Program advertises, for example, free informational consultations on "labor issues," but it also offers sessions related to immigration, criminal, civil/ family, and other administrative issues. In the midst of the COVID-19 pandemic, this outreach material was paired with flyers from the Farmworker and Landscaper Advocacy Project encouraging individuals to get vaccinated and informing them about where to seek emergency funds (Consulado General de México en Chicago 2022). Outreach activities happened both within and beyond the consular office. For example, the Chicago consulate hosted events at local churches in the communities of Cicero, Bensenville, South Chicago, and Waukegan (Consulado General de México en Chicago 2011).

Local stakeholders are by far the most significant actors in these consular coalitions, many staff confirmed. To be sure, the landscape of local industries and civil society shaped outreach efforts. For example, in California's Central Valley agricultural region, field safety and collaboration with the United Farmworkers predominated. In Chicago, local chapters of national unions such as UFCW, United Electrical Workers, the SEIU, and United Auto Workers, alongside several prominent worker centers, kicked off the week's events. Consular activities in Washington, DC, included the pan-Latino advocacy group VACOLAO (Virginia Coalition of Latino Organizations) and legal aid groups such as Maryland Legal Aid and the Legal Aid Justice Center. In Atlanta, partners included not only the local Georgia Immigrant and Refugee Rights Coalition but also a business group—the Hispanic Construction Association. And in "new destination" communities such as Omaha, Labor Rights Week relied on a tight community of nonprofit and faith partners such as Catholic Charities, the Heartland Workers Center, Justice for Our Neighbors, the Latino Center of the Midlands, Nebraska Appleseed, One World, and the University of Nebraska.

As one Mexican embassy staff member explained, some offices may rely almost exclusively on information sent by Mexico City offices, which they then translate into public service announcements distributed locally, while others utilize far more autonomy and tap into local resources.[49] A consulate's collaboration with local decision makers is, however, dependent on the extent to which they have developed relationships with and educated local officials about their role, as one official noted. From this perspective, embassy staff stressed the need to be nimble rather than to apply strategies uniformly at the local level: "It's important that each consulate has the space to develop strategies and methods in their annual programming . . . and to work with the most pertinent agencies."[50] As such, local civil society (e.g., churches, day labor centers, hometown associations, civil rights advocates, legal service providers) provides "natural communication channels," which consular officials use to disseminate information and to dialogue with local communities. These groups are critical logistically as well for everything from organizing mobile consulate days to conducting outreach to agricultural camps to visiting prisons: "They multiply our capacity to see and hear what is happening in our communities across the country," this staff member explained.[51]

In places where the Mexican consulate is part of a much larger consular corps (as in New York, Washington, DC, and Los Angeles), it also plays an important role as a convener for other Latin American consulates. In many cases, MOU signing ceremonies were jointly held with the US labor secretary and a collection of ambassadors from other countries, in conjunction with the agency's Consular Partnership Program. For example, at the tenth anniversary of the EMPLEO program in Los Angeles, the Mexican consul general was joined by counterparts from several Central American consulates. And that same year, DOL representatives in Los Angeles met with consular officials from the People's Republic of China (ILAB 2014b). During Labor Rights Week, agencies also coordinate outreach efforts across consular partners, either to cosign material to be distributed or to rotate workshops throughout the various consular offices.

While the diplomatic standing of consular officials permits them to sign official bilateral MOUs only with national counterparts, several consulates have also coordinated with state and sometimes local agencies. For example, Chicago's 2009 Semana kicked off with remarks by an official from Illinois's DOL and Department of Human Rights, who spoke alongside the US DOL (Consulado General de México en Chicago 2009). In Fresno, California, consular officials have worked with California's Agricultural Labor Relations Board, the sole state-level agency in the country focused on implementing the collective bargaining rights of farmworkers, who are excluded from federal protections. Across that state, the California Board of Workers Compensation, the Division of Labor Standards Enforcement, the Department of Fair Employment and Housing, and Cal-OSHA all enforce protections that surpass federal minimums, highlighting the importance of consular-state collaboration. In Orlando, Florida's Department of Economic Opportunity, Division of Workforce Services, and the Department of Agriculture and Consumer Services have provided consular outreach, as have Arizona's Division of Occupational Safety and Health in Phoenix and the New York State DOL human trafficking initiative in New York City. Finally, even though it was not an official signatory to the Justice and Equality in the Workplace Partnership in Houston, the Texas Workforce Commission has been a key option for immigrants pursuing wage theft claims. All of these cases demonstrate why consulates must work with state and local agencies as well as federal ones.

CONSULAR LABOR INTAKE STATISTICS

Like any bureaucratic institution, consulates are required to report how many events were held, the type of event, how many people attended, and how many cases were referred to enforcement agencies. According to SRE records, from 2010 to 2018, labor case intake fluctuated, decreasing in some years and then rebounding. Beyond general inquiries, the largest segment of case intake was classified under "wage theft," followed by workers' compensation. Far fewer cases involved discrimination or labor trafficking (see table 3).

Case statistics over the last two years reveal a predictably disproportionate number of cases (three-quarters) brought by men. In some regions, this disparity is even greater: for example, in Milwaukee 271 of 278 cases in 2020 were filed by men. Furthermore, while some consulates are registering dozens of cases each year, other large cities (such as Boston, Miami, and San Jose) have only a handful, though caseloads vary substantially from year to year. It is likely that these generally low numbers reflect a robust system of referring cases to community-based resources. All told, there were 1,154 total cases in 2019 and 1,121 in 2020, reflecting the general reality that the Mexican consulate plays a very small role as a direct service provider to its diaspora of 10.9 million people living in the United States in 2019 (Israel and Batalova 2020).

According to its internal reporting for its recorded highs, consulates collectively hosted 947 events in 2016, served 72,156 individuals (2017), worked with 852 "participating agencies" in government and civil society (2015), and conducted 661 media outreach spots (2012). The number of participating consulates (including and beyond Latin America) had risen to eighteen in 2017.[52] But as SRE staff admit, the growth and success of the annual Labor Rights Week have not translated into enough tangible actions:

> The main challenge for Labor Rights Week is to get the Mexican community to make it to the events held at the consulate and beyond—take advantage of labor agencies who are present and the organizations and lawyers who could take a look at their cases. It's not uncommon for attendees to show up to the consulate . . . this week to deal with their *matrícula* or passport but not necessarily bring with them all the necessary documentation [for their labor case] such as pay stubs and other evidence that would facilitate a more effective consultation. . . . We haven't managed to transform a purely informational event into one that addresses cases. While the number of participants [of the Semana] goes up every year, the number of cases attended [to] does not reflect this.[53]

This problem persists despite the week's success in striking up collaborations with federal and state agencies and labor lawyers.[54] Furthermore, there is a clear imbalance in the types of cases processed by consulates. Consular reports reveal an overwhelming focus on workplace injuries and wage theft. These are certainly two of the most difficult arenas in which to enforce protection, but there are other complex legal arenas such as discrimination and collective bargaining that are not represented in the consular caseload.[55]

CONSULATES THROUGH THE LENS OF COOPERATION AND CONFLICT

In sum, the US labor standards enforcement system is a maze that leaves potential claimants searching for allies who will help them navigate it to secure resources. For Mexican immigrant workers, the local consulate has become one of these key brokers, helping to coordinate the confusing and siloed enforcement arenas. It uses its diplomatic standing to connect with federal counterparts—leveraging this influence to access state and local bureaucracies where possible—in order to help workers identify the best way to file a viable claim and (when relevant) manage the anxieties created by the ever-looming immigration enforcement regime.

Consular staff seek to foster community goodwill but, more important, to build on supranational and bilateral obligations, commitments espoused by recent labor reforms in Mexico and the country's relatively recent turn toward "diaspora diplomacy." Yet Mexico's role in advancing the rights of its export labor is not simply a response to top-down mandates; rather, it stems from demands initiated by domestic and transnational civil society groups. Indeed, labor unions and immigrant rights activists planted the seeds for the Ventanilla Laboral, the yearly Semana, and dozens of partnerships that have become firmly rooted in everyday consular practice today. To be sure, these modestly successful state-society partnerships build on the successes of an increasingly visible transnational-oriented migrant civil society. These advocates managed to institutionalize a now-defunct collective remittance-matching fund to address rural development needs (the famed Tres por Uno program, 2002–20)[56] and achieve the significant restitution of electoral voting rights for all Mexicans living abroad (Pintor-Sandoval 2021).

The annual Labor Rights Week has become a defining consular function and a major coordination feat, as it requires signing LOAs with many federal agencies, maintaining relationships with state and local agencies that are fighting for stronger protections (despite the lack of diplomatic relations), and creating referral networks and working partnerships across the variety of civil society groups in each consular jurisdiction. These events and the accompanying signing ceremonies are critical to ensuring consistent participation, as consular staff inevitably turn over and must juggle various competing federal and state mandates. However, the exact ways in which these partnerships materialize depend on the demographic makeup of the diaspora in a community, the economic and industrial landscape, and the conglomeration of immigrant worker advocates. Moreover, while such elaborate annual public campaigns have become part and parcel of consular protection—and have been formalized through a series of federal memoranda—the realities of these agreements differ radically on the ground.

The institutionalization of Mexico's migrant labor protection program is a major accomplishment and reflects a telling shift from (or ongoing contradiction with) state efforts to interfere with and sometimes actively stifle advocates working to build worker power. Official programming also faces a series of logistical challenges, including the rigidity of diplomatic institutions and personnel. These obstacles call into question the ultimate sustainability of a tripartite enforcement regime in which the sending state is a key actor. Nevertheless, Mexico's shift has paved the way for a long list of other diplomatic actors (from Latin America and beyond) to similarly provide other immigrant communities with a framework for demanding commensurate protections and resources.

The question remains, however, how much practical impact these investments will have, despite the symbolic importance they hold for managing bilateral relations and the demands of a transnational civil society. It is still too early to predict if the two main actors, Mexico's SRE and the US DOL, faced with limited requests from civil society advocates for offering transparency and accountability to direct service government programs, will have the capacity to measure and evaluate the real impact of Labor Rights Week in preventing and/or addressing labor standards violations of Mexican migrant workers in the short, medium, and long term.

3

The Sending State and Co-enforcement

Mexico's Role in Brokering Immigrant Worker
Claims Making

Mexico is an emblematic case of the increasingly active role of origin countries in managing the rights of their diaspora. Yet as described in chapter 2, Mexico's diplomatic presence across North America is in many ways unique. With fifty-seven consular offices across Canada and the United States, it is by far the most imposing actor in the diplomatic corps. And while reports have shown increasing activity of other migrant groups (Indian and Chinese in particular), Mexico is still the top origin country of immigrants in the United States, and almost 97 percent of all emigrants from Mexico reside in the United States (Israel and Batalova 2020; Budiman 2020). Reflecting this demographic strength is the robust bureaucratic apparatus that serves the estimated 10.9 million Mexican migrants living in the United States and the US-born descendants of Mexican citizens who have been eligible to also naturalize since 1997 (Mendoza 2021). This bureaucracy has become an important political actor and resource in cities across the United States. While other countries have an important presence in the United States as well, no other diaspora has the same combination of population size and distribution, relatively amenable bilateral relations, institutional capacity, and a pressing need for institutional support. (Figures 2, 3, and 4 provide an overview of the dispersion of the Mexican population in the United States.)

Mexico's consular offices—the prime instantiation of a foreign country's diplomatic presence—have thus become key actors in labor regulation, at least in places where they have developed relationships with US agencies and civil society partners. Many of these same community partners pushed for greater accountability, an effort that eventually led to the working relationships and legal instruments (national and bilateral) seeking to ensure that Mexico respects migrant worker rights. (Refer to chapters 2 and 5 for the full history of civil society's role in demanding these mandates.) While the 2008 memorandum of understanding on worker rights was struck between Mexico's Secretaría de Relaciones Exteriores / Ministry of Foreign Affairs (SRE) and the US Department of Labor (DOL) (primarily responsible for enforcing protections such as minimum wage and health/safety), other key agencies such as the Equal Employment Opportunity Commission (which sets antidiscrimination standards) and in some cases even the National Labor Relations Board have followed suit with their own agreements.

Yet despite its outsized role, the Mexican consular network is far from the only organization with which these agencies must engage. In fact, in jurisdictions across the United States, states and localities add another layer of enforcement complexity. For example, as of 2021, twenty-nine states and Washington, DC, have more robust minimum-wage laws than federal law mandates, and forty-one localities have set a minimum wage higher than their state minimum wage (Economic Policy Institute 2019). Other jurisdictions have gone even further to institute living-wage laws (Luce 2004) and have instituted their own enforcement bureaucracies that work openly with community partners (Fine and Bartley 2019). While many researchers have highlighted the simultaneous necessity and inadequacy of an individual workplace rights approach in the face of declining collective bargaining and rampant neoliberal policies (Lichtenstein 2002), workplace regulation remains one of the few tools available for checking employer power and defending worker well-being. Local Mexican officials looking to address the workplace rights of their emigrant workforce in those communities must become knowledgeable about every layer of this complicated regulatory apparatus.

The Mexican consulate performs a varied set of functions in the labor standards enforcement process year-round, though it is especially active during the long-running Labor Rights Week. In this annual fall event, many consular offices transform into hubs for disseminating information to local communities about their rights in the United States or in their particular states and localities. They host "Know Your Rights" workshops (on- or off-site) and disseminate pamphlets and flyers to attendees who pass through the office. These efforts are by no means a uniform corrective to the structural imbalances in the low-wage labor market. However, such worker outreach is an ostensible action to boost the efforts of government agencies (which often struggle to reach immigrant communities) and of labor advocates (whose resources are also limited).

In addition to in-person programming, many savvy consular offices have developed a significant media presence, releasing information on their Facebook feeds or through local public service announcements on ethnic media; some even host telethons. (Official websites for consular offices tend to be maintained with varying regularity, and social media have been increasingly used as information portals.) Beyond the week dedicated to labor rights—which many argue is a largely symbolic affair—the most proactive consulates cultivate relationships with other co-enforcement actors. These include not only federal and state agency officials but also community advocates who are attuned to community needs and whose experience often far eclipses that of consular officials, who tend to serve short-term assignments in a given city.

A handful of consular offices have gone so far as to host hotlines and contract with private attorneys to provide assistance "in house" to workers seeking help, but most consular offices refer out the vast majority of cases. Nonconsular advocates often guide workers to a US agency or refer them back to a consular office to obtain documentation or additional help in pressuring employers or making inquiries to regulatory agencies. This merry-go-round process frustrates workers, who are spun around to various agencies and organizations before hopefully finding a viable way forward to file a claim. Rare is the consular office that is able to fully and singlehandedly meet the goals laid out in the 2004 memoranda of understanding. Interestingly, a stronger civil society apparatus might actually decrease direct consular involvement. In their assessment of Mexican consular network administrative data (the Sistema Integral de Protección Consular / Comprehensive Consular Protection System), Martínez-Schuldt (2020) finds that in places where the density of local organizations is higher, the consulate directly takes on significantly fewer cases; that is, the burden falls on civil society. While this finding is not robust for labor cases specifically, the association remains negative, suggesting a differential role for consulates depending on the presence of other partners in their respective jurisdictions.[1]

Given these deep community entanglements, this chapter offers a more refined organizational lens for understanding how the Mexican government has collaborated with worker advocates across a range of regulatory arenas and jurisdictions in co-enforcement arrangements. In line with other critiques of "responsive regulation" efforts to keep state and market forces in check (Parker 2013) and protect worker rights, we reject approaches that either disparage or celebrate consular support; instead, we are interested in what does or does not work, and why. We thus offer a bottom-up organizational analysis of sending-state co-enforcement efforts. While this approach implicates a wide range of civil society actors, we focus here on those most engaged with labor education and organizing (labor unions and some worker centers) and access to justice (legal service providers). In chapters 4 and 5, we discuss the wide range of other outreach and rights mobilization efforts advanced by advocates working across national borders to contest state power.

We begin by examining the co-enforcement process and how labor unions and other worker-led organizations have engaged the Mexican government in it. In doing so, we do not aim to glorify this process: indeed, despite its clear benefits, it is not a panacea, given the various challenges we discuss below. However, the co-enforcement of immigrant worker rights provides a useful lens through which to view attempts to increase state accountability across borders, as well as the various ways migrant-serving organizations are leveraging consular obligations to improve labor standards regulation in the United States. For the labor movement, we identify at least three benefits to collaborating with the Mexican government: (1) it gives them access to a broader set of power brokers; (2) it provides them with a captive audience (i.e., consular visitors) for labor education; and (3) it facilitates organized labor's shift to a regional strategy. Our aim is not to conduct a policy evaluation but to understand how these processes get to be implemented and by whom.

In the second half of the chapter, we examine the collaborations between public interest law organizations and Mexico's consular network. We argue that the impact of these coalitions depends on the local civic and political context. While we document many benefits, we also reveal persistent challenges across the consular network. We conclude by reconsidering the sending state's potential within the co-enforcement framework, both as a lateral collaborator and, more typically, as a bureaucracy that must act forcefully, but with diplomatic restraint, to defend the limited rights of Mexican citizens.

REVISITING LABOR CO-ENFORCEMENT THROUGH A CROSS-BORDER LENS

The Mexican government's shift to begin advocating on behalf of its emigrant workforce can be tied to both homeland politics (i.e., efforts to regain migrant loyalty and attract family remittances) and bilateral relationships that Mexico has cultivated (chiefly with the United States). Yet we know that these migrant rights advocacy efforts have remained largely aspirational (Gordon 2006), in large part because of the complexity and costs required. Not only does such advocacy require expending tremendous resources above and beyond everyday consular staff functions, but delicate homeland politics can frame investments in the diaspora as directly competing with the needs of those workers who remain in Mexico. Moreover, Mexico's more proactive stance emerged after a long history of direct antagonism to emigration, and despite years of failing to pay restitution to Bracero guest workers, whose wages were garnished by the Mexican state, supposedly to fund savings accounts to be accessed upon their return (González 1999). Given this history, Mexico's claim of renewed devotion to its diaspora has been viewed with suspicion, and its recent efforts could rightly be written off as "junket affairs" of politicians making empty promises while wasting taxpayer dollars (FitzGerald 2008). Nonetheless, understanding the Mexican government's attempts to engage in the co-enforcement of migrant worker rights is analytically useful. Domestic labor agencies in the United States—federal, state, and sometimes local—provide a regulatory framework for the sending state's immigrant worker advocacy, as US agencies are also engaged in co-enforcement efforts with a wide variety of other civil society stakeholders. By focusing on two key organizational fields— the labor movement and access-to-justice advocates—we consider how sending states' promigrant narratives become institutionalized in local communities and are interpreted by existing civil society. To this end, we revisit traditional theories of co-enforcement, which focus largely on the state's relationship to worker organizations, through the lens of the sending state.

In the classical model of tripartite enforcement, Ayres and Braithwaite (1992) explain, the firm, the state, and worker organizations should all have equal standing under a "responsive" regulatory framework (Amengual and Fine 2017). The core argument of "responsive regulation" is that the third leg of tripartism— worker organizations—is necessary to keep state and market forces in check. Several analysts have critiqued the feasibility and efficacy of the responsive regulation approach to labor co-enforcement in the United States and beyond (Weil 2016; Marsden, Tucker, and Vosko 2021; Parker 2013; Berg 2016). Criticisms aside, this institutional model has been adopted (with varying degrees of success) across many migrant destinations and with increasing sending-state involvement. While other grassroots worker-led models have emerged to advance worker rights (sometimes even outside formally sanctioned processes) (Fine et al. 2018), our focus here is on efforts to shore up formal, worker-driven claims-making channels in the United States.[2]

In one study of these formal channels, Amengual and Fine (2017) examine the case of Argentina and the United States to highlight the unique collaborations that can emerge between regulatory agencies and worker organizations, each of which must also navigate context-specific political realities. As they argue, tripartism is not merely concerned with "guarding the guardians" in labor regulation. It also serves to feed claims to regulators and inform their proactive strategies. However, for a functional partnership to emerge, there has to be a give-and-take. State agencies have to be willing to share information, collaborate in decision-making, and risk being viewed by the business community as biased in the workers' favor. Worker organizations must collaborate with entities with whom they have often had an adversarial relationship and be willing to follow the logic and time lines of a frustrating, slow-moving bureaucracy (132).

Tripartite models of co-enforcement have increasingly incorporated the sending state as origin countries expand their notions of migrant governance, often in response to the explicit demands of their diaspora (Margheritis 2016). However, the relationships between host country governments (who seek outreach partners) and origin country governments (who seek legitimacy) vary substantially from place to place. Oswalt and Rosado Marzán (2018) distinguish between "side-to-side" co-enforcement partnerships that rely largely on "agency-agency" collaboration (e.g., between federal and state departments of labor) and "up-and-down" or "agency-to-advocate" collaborative models with civil society, such as those where union officials are deputized to assist in regulation (Fine and Gordon 2010). The consular network's participation introduces a hybrid model to this typology. Purely bilateral cooperation between two government entities is uncommon; more typically, these partnerships also incorporate an outward-facing component of collaboration with civil society, as with the "Chicago-Area Interagency Workers' Rights Roundtable" that Oswalt and Rosado Marzán profile in their study.

As this overview shows, consular bureaucracies do not exist in a vacuum. They operate in an established system of enforcement actors, where they can help fill enforcement gaps. Thus the utility of consular advocacy in the co-enforcement process depends on jurisdiction and the characteristics of the local immigrant community. Furthermore, NGOs constitute a heterogeneous sector with different aims and tactics (as we describe in chapter 4). Focusing on the co-enforcement of labor standards, we examine the nature of consular collaborations with labor organizations and legal service providers. In doing so, we highlight the importance of meso-level differences for analyzing relations among state actors and between Mexico and its emigrants settled across the United States. Finally, we assess the critical role of consular leaders and the relationships that emerge with their bilateral government counterparts and with community actors.

MAPPING CIVIL SOCIETY ONTO
THE CO-ENFORCEMENT PROCESS

In a claims-driven regime where those most vulnerable to labor violations are also the least likely to bring forth a claim, the fraught process of brokering immigrant worker rights becomes essential. These claims are the core mechanism for triggering regulatory responses, but they can be incredibly costly for workers, in terms of both time and opportunity costs and the psychic burden that these confrontations can entail (Lesniewski and Gleeson 2022). But of course many workers and their advocates do come forward, adopting an array of strategies. Moreover, new alt-labor advocates have cultivated impressive models for participatory enforcement to compel employer compliance (McCartin 2009; Fine 2011; Vosko 2020; Kader 2020).

However, government regulation remains the most widespread mechanism for overseeing the low-wage labor market. This regulation can include, for example, filing a claim with the DOL for nonpayment of wages or breaks violations, submitting a complaint to the Occupational Safety and Health Administration regarding unsafe work conditions, filing for workers' compensation after an injury, or approaching the Equal Employment Opportunity Commission for ongoing sexual harassment. In each of these arenas, co-enforcement models (buttressed by community partnerships) have emerged. Here we focus on these attempts to navigate official US labor standards enforcement processes, attempts often brokered by key advocates such as labor organizations, legal service providers, and sometimes a consulate.

The benefits of this supported claims-making approach are many. For workers themselves, securing the help of an advocate can greatly increase their ability to file a claim and ultimately win restitution (Gleeson 2009). For enforcement agencies (or any government entity), collaborating with civil society groups can be an effective way to multiply their reach to immigrant communities (de Graauw 2016). In this regard, the consular network functions as an ancillary both to US labor agencies and to civil society groups advocating on behalf of immigrant workers. In this crowded landscape of labor standards enforcement, the costs and benefits of collaborating with the consulate network will vary substantially depending on the type of organization in question (whether a labor union, a legal aid organization, a worker center, or an immigrant rights organization) and its location.

These demand issues aside, many factors have compelled the Mexican government to aid in the enforcement of immigrant worker rights. To be sure, the bilateral agreements between Mexico's SRE and various US agencies have provided a workable framework for intervention. However, these very instruments are (as we described in chapter 2 and discuss at length in chapter 5) the result of long-fought transnational advocacy efforts for broader accountability. Moreover—and in part responding to demands from US labor advocates—US labor agencies have increasingly invested in community liaisons in order to more effectively inform workers about their rights and gain the trust of marginalized communities (Gleeson and Bada 2019). The DOL's Wage and Hour Division, for example, initiated a Community Outreach and Resource Planning Specialist (CORPS) position, which has now been staffed in many offices across the country (Wage and Hour Division 2021). CORPS staff make it a point to connect with a wide array of community groups and often work in conjunction with the International Bureau of Labor Affairs' Consular Partnership Program. Meanwhile, Mexico's recent outward shift is part of a growing trend of "diaspora diplomacy," in which sending states address key issues related to their export labor, including trafficking and fraudulent international labor contracting. Labor standards enforcement is premised almost entirely on worker-driven claims (especially those of the most vulnerable workforce, including low-wage migrant workers). Thus both origin and destination countries clearly have an incentive to collaborate, and in the Mexican case the wide geographic dispersion of their consular network places them in the unique position to establish co-enforcement partnerships across states that no other origin country with a large population of emigrants has been able to replicate.

Yet these collaborations are only as successful as the parallel partnerships they can create with community organizations with a proven track record of working with immigrant communities. As many of these community groups work directly with immigrant workers, they must consider the potential value added (or the burden) of collaborating with the consular network. Consular staff can offer key assets such as language access, legitimacy with local Mexican immigrant communities, diplomatic access to local regulatory agencies, and the organizational capacity to host programs and conduct outreach. For some community groups, these are coveted advantages; for others, they are simply duplicative functions given their existing community partners and their own organizational capacity.

While the Mexican government has rhetorically staked a claim in the work-ers' rights enforcement arena nationally, in practice its ability and willingness to collaborate depend on its local capacities and civil society's willingness to engage. This potential for partnership often hinges on local organizations' central mis-sion and service focus. Some mobilizing organizations are primarily involved in providing initial outreach and referrals to workers, others in direct service and claims processing, and still others in pushing for workers' rights reforms through policy advocacy. Consulates are differently useful in each of these arenas. While consular offices can indeed become a one-stop shop for distributing information about workers' rights, they are more limited as long-term service providers and are useful only in very select policy advocacy endeavors because of their severely curtailed ability to intervene in domestic affairs. Materially, consulates can provide space and personnel, but symbolically they can also offer advocates leverage and legitimacy. This unique influence—exerted through a phone call, a letter, or even a rare visit from consular officials—can be wielded strategically in dealings with US counterpart agencies and sometimes even employers. Yet this same formalism and symbolic heft can be counterproductive in outreach to vulnerable communities that feel disenfranchised by or distrust their own home government.

Indeed, consular collaboration poses challenges. It requires time and resources, and it is variably practical and effective, depending on the issue at hand. Labor and employment law is divided into siloed statutes and agencies (wage theft, occu-pational safety, discrimination, gender equity, etc.), and community groups dif-fer in their capacity and in the strategies they deploy to address each. Some have full-time staff dedicated to casework (occasionally even lawyers), while others see legal claims as merely a stepping-stone to a loftier organizing or policy advocacy goal (Fine 2006). Thus depending on claim types, industries, and the categories of workers involved, a consulate is more valuable in some co-enforcement arenas and contexts than others.

Civil society is also not a monolith, and many complex organizations must juggle a number of mandates. We build on Bloemraad, de Graauw, and Gleeson's (2020, 292) characterization of immigrant organizations as the "civic infrastruc-tures of immigrant communities, that is, the set of somewhat formalized and orga-nized groups that are neither public institutions nor for-profit businesses and that serve or advocate for these communities."[3] Here we focus especially on two groups that frequently engage with workers' rights co-enforcement and the claims-mak-ing process: labor organizations and legal service providers.

We begin with labor unions, which in the United States are a waning institu-tion but remain the best predictor of job quality and immigrant worker power in many jurisdictions (Thomason and Bernhardt 2018). Unions played a primary role in establishing Labor Rights Week. They steward their existing members' col-lective bargaining contracts and have increasingly engaged in organizing immi-grant workers and advocating for policies to benefit all working people across the globe (Adler, Tapia, and Turner 2014). We also pay attention to the role of alt-labor groups, which are nonprofits that lack the power to collectively bargain but are assuming an increasingly important role in the co-enforcement process and migrant worker advocacy efforts writ large (Fine et al. 2018).

We then turn to legal service providers, another key partner in consular efforts to advance migrant worker rights. The Mexican consular network is an important resource for helping workers lodge a claim, and the consulate staff turn to lawyers for training and for referrals when workers come to them seeking legal assistance. While many types of organizations provide some form of rights training and "low-touch" legal orientation, here we focus especially on organizations pushing for access to justice via formal legal service regarding labor and employment issues (Rhode 2004).

ORGANIZED LABOR AND IMMIGRANT WORKERS

The Labor Movement's Legacy with Immigrants

Labor unions have long played a critical (and often complicated) role in advo-cating for immigrant workers. In 1986, the AFL-CIO argued in favor of punitive employer sanctions for hiring undocumented workers, which have since proved to be a major detriment to immigrant workers seeking work and a boon to immigra-tion enforcement efforts. However, since 2000, the AFL-CIO has vocally thrown its support toward an amnesty for undocumented workers, alongside other interim quasi-legalization efforts. For the biggest "immigrant unions," this stance is a key survival strategy. Private-sector union membership in the United States is at its lowest point in decades, at 6.4 percent nationwide in 2018, compared to 24.2 percent in 1973 (Hirsch and Macpherson 2020). Among immigrant workers mem-bership is even lower, and on average over the last decade Mexican immigrants have the lowest unionization rates, partly because of their disproportionate repre-sentation in low-wage, nonunion jobs (Milkman and Luce 2020). In this context, supporting immigrant worker rights and strengthening immigrant worker unions go hand in hand.

The Mexican state assumed a more "active" role in the well-being of its diaspora in large part thanks to the demands of immigrant civil society, many of whose leaders had deep roots in the US labor movement. These leaders were the key architects of strategic organizing campaigns in high-immigrant industries such as UNITE-HERE!'s "Hotel Workers Rising" (UNITE-HERE! 2006), the iconic Jus-tice for Janitors campaign of the Service Employees International Union (SEIU) (SEIU n.d.), and various campaigns by United Food and Commercial Workers International Union (UFCW) for sectors ranging from meatpacking (UFCW n.d.) to ethnic grocers/*mercados* (Bend the Arc and UFCW Local 5, 2013). Each of these efforts included community alliances, for instance UFCW's work with the Frente Indígena de Organizaciones Binacionales in central California's agricultural industry and the Federación de Clubes Michoacanos en Illinois, located in Chicago. Furthermore, well-organized migrant leaders across the United States (as we describe in chapter 5) were actively involved in transnational labor solidarity campaigns with Mexican unions.

To be sure, unions have diverse memberships and aims, and despite the declarations of national leadership in favor of immigrant worker rights, local affiliates are often less receptive. Moreover, even in some places where immigration is significant, union leadership remains largely white and native born and is sometimes opposed to proimmigrant policies (T. Lee and Tapia 2021). There is no doubt, though, that the labor movement has been a critical proponent of immigrant worker rights, from outreach to collective bargaining to policy advocacy (Delgado 1993; Milkman 2020).

The labor movement's advocacy around immigration reform has been undeniable at the national level (Wong 2017; Nicholls 2019), but it has also played out in state legislatures and local government chambers. For example, Chicago unions worked in conjunction with the Illinois Coalition for Immigrant and Refugee Rights to back a bill that now allows undocumented immigrants to secure a driver's license.[4] In San Jose, the SEIU worked with a broad coalition (brought together by the AFL-CIO–affiliated Working Partnership USA) to back a ten-dollar minimum wage (Partnership for Working Families n.d.).[5] And in Houston, the Harris County AFL-CIO incubated and partnered with the Fe y Justicia Worker Center (originally incubated by the Interfaith Worker Justice network) to spearhead the ultimately successful "Down with Wage Theft" campaign (Houston Interfaith Worker Justice Center 2012).[6]

Throughout these campaigns, unions partnered with various community coalitions (Turner and Cornfield 2007; Milkman, Bloom, and Narro 2010; de Graauw, Gleeson, and Bada 2019) but also strategically courted the Mexican consular network to boost their own efforts to improve the conditions of immigrant workers (many of whom hail from Mexico). Though consular staff must remain formally neutral, they can provide the political legitimacy that many unions lack in an environment increasingly hostile for organized labor. Further, especially in jurisdictions where unions are resource-strapped, a consulate can offer unions the help of an established staff as well as a physical space from which to broadcast their labor education outreach. For example, during an organizing campaign in a local grocery chain, the Mexican consulate in Chicago offered their space to UFCW to meet with workers on weekends.[7]

Building on the many long-standing, ad hoc collaborations that arose in popular Mexican immigrant destinations, labor leaders were key players in founding the annual Labor Rights Week. In fact, several union leaders we spoke with argued that their local efforts provided a template for what would later become the national weeklong model. What began as daylong, one-off workshops culminated in a regular collaboration with the San Jose consulate, explained one UFCW leader. This and many other success stories—in Houston, Los Angeles, Chicago, and beyond—became part of the pitch for greater investment in labor rights outreach that labor leaders made to officials at the Mexican embassy in June 2009.[8]

Unions have not always been willing to work with consular staff, given the Mexican government's sordid history of union busting and still-rampant classism (González 1999). Yet several unions were key architects of the 2004 labor agreement between Mexico and the United States and have played an important role in Mexico's Instituto de los Mexicanos en el Exterior / Institute of Mexicans Abroad, which aimed to provide the Mexican diaspora with a political voice. For example, as we describe in chapter 2, Esther Lopez, a former UFCW vice president, and Eliseo Medina, a former SEIU vice president, were appointed by the institute to serve as organizational delegates advising Mexico's government on migrant affairs, and Moises Zavala, a UFCW organizer from Chicago, was elected to serve on the institute's advisory board.[9] These leaders pushed to center worker rights in the Mexican government's platform.

Once Labor Rights Week was institutionalized, several immigrant unions such as the SEIU, UNITE-HERE!, UFCW, and United Farmworkers continued to team up with the consular network on everyday outreach. The annual Labor Rights Week was eventually rolled out to twelve pioneer cities in the first year, then to almost thirty cities in the following year, and eventually nationwide. These collaborations have been especially productive in jurisdictions where there are few other available resources for workers seeking to make claims to defend their rights (as we describe in chapter 4). For any organization interested in proactive worker education, a consular office provides a "captive audience" for labor outreach, given the throngs of individuals who must pass through its massive bureaucratic institution for identification documents or consular services. To offer an estimate calculated by UFCW, during the first five years of Labor Rights Week, union outreach trainings offered at the Mexican consulates of Los Angeles and Dallas benefited one hundred thousand workers. In Houston, it is estimated that three thousand workers were served during such Labor Rights Week trainings.[10]

However, the reach of labor unions themselves should not be overstated, as alt-labor groups, for whom formal unionization was not a key goal, also played a major role in connecting workers to labor agencies and other forms of restitution. Many worked closely with labor unions, while other took notably different approaches. Not bound to the same national policy battles and binational campaigns for worker justice, these worker centers were often more nimble and opportunistic in evaluating the value added by consular collaboration (as described in chapter 4).

What the Consular Network Offers Organized Labor

Partnerships between labor organizations and consulates can take many forms, but we identified at least three modes of collaboration—sometimes operating in combination—across the country.

Consuls as Influential Conveners.   In the first mode, unions look to consular staff primarily as conveners who head a respected institution that wields influence in ways that labor unions cannot. That is, in addition to opening their doors to unions to conduct outreach, consuls help bring together a range of US agency counterparts to shape the annual Labor Rights Week. For unions, most of these labor agencies (the DOL's Wage and Hour Division, the DOL's Occupational Safety and Health Administration, the Equal Employment Opportunity Commission, and sister state agencies) provide limited direct protections for their represented workers, who have a collective bargaining contract to fall back on. However, these agencies *are* key actors in terms of regulating industry conditions that put nonunion workers especially at risk. In several places, the National Labor Relations Board—the agency that directly regulates unions—has been part of these convenings: in Houston, for example, where the Justice and Equality in the Workplace Partnership brought all these stakeholders together through a community hotline (though we should note that this was a unique strategy not easily replicable in other cities).[11]

Central labor councils—the local bodies of the AFL-CIO federation that incorporate various affiliate unions—are a primary vehicle for convening labor leaders. However, consular convenings have also allowed worker advocates to explicitly focus on the issues facing Mexican immigrant workers, which has often also meant highlighting immigration challenges. Even after the historic 2006 split between the AFL-CIO and the newly formed Change to Win coalition—for which organizing immigrant workers was a central sticking point (Cornfield 2006)—the Mexican consulate's Labor Rights Week relied on collaborations with union affiliates in both factions.[12]

Finally, in big cities with large and diverse Latino immigrant populations, these union-consulate partnerships have also involved the entire Latin American consular corps. In Chicago, for example, the consulates of Brazil, Colombia, Ecuador, El Salvador, Guatemala, and Honduras, among others, are all active.[13] By far, the Mexican government has always been considered the "elder brother" among these diplomatic bureaucracies. In 2017, shortly after the inauguration of Donald Trump, the Chicago Association of Latin American Consulates, led by the Mexican government, sponsored a massive labor and immigrant rights training at a large-capacity auditorium at the University of Illinois at Chicago. Every Latin American consulate invited its constituents from its jurisdictions (including neighboring states such as Indiana and Wisconsin) to listen to labor rights educators from UFCW and staff lawyers from local immigrant rights organizations.

Consular Offices as Captive Audience Outreach.   In practice, labor unions most often play the role of on-site educator, offering information sessions to the captive audience of individuals waiting to receive services at consulates. As a Harris County AFL-CIO staff member described the immense "foot traffic" in Houston's consulate every day: "Every time I go there, that place is packed. I mean it's in a big enough area where there's two hundred to three hundred people in there on any given day at any time." The consular office also provided unions with a high-profile setting for broadcasting their outreach to the wider community, especially in Spanish-language media.[14] To be sure, a core aspect of union outreach includes encouraging workers to organize. However, as one UFCW leader in Phoenix explained, this particular know-your-rights training ran the gamut from "information regarding labor rights [to] human rights [to] civil rights." For UFCW, holistic training for workers was crucial, and their typical outreach included information about occupational health, disease prevention, and health care access.[15] These union presentations served to build community trust.

Perhaps the biggest issue facing immigrant workers, though, involves federal immigration enforcement efforts. Our interviews with consular partners took place during the height of the Obama administration's policy of carrying out "silent raids" (Griffith and Gleeson 2019). During this period, workplace audits were rampant, which caused problems for nonunion and union worksites alike. "No-match letters"—delivered when there was a mismatch between an employee's name and the Social Security number provided by the employer—that often followed audits were a key impetus driving unions to foster a relationship with consulates. When we spoke to a representative from the Teamsters Local 743 in 2013, they highlighted the problems caused by no-match letters, which were thwarting many organizing campaigns and fueling deportations under the Obama administration.[16] In Chicago, as in other cities across the United States, these letters became one of the main foci of the emerging partnership between unions, service providers, and consular staff.

Workers' rights outreach was particularly important for UFCW 99 in Phoenix, its leaders explained, because they operated in a "right to work" state (i.e., a state where organizing efforts were hampered by state rules limiting member dues). Getting consular staff on board for this work was important symbolically. "In the last event we held, consular representatives were there to give out information to people, chatting with co-nationals about their labor rights," one union leader explained. "I saw in that last event a much more direct participation than I had in times past."[17] Consular staff were not always directly involved in these efforts,[18] but establishing the consular office as a welcoming hub for labor rights outreach was consequential, especially in settings where unions held less power.

Consulates as Regional Actors.   Third, consular activities, as inherently regional, can target very large jurisdictions. The federated structure of the consular network in many ways mirrors that of labor unions. Moreover, just as unions make strategic decisions around where to concentrate their resources, the Mexican consulate can become an anchor point for much of their regional outreach. Although consular offices are often located in central cities, their vast reach (potentially across dozens of counties and states) makes local consulates important partners in unions' regional organizing. As explained in chapter 2, UFCW had significant leverage when the Mexican embassy was selecting the cities in which to launch the pilot of Labor Rights Week, suggesting sites where they had significant local resources to mobilize for this collaboration. One national UFCW leader explained how the union's outreach around labor and immigrant worker rights was concentrated in "eight or ten cities across the country. . . . Very specifically, we go and we set up stations at the Mexican consulate. We provide information on a range of issues, health and safety for workers, information around verification employment, rights in particular that workers have."[19] Like unions, who often cover vast jurisdictions themselves, local consular offices have significant discretion over where to conduct their programming. "Each consulate makes their own programming. Some venture out beyond the consulate," another UFCW leader told us.[20] As such, the mobile consulate provides unions a reach they wouldn't otherwise enjoy, and some consulates have partnered with churches and elementary schools in the metropolitan area of Chicago to increase visibility and foot traffic during Labor Rights Week.

To be clear, the mobile consulate program is on the whole a woefully inadequate attempt to reach isolated migrants in the far reaches of the given region, and its impact should not be overstated. Outreach is infrequent, staffing is limited, appointments (which must be scheduled through the infamous and overstretched MEXITEL system—now rebranded as Mi Consulado) run out quickly, and given time pressures, consulates must often prioritize the most pressing matters (mostly processing bureaucratic documents for citizens who cannot safely or practically travel to the central consulate repeatedly). Yet these challenges are not a unique feature of the Mexican bureaucracy. Indeed, many of the bureaucratic limitations facing consulates (and their mobile functions) also plague US federal and state labor agencies. And despite their flaws, the mobile consulates have allowed advocates to leverage bureaucracy in service of their aims.

Because of their regional jurisdictions, unions help inform consulates on where to dispatch resources outside of central cities. As one union leader explained: "We work with [consular officials] to bring the Mexican consulate to communities like Dodge City, Kansas, those kinds of things where services are a little bit more limited and far away. . . . And certainly on the immigrant rights front—to be able to provide timely information to the immigrant communities—we worked closely with the Mexican consulate."[21] In western Kansas, the leader went on, the union had eight thousand members, yet the closest big city was Wichita (three hours away), and the closest consular office was in Denver, Colorado. Thus, in a place where "there's not a whole lot of support . . . maybe the Catholic Church and the union,"[22] a collaboration between labor leaders and consular officials can be particularly fruitful. This collaboration might include, for example, events that provide health and safety or I-9 employment verification training, followed by the offering of consular services. The benefit is mutual, as unions can extend the reach of a consular office in rural communities in particular. For example, the Dallas consulate often relied on union halls as a base when providing services in more rural areas like Lubbock and Plano.

Depending on union density and reach, consular collaborations are most useful for unions in places with scarce resources serving local immigrant communities. These partnerships are often the only opportunities isolated communities have to access not only legal assistance across many arenas but also worker training, immigration law consultations, and recently even COVID testing. In contrast, in places with an already robust infrastructure of civic organizations, union-consular partnerships offer a good opportunity to make new alliances or solidify existing ones with diverse community organizations such as elementary schools or churches serving immigrant neighborhoods.

Benefits to Labor Organization–Consulate Collaboration

All told, labor unions benefit from working with a consulate in several concrete ways. For one, they provide a means of reaching the broader, especially nonunion workforce with whom unions do not have a direct line of communication. Such collaborations allow unions to surmount certain geographical barriers and build relationships and trust with immigrant workers who may not otherwise encounter unions in their daily lives. This is true especially with more recently arrived immigrant communities, such as Oaxacan indigenous immigrants. Union leaders described needing to gain their trust, often by working with community groups such as the Frente Indígena de Organizaciones Binacionales. The end goal was for these workers to "also feel confident in coming to the unions for help when they find themselves in a bad situation at work."[23]

In advocate-dense places like the Bay Area, a consulate is only one of many community actors, each of which has cultivated its own relationships with vulnerable communities. Yet as one building trades leader explained of this region, the Mexican consulate was also an unavoidable bureaucratic reality that everyone had to contend with at some point, given its political significance and broad reach. When doing outreach, he often brought literature from the Mexican consulate to lend weight to his message: "When you hear from your . . . native government, that these are your rights in the United States, that makes it very official to say, 'Okay, the Mexican consulate is telling me that I need to have these rights in the United States.'"[24] During the COVID crisis, union-consular collaborations kicked into high gear. The Mexican consulate in Chicago quickly joined forces with the Chicago and Midwest Regional Joint Board of Workers United, United Electrical, Radio and Machine Workers of America, the SEIU, UFCW, and the Occupational Safety and Health Administration to create a special digital guide for Illinois essential workers in Spanish and to disseminate information about occupational health rights and other basic protections during Labor Rights Week in 2020 (SRE and Consulado General de México en Chicago 2020).

Consulates—and specifically the consul in charge of the Departamento de Protección—can also grease the wheels of arcane regulatory bureaucracies to which unions are not always granted access. As one Bay Area UFCW leader noted, "You know, we [union leaders and consular officials] feel very comfortable being able to call one another if we are in need of some assistance."[25] She admitted that her experience might be unique given the centrality of the Bay Area (home to three Mexican consulates), but regardless, the reciprocal relationship she had built with the various consulates helped make some of her advocacy work more effective. Consulates are also important in places where few civic partners exist and the political climate is markedly more hostile. For example, a Harris County AFL-CIO leader frankly described the vacuum left by underresourced and understaffed US labor agencies in the Houston area: "It's really important that those governmental agencies figure out a way to have a much broader enforcement program. It's absolutely essential . . . because they're understaffed now, [and] when you're understaffed, you're kind of leaving it to the goodwill of employers. . . . You just can't bet on that goodwill."[26]

While unions do seek to make connections with workers passing through the consulate, this is not necessarily the most important strategic goal of union-consulate partnership. As one UFCW leader in Phoenix described, "Our most important success is the relationship with the consulate. . . . It is very important for us to know that we can pick up the phone and talk with someone at the consulate and that they know someone here at the union. . . . I think that the direct relationship with the consulate and this working relationship that we have is very important because we have a place to which we can return and know that they are going to help people."[27] Unions have worked hard to cultivate these positive relationships, which they have also been able to leverage at the national level.

This direct line of influence with consulates is also important because the union itself is often seen as a one-stop shop for its members, who come seeking help with a variety of issues far beyond work grievances. For example, in California, Assembly Bill 6 made driver's licenses available to undocumented individuals, though it required them to present official identifying documents to obtain them. If these documents were lost or had expired, undocumented applicants had to rely on the Mexican government to reissue them. Having a consular official come to their unions' AB6 workshops was therefore a crucial benefit, one SEIU leader explained,[28] allowing their members to resolve documentation problems along with other issues.

While both unions and consulates seek to develop ties with the community, both often struggle to surmount perceptions that they are complex, hierarchical organizations that cannot necessarily be trusted. Yet this liability can also be a benefit, as precisely this shared, top-down organizational nature facilitates their collaborative work and allows all actors to rally around a common goal. (By contrast, grassroots organizations typically lack such rigid leadership structures and in some cases lack even the physical space to legitimize their presence.) For example—and without discounting the efforts of local community leaders—the binational accord between the US DOL and Mexico's SRE set the tone for the work of consulates on the ground. This centrally managed but locally implemented organizational front created a sense of continuity that worked in unions' favor, as one South Bay building trades leader was amazed to find over the years: "To my surprise, every single one of them has been very supportive."[29]

Finally, much of the labor union organizing in immigrant-dense cities such as Chicago is decidedly transnational (Galvez, Godoy, and Meneima 2019; de Graauw, Gleeson, and Bada 2019). Working with the consulate not only unlocks much-needed resources but opens up another avenue for holding the Mexican government accountable. These labor advocacy efforts have extended far beyond organizing passive educational outreach one week out of the year; rather, unions like the UFCW consistently work with *and against* the Mexican government on both sides of the border and across North America. Even benign outreach programming has often been leveraged to demand or offer accountability, as in 2014 when the Chicago Regional Council of Carpenters called on the Mexican consulate to facilitate a joint professional training program with a group of carpenters from a Mexico-based sister union that had also been pressuring Mexico for reform. The consul obliged, and the cross-border training program thus became a demonstration—even if largely symbolic—of the Mexican government's commitment to advancing labor rights in Mexico.[30]

In sum, union-consulate collaborations ideally allow labor leaders unfettered, yearlong access to large groups of captive, Spanish-speaking immigrant workers who can benefit from informational workshops while they wait for consular documents. These collaborations give unions a strategic partner and an ally to support organizing campaigns and provide direct services frequently needed by many union members. Making alliances with consulates has also allowed unions to deliver more holistic services to marginalized immigrant constituents, while simultaneously leveraging transnational union networks to push the Mexican government to be accountable for the labor rights of its workers back home.

Challenges to Labor Organization–Consulate Collaboration

All told, unions described many benefits to working with local consulates. Yet many were also quite candid about the challenges they encountered while cultivating these relationships. For one, like all collaborations, they required a continual investment of time and energy, resources that were not always readily available. For example, a national leader for the UFCW recalled how difficult it was to make "the Mexican consulate recognize the need for labor rights education and access to labor rights information." Speaking candidly, she admitted that "sometimes those relationships get kind of dicey" and could come with "some hesitation and some tension and some nervousness." Over time, these tensions were eased, and subsequently there was a "real growth in understanding and a real apprecia-tion of the need to provide labor rights education to Mexican immigrants."[31]

These relationships also had to be cultivated and maintained, according to one labor leader with the Roofers Union in San Jose who had a long-standing relation-ship with the Mexican consulate there and had seen many consuls come and go. Each official had to be dealt with differently: "Some consuls are very approachable, some other ones are not." Referring especially to the class (and often political) dif-ferences between consular staff and union leaders and members, he admitted that not all of his members had had great experiences at the consulate office. The qual-ity of the relationships depended largely on the particular interests of the assigned diplomat and on labor leaders' ability to facilitate them. Sometimes leaders simply didn't have time: "They [consular officials] do a good outreach. . . . [But] I don't have time to go around to all the meetings they have and all the community events they have. I just don't have time for that."[32] In this case, limited resources led to a less than optimal collaborative environment.

Another San Francisco Bay Area UFCW leader similarly confirmed the need to quickly "develop a relationship with the consulate" so that their concerns would not take a backseat to the consulates' many other campaigns and initiatives that "have nothing to do with the issue of labor." Indeed, labor unions had to not only maintain communication with consular officials but also convince them to inte-grate labor issues into the other services they offered, such as women's rights and children's needs. The onus, he explained, then fell on unions to bring labor rights into focus while stressing that the worker was also a "father, mother, son, daugh-ter"—that is, the union had to make a broader case for labor rights as affecting every aspect of immigrant lives: "We need more understanding about what the labor movement [is]," the UFCW leader explained.[33]

This relationship building involved training the consular staff to be effective advocates. While many leaders noted that working with a Mexican consulate (as opposed to US labor agencies, for example) offered more opportunities for estab-lishing cultural ties and trust with the community, not everyone was convinced that this made consulates uniformly better advocates for workers. One SEIU leader in San Jose explained her ambivalence over consular collaboration: "I don't think it differs much. It has its bureaucracy and [red] tape that it has to go through. It maybe has more credibility with people. And it's seen as . . . an extension of the government or the country, which could go either way in terms of trust. Yeah, so I think that could be good sometimes and sometimes not."[34] A Teamsters leader in Chicago similarly noted that the majority of consuls were "very bureaucratic," a quality that explained the "terrible impression that people had of the Mexican consulate," despite their utility to the community.[35] Unions reported struggling to convince consulates that they needed to take actions to reverse this reputation.

Indeed, not only immigrant communities but also many labor leaders them-selves were skeptical of consulates. For example, a leader with SEIU 1877 in San Jose reflected on the irony of working alongside other labor colleagues with local consulates when they had just a short time prior worked in solidarity with the Union of Mexican Electrical Workers in their strike in Mexico City, even organizing a demonstration at the consular office: "They [the consulate] got a lot of bad press. We had organized a march at the consulate, things like that, just last year. And so, when I heard that they were doing Labor Week, I was really shocked. . . . It felt like a PR thing to me."[36] While many union leaders were similarly leery of big-government bureaucrats, some, like this SEIU 1877 leader, had a more optimistic view of future consular interactions: "The government of Mexico right now, the way it's so conservative and business oriented, and has been for what, eighty years, one hundred years, you would [expect to] see that in the way they treated people. I think now that they're becoming more service oriented and more focused on rights, whether they be legal or *laboral* or what have you, I think it's a good thing. And it's very shocking, in a good way."[37] But this shift, the leader conceded, would take time.

For many labor leaders, working with a consulate was largely symbolic and confined to Labor Rights Week in September. As a Teamsters leader in Chicago explained, "Unfortunately, we can't really say that the impact on the people has been worth much because a lot of times people go as if it were a book fair, rather [than] a labor fair. They come but they don't stay." Moreover, making the community view a consulate office as a place where they could "go and learn about your worker rights . . . about the community services available to you" was an inherently difficult task given how consulates are structured.[38] With the exception of the Chicago office, Mexican consulates do not have a specific division dedicated to worker issues, and thus most consular outreach remains limited and dependent on the specific priorities of the General Consulate and the Consulate of Protection (legal protection section), which often have little to do with labor issues. During Labor Rights Week, labor leaders often pleaded with consular officials to publicly leverage their influence: "I'd like them to spread the word using their media connections. Because they do speak out on the radio. . . . Everybody's listening to the radio at work."[39] Yet these media campaigns typically waned soon after Labor Rights Week ended, rarely persisting year-round.

Finally, in addition to pushing for year-round programming, many labor leaders stressed that promoting worker rights was not the same as advocating for workers' rights to organize. A UFCW leader surmised that this disconnect ultimately had to do with the politicization of worker rights in the United States and the US government's initial fear that Mexico would "promote unionization." Over time, these anxieties pushed unions out of the central planning of Labor Rights Week, he explained. "The consulate will not talk openly about the issue of unionization," opting instead to focus on ensuring wage payments, even if they are poverty wages with no benefits. Ultimately, then, consulates could never be advocates for labor reform, he admitted. "Because of their diplomatic nature, the consulate won't do it. They can't do it."[40]

In sum, the Mexican consular network can be a valuable though imperfect partner for pursuing the core agenda of labor unions. Difficulty arises from the sovereignty constraints of the diplomatic corps and the directives binding staff to be neutral actors in advocating for the labor rights of Mexican immigrants under US labor laws. Moreover, Mexican consulates have a long history of engaging in discriminatory practices and have not always acted in the best interest of immigrant workers in need of protection (González 1999; Goodman 2020). This has eroded community trust and hampered collaboration. Labor union leaders are well aware that consuls must navigate the complex bureaucratic layers in the Mexican government before advocating on behalf of their emigrants in any meaningful way. Furthermore, consulates typically have no department dedicated exclusively to worker advocacy. The protection of labor rights is assigned to the legal protection section, a department in charge of multiple issues including family law, criminal defense, and corpse repatriation.

Ultimately, consulates have limited resources to provide legal services to workers with labor grievances because a significant part of their budget for legal services is devoted to other obligations such as advocating for incarcerated citizens or supporting family repatriations. Consequently, union leaders have to compete for consuls' attention and convince them to increase awareness about the importance of workers' rights.

INCREASING ACCESS TO JUSTICE
FOR IMMIGRANT WORKERS

In addition to labor education and outreach, consular involvement in co-enforcement involves broadening access to legal services. Access to a legal advocate is a critical aspect for individual claims making, the engine of labor regulation in the United States. Legal services providers in this arena include private attorneys, many of whom also work with nonprofits. They may work on a contingency or volunteer basis, and on rare occasions may formally contract with a consulate, as described in chapter 2. Below we outline this aspect of consular collaboration and how legal advocates worked with consuls to advance worker claims.

The Critical Role of Legal Services for Worker Rights

Beyond general outreach and education, Labor Rights Week aims to help aggrieved migrant workers file claims. Key partners in this regard are public interest law organizations, who provide critical services while facing a number of resource constraints. An attorney at the Community Justice Project in Reading, Pennsylvania, for example, explained how funding limitations meant that their caseload was limited to those involving "survivors of domestic violence, victims of crime, and . . . people who are eligible for renewing Deferred Action for Childhood Arrivals."[41] They simply did not have the resources to handle labor and employment cases as well.

Funding in large part determines the type of clients that legal service providers can serve. According to a survey of a random sample of public interest law organizations, about a quarter of these organizations rely on federal funding from the Legal Services Corporation (Albiston, Li, and Nielsen 2017), which precludes grantees from serving undocumented immigrants (Legal Services Corporation 2020). Consequently this population is in dire need of services, even in regions with long-standing Mexican and undocumented communities. For example, outside of Sacramento, California, in Solano County, "there are no legal service organizations that support undocumented workers. . . . There never have been," explained the lead attorney for the newly created Center for Workers' Rights. While in fact several regional groups serve undocumented workers, this perception nonetheless reflects a very real service gap. Furthermore, many of the area agencies that do serve undocumented clients do not wade into labor standards enforcement territory, "even for legal permanent residents and others who are able to legally work in the United States."[42] Some legal aid organizations will create sister organizations with separate funding streams that can serve undocumented clients, but these often have far less capacity.[43] This inequity is especially pronounced in places with a thin civil society presence and with state and local governments that do not support labor standards enforcement efforts (Fine and Bartley 2019).

Legal service providers are also often constrained by their specific organizational mission, as not all of them have the same mandate when it comes to worker rights. For instance, some of these legal groups, such as the Southern Poverty Law Center in Atlanta, focus on impact litigation around "wage and hour abuses . . . harassment, discrimination, racial profiling . . . and anti-immigrant laws," rather than on processing individual claims throughout the Southeast.[44] In some of these cases, the Mexican government has issued formal rebukes of US policy or has even collaborated on legal challenges as a friend of the court, as in the October 2019 amicus curiae brief filed by the Mexican government to the US Supreme Court of the United States in a case regarding the rescission of the Deferred Action for Childhood Arrivals (DACA). This brief stressed how terminating the program would return its beneficiaries to a state of vulnerability (SRE 2011b; SCOTUS 2012; Associated Press 2019).

Regional differences and funding priorities each shape the services available to workers. In the Southeast region, for example, the Southern Poverty Law Center's Esperanza Project focuses especially on workplace sexual abuse and harassment targeting immigrant women in fieldwork (SPLC 2006). The office of the Equal Justice Center in Dallas concentrates primarily on "litigation in state and federal court on behalf of low wage employees." It has "a special interest in representing immigrant workers," who largely hail from Mexico and Central and South America. And the "migrant offices" of the California Rural Legal Assistance network have an even more focused aim: they can only help agricultural workers such as "farm workers, dairy workers, packing house workers."[45] Moreover, driven by support from the Department of State (US Department of State 2021) and philanthropic interest (NEO Philanthropy 2017), legal service provision has increasingly focused on "human trafficking" (one of the few exceptions to serving undocumented clients).[46] These complex cases involving U or T visas require labor and employment attorneys to work in conjunction with immigration lawyers, who must then cooperate with law enforcement to establish a basis for the case.[47]

We found that legal service providers seldom focused solely on workplace issues; they could, however, use their resources and programs dedicated to other issues to perform some worker outreach as well. Catholic Migration Services in Queens, for instance, was contracted to run the labor hotline for the Mexican consulate in New York City. As one of its employee noted: "We have a very strong immigration and housing program . . . so people sometimes come for . . . consultations. Then they find out about the workers' rights programs and later they might come back and just walk into the office and ask to talk to a lawyer. We're pretty flexible about that." Many of the worker cases they received came in through this *línea laboral* (labor hotline), as well as via referrals from other legal clinics. An estimated one-third of these calls were from Mexican immigrants, with the rest of the callers being immigrants from the long list of countries of origin of New York City's diverse Latino population.[48]

Legal services are often provided by complex organizations engaged in a wide array of organizing and advocacy projects, such as the Services Immigrant Rights and Education Network (SIREN) in San Jose, California. Arguably the most prominent immigrant rights advocacy organization in Silicon Valley, SIREN provides immigration legal assistance, including in some trafficking cases.[49] Other organizations such as the Wage Justice Center in Los Angeles—known for its Day Labor Hotline—are specialized legal service providers focusing on wage theft.[50] The collaboration networks among these organizations are diverse, varying significantly from place to place. For example, in cities with law schools, law students supply a crucial volunteer base for legal aid clinics. In other places where there are few law schools and attorneys are hard to attract, paralegal staff are the primary service providers.

The range of services that public interest law organizations offer vary. Many legal advocates lead "Know Your Rights" workshops or health and safety trainings. Some legal service providers primarily provide representation for clients filing a formal claim. In California, relevant agencies may include, for example, the Labor Commission or the Department of Fair Employment and Housing,[51] or their federal counterparts in places with no state regulatory apparatus. Legal service providers may even provide technical advice or translation assistance in small-claims court (a popular, though some argue fraught, site for demanding small-scale restitution) (Thomas 2020).[52] Some groups work with other larger volunteer firms for more specialized cases, such as those involving workers' compensation, to provide direct representation to injured workers.[53] Still others are engaged in policy advocacy and capacity building with community organizations, including the local consulate.[54]

Clients who work with nonprofit legal service providers often have to meet low-income guidelines. These groups are especially important for immigrant workers, who tend to lack the language and bureaucratic know-how to navigate the labyrinth of regulatory agencies (Gleeson 2016). They are typically the only option for undocumented workers in particular. According to the Farmworker and Landscaper Advocacy Project in Chicago, "Of the cases that we get following Labor Rights Week, I can tell you that about 95 percent are from people who are neither US residents nor citizens."[55]

While most organizations affirmed that they did not formally collect data on their clients' immigration status, many anecdotally reported that undocumented immigrants made up a large proportion (in some cases nearly all) of their client base. Yet even in immigrant-friendly jurisdictions it was not always easy for these organizations to reach out to the undocumented, which was why events like the Semana de Derechos Laborales were so important. A staff member from the Legal Aid Society's Employment Law Center (one of the largest networks of legal advocates in California, now known as Legal Aid at Work) explained the necessity, and challenges, of helping undocumented workers claim their rights:

> In California, your status . . . actually has little relevance as to your rights except when it comes to the area of unemployment. You can't get unemployment benefits if you're undocumented, but everything else you're entitled [to]. You're entitled to workers' comp. You're entitled to be paid the minimum wage. You're entitled to overtime. You're entitled to time-and-a-half or . . . lunch and meal breaks and health, everything. . . . Low-wage workers who are undocumented have that extra fear factor of "Oh my God, if I complain they're gonna call ICE on me, and then I'm gonna be deported and my whole family's gonna be in trouble."[56]

Another paralegal explained that beyond this pervasive fear, many of the undocumented clients her center saw doubted whether they were actually entitled to compensation: "Because of their legal status, they feel they don't have any rights, first of all. . . . They're threatened [by employers] that because of their legal status they don't deserve these rights. . . . They basically live under feeling threatened [sic] that . . . their wages are not gonna be given to them, or that they'll be reported to the immigration office or to the feds." These challenges, she added, were further compounded by language barriers, educational limitations, lack of access to technology, and the inability to get time off work to pursue a claim.[57] Each of these outreach considerations shapes how legal service providers consider the costs and benefits of collaborating with a consulate.

What a Consulate Offers Labor and Employment Lawyers

The relationship between an area consulate and legal service providers varies widely. Much like labor unions, legal advocates are often called upon to facilitate "Know Your Rights" trainings for consular audiences during Labor Rights Week and beyond. They may also host a table inside the consular offices where they distribute informational flyers and brochures. On some occasions, a consulate may even physically host an organization's legal aid clinic. While some pioneer consulates regularly contract with lawyers who provide on-site consultations (for example, in Chicago) or sometimes even long-term representation, the vast majority of consulates rely on outside referrals. A group like the Farmworker and Landscaper Advocacy Project in Chicago, which focuses on a particular subset of workers, is able to tap into a consulate's lawyer network to refer out cases it receives. As one of its advocates explained, "For example, a construction or restaurant worker—we can't take those cases directly, but we can refer out to one of these [other] organizations or lawyers who can help."[58] In exchange, such organizations help expand the consulate's reach as well.

Consulates have a limited budget with which to retain a small group of lawyers to support the most vulnerable cases that come before the desk of the Consul de Protección (the consul heading the Legal Protection Section). Staff here keep a directory of reputable lawyers that community members can use to obtain a referral to a specialized practitioner with a solid track record. However, there is not much transparency around how a local lawyer gets added to this directory or is chosen to serve as a consulate lawyer. Sometimes, the SRE hires a specific law firm to produce a report on how to improve the delivery of legal services, but there is no formal bidding process. Rather, the perception among many is that personal networks determine which lawyers eventually secure contracts, which has sown significant distrust among community groups critical of consular dealings.

As part of its legal representation function, the consulate works with legal advocates in the community. The SRE sponsors the national Programa de Asistencia Jurídica a Personas Mexicanas a través de Asesorías Legales Externas en los Estados Unidos de América / Legal Assistance Program to Mexicans by Attorneys in the United States, an initiative that has been deployed to the fifty-two consulates throughout the United States to provide basic legal services in multiple legal arenas including administrative, human rights, criminal, civil, labor, and immigration law. This program is complemented by JURIMEX, a hotline organized in collaboration with several groups of US lawyers that offers free and confidential legal advice in Spanish on issues related to certain areas of US law across several consulates in Florida and California. This hotline is staffed twenty-four hours, seven days a week, and typically handles cases involving car and work-related accidents. Within this structure of legal advocacy, only a small portion of the cases received concern worker rights.

The Equal Justice Center of Dallas, an organization selected to receive funding from the local consulate for legal services, described the extent of consular support: "Yes, it's not a lot of funding. At the moment, it's pretty limited. As I understand it, when they get approval from Mexico City to add a legal organization to the group that they utilize, they . . . want to sort of wade into it and sort of get a little bit of experience with that organization first and see what they're able to help with. . . . I don't know if that's a funding source that . . . can be expanded."[59]

In sum, consular resources for legal services are typically very limited, and Mexico doesn't usually increase them except during crises. For example, when the threat of massive deportations to Mexico became apparent shortly after President Trump's inauguration, Mexico's then-president Enrique Peña Nieto announced the creation of a $50 million defense fund to be distributed across the consular network to pay for lawyers and to post bail for undocumented workers. Upon closer inspection, however, this initiative was met with significant cynicism from longtime immigration advocates. A quick back-of-the-envelope calculation about how many immigrants were at risk—and how many lawyers would be required to work all the cases—revealed that $50 million across the fifty-two office consular network was in fact a paltry sum.

Beyond this in-house assistance funded by the Mexican government, each consul of legal affairs maintains the previously discussed list of attorneys for referrals. In some jurisdictions, legal service providers have negotiated discounted rates for consular referrals.[60] Furthermore, there are instances in which the consulate invests in hotlines, like the Linea Laboral run in New York City by Catholic Migration Services, to buttress legal support. This program receives a modest $10,000 a year that can go only toward the salary of a Mexican national and the maintenance of the phone line and outreach materials.[61] But we found that this was a unique paid collaboration that did not exist uniformly across the consular network.

The direct relationship between a consulate and legal advocates goes both ways: that is, consulates refer clients to legal advocacy groups, and these groups supply information and provide other resources to consulates. A worker at the Women's Employment Rights Clinic, a small university-based organization in San Francisco, recalled: "Periodically I'll get an email . . . from someone within the San Francisco [consulate] office asking if I can talk to someone. . . . If I have a question . . . I know I can call them for the same." Similarly, Catholic Migration Services in New York City described how their organization provided information to consular officials across a range of issues: "I think it's really been good for the staff at the Mexican consulate. When they have a problem that they can't handle in house that they need to be able to speak to an attorney [about], they're able to put that person in contact with us."[62]

In jurisdictions where the Labor Rights Week has expanded to a year-round partnership, the communication between legal service providers and consular officials is more formalized. In New York City, Catholic Migration Services sent the local consulate regular reports: "We keep them notified about our litigation when we're representing workers in federal court . . . mostly just to let them know that we appreciate the support that we've gotten and that we want to keep them in the loop. And we want them to know that we're working very diligently on these issues."[63] In Houston, the Justice and Equality in the Workplace Partnership allowed the local consulate to cross-file claims across the disparate claims bureaucracies that seldom communicated otherwise (Gleeson 2012). In all these cases, more communication increases the odds of better outcomes.

Some consular relationships with legal service providers are more formal than others. Yet formalizing these relationships requires negotiation, a well-resourced legal services community, and the political will of the local consul. Only certain areas meet these conditions. For example, in Philadelphia, one provider explained, "There are some other organizations that have more formalized agreements where they have a contract to accept a certain amount of referrals from the Mexican consulate. . . . We have gotten referrals from them over the years, more or less regularly, and then when there was some staff turnover . . . the referrals went down. So we recently met with them again to figure out how to work more closely together again, and we are now sending a paralegal there once a month to do presentations and have gotten a few recent referrals."[64] As this provider's account indicates, establishing and maintaining these relationships can be a dynamic, time-consuming process.

Ultimately, consulates play varied roles in dealing with legal service providers. For some, the local consulate is part of a "co-counseling relationship" that "bring[s] resources that the client might need."[65] A lawyer with the California Rural Legal Assistance in San Francisco described the consulates as a kind of "microphone amplifying the voices [of providers]" that offered "outreach and [lets] everybody know about the resources that are available." In other cases, legal service providers viewed the consulate as a competitor for cases or as just another bureaucratic barrier.

Benefits of Legal Service Provider–Consulate Collaboration

All told, there are many benefits of collaborating with a consulate. Principal among them is gaining access to staff who can help translate for their Spanish-speaking clientele, an absolute requirement in legal proceedings (and a resource that is frequently in short supply, even in heavily Latino regions). Whereas labor unions and other community organizations almost always have Spanish-speaking organizers, the staff attorneys at legal aid organizations or government agencies are very frequently not bilingual.[66] This was the case in California's Central Valley, for example. One legal service provider staff member in that region—a bustling farmworker community—said that because an estimated 90 percent of her clients were monolingual Spanish speakers, the local consulate was a vital resource: "So that's why the partnership with [the consulate] . . . is so important, because . . . for every clinic, they send out two to three translators. . . . They're not lawyers—or some of them are actually lawyers in Mexico—but it's irrelevant for [these cases]. They go in, and they sit with an attorney who doesn't speak Spanish, and they translate for them."[67] Moreover, when holding workers' rights clinics in this region, consular staff provided additional help with intake: "They really help to speed everything up because people aren't waiting because there's no one to translate."[68] In this context, consular staff became, in essence, a force multiplier.

Furthermore, especially in places without an extensive support structure for vulnerable workers, a consulate can help legal aid organizations to disseminate workers' rights information. In Raleigh, North Carolina, for example, the local legal aid organization credited the consulate with helping them gain access to guest workers fearful of being blacklisted for coming forward: "They [the consulate] lent us a little bit of their credibility, because . . . they don't want to be blacklisted and not be able to come back. . . . We've really cut down on that in North Carolina because we were able to get enough clients to complain about it, and we actually got a copy of the blacklist."[69] This collaboration was particularly striking given the consular network's discouragement of union membership in California's early agricultural unions in the 1930s (García y Griego 1988; González 1999) and its recent history of facilitating the deportation of its citizens in North America (Vosko 2016, 2018; Goodman 2020). (Some would argue that even today consulates abet such practices through benign neglect veiled as diplomatic neutrality.)

Lingering mistrust notwithstanding, the credibility that consulates provide is especially important for new providers looking to build their base in a community. As the founder of the Center for Workers' Rights in Sacramento noted about consulates:

> The sheer volume of contacts that they get from workers reaching out for assistance is more substantial than any individual organization. So they are able to kind of direct individuals to our services . . . since the workers are already contacting them. It also is a comfortable place for the workers to contact, because they feel like we dealt with the consulate already and are familiar with who they are and what they do. So since we're a new organization, we want them to know that we have kind of the stamp of approval of an organization they already have worked with before.[70]

Even in arguably the most progressive jurisdiction in the country, San Francisco, the consulate played an important role in reaching out to the still-vulnerable undocumented community. This made sense given the consulate's centrality to the daily life of Mexican immigrants, who had to navigate its bureaucracy in order to access key services and documents. Because of these necessary and repeated interactions, however, some immigrants had accumulated deep resentments toward this mega-bureaucracy, which had a reputation for being classist and racist. In this sense, the Semana de Derechos Laborales (with its related media blitz and outreach push) served to break down perceptions of the consular network as rigid and to revamp its community reputation. According to one San Francisco advocate, "I think that this Labor Rights Week—the media attention and coverage and outreach that they've done—has built a sense in the community that they can go there for other things. And those things may not be directly something that they can help them with, but . . . they have developed ties and collaboration with community groups to ensure that when something comes their way, they know where to send people and they will try to help. I think that's significant."[71]

Widespread exposure to the consulate also means that some migrants are comfortable and familiar with the institution in a way that they are not with other US-based organizations. "There are always complaints," one service provider in Chicago explained. "But you also find people who speak well of the consulate, [saying] that it has supported and helped them . . . that they had a case and it helped them find free legal assistance. Or, for example, say a family member died and the consulate helped then send the body back to Mexico."[72] In the most extreme cases, community members relied on the consulate "to try to find their loved ones or family members when they can't find them, when they are either crossing or have been detained."[73]

As we will see in chapter 4, many grassroots and worker centers can vouch for a consulate's efficacy in solving emergencies for precarious workers. We should remember, though, the clientelist nature of the Mexican government in relation to its offering of bureaucratic services. Only those who have leverage (*palanca*) or the support of certain advocates tend to benefit from this efficient help. For the masses who show up every day at consular doorsteps facing an emergency without an advocate referral, services may not be delivered as swiftly as needed.

On the whole, legal providers reported varied experiences working with consulates. Some, like the following provider in San Francisco, were very pleased: "They're a lot like all the other partners . . . They're just like, 'Roll up your sleeves. What do we need to do to get to work here?' . . . I love that about them. . . . It works perfectly because they're ready to do whatever it takes, just like all of our other collaborating organizations that host our clinics."[74] Legal advocates also understood that—like them—the consulate was bound by bureaucratic procedure. As one Washington, DC, lawyer explained, the local consulate's formal role was not to help work out "a labor dispute between a private employer and an employee."[75] Many providers thus had limited expectations of the consulate when it came to aiding with legal advocacy.

Consulates can be especially useful to legal service providers in gathering the required documents for the claims process. Especially during the era of REAL ID, which prohibited migrants from accessing government-issued IDs, migrants needed Mexican identity documents if they were to seek restitution in their workers' rights cases.[76] Most commonly, workers visited a consulate to procure their Mexican passports and the *matrícula consular*. These documents were also important for obtaining local forms of identification (like municipal IDs) that had emerged in proimmigrant jurisdictions like San Francisco and Chicago. They were especially critical for negotiating encounters with local law enforcement and for gaining entry into, for example, a labor standards government agency building or for collecting restitution. From 2003 to 2019, the Mexican government issued an average of 910,000 *matrículas* throughout the world, with a notable pandemic-era dip to only 502,635 in 2020. At its height, over 1,100,000 such documents were issued in 2015 (SRE 2021e), coinciding with the massive push to prepare for the landmark Deferred Action for Parents of Americans and Lawful Permanent Residents (NILC 2015),[77] which placed enormous pressure on consular documentation services as hopeful immigrants rushed to get the required paperwork in order.[78]

Certain categories of immigrants also relied on the consulate to obtain the necessary documents for seeking immigration relief. These consular documents were essential for basic survival, as they were needed to obtain housing, turn on utilities, or access immigration resources. For example, DACA applicants seeking a work permit often had to visit the consulate to obtain a birth certificate, as did parents returning to Mexico with a child who needed similar identity documents to "reintegrate" into Mexican institutions.[79] These consular services were especially important for adults. As a lawyer with the Community Justice Project in Reading, Pennsylvania, explained, "Usually, children in Reading will have a school ID, so they'll have some sort of photo ID, but [for] adults it's often a huge problem."[80]

As with unions and worker centers, many regional and statewide legal aid organizations are able to piggyback on the outreach infrastructure of mobile consulates. Legal service providers in particular are typically concentrated in dense urban centers like New York City, with limited reach to underserved immigrant regions like upstate New York and Long Island where there is tremendous need. These imbalances are compounded by the lack of significant and dedicated funding, which hampers the outreach capacity for rural communities in particular.[81] Such outreach also requires building a knowledge base about the resources in those communities, which are often very different from those of the city where a consulate is based.[82] Rural (and sometimes suburban) workers are doubly vulnerable given their geographic location (de Graauw and Gleeson 2020) and their concentration in high-violation informal jobs like domestic work and construction.[83] Not only are organizations few and far between in these more remote places, but the organizations that do exist tend to be younger and have fewer resources. Consulates often serve as incubators and anchors for these newer organizations. For example, the Employment Law Center, based in the San Francisco Bay Area, established itself in Fresno, California, as well with the support of the Mexican consulate (Legal Aid at Work 2012).

A consulate can also extend legal service providers' reach across borders. Under US law, workers are often still eligible to receive restitution even if they have returned (or been deported) to their country of origin. This is typically the case with guest workers who travel seasonally,[84] but it is also true for immigrants who for whatever reason are no longer able to stay in the United States (because of deportation or voluntary return, for example). In these cases, government agencies and legal service providers often struggle to reach workers who have either initiated or won a claim, a reality that employers often bank on in order to avoid having to pay restitution. A consulate can assist in bridging that gap by helping to locate workers across Mexican states and facilitate payment. For example, the Equal Rights Advocates, a women's rights legal aid organization in San Francisco famous for its impact litigation, worked with the local consulate in a class action suit against supermarket labor brokers to secure restitution for workers who had returned to Mexico: "The Mexican consulate was very involved. . . . They were very helpful to us when we were doing outreach in Mexico, trying to find workers."[85]

In the best-case scenario, a consulate acts as a convener for legal service providers (as they also do for labor unions). As one service provider in Chicago explained, "The consulate has also facilitated communication and made it possible for us to have a seat at the table. . . . There [are] often many differences [among organizations]." From her perspective, the local consulate had, through Labor Rights Week, succeeded in bringing advocates together toward a common goal.[86] Similarly, the New York City consulate, one of the largest and best staffed in the country, has successfully convened and worked with the broader Latin American consular corps, further expanding collaborative possibilities.[87] The sustainability of this model throughout the entire year—and not just during Labor Rights Week —remains limited.

In sum, legal service providers play an important role as brokers for victims of labor law violations seeking restitution, helping workers navigate the complex bureaucratic layers of labor regulation and co-enforcement. Collaborating with consulates provides valuable information to legal aid providers in their efforts to locate returned immigrant workers who are owed restitution in labor violation cases. For legal aid providers with enough resources to serve clients, the Mexican consulates also offer an excellent opportunity to educate the public about the services and solutions they can offer to workers with grievances. Furthermore, consulates can filter out disreputable providers and support (through collaboration) honest brokers. This has the potential to reduce the incidence of fraud related to *notarios públicos*, predatory offices common in communities with limited access to legal aid organizations. These collaborations are highly synergistic and mutually beneficial, as consulates have the opportunity to establish formal contracts with legal aid organizations, expand the range of services offered to constituents, and transform consulates into one-stop shops for immigrant workers in need of consular documents and legal services.

Challenges to Legal Service Provider–Consulate Collaboration

Despite these myriad benefits, one of the biggest challenges for legal service providers is finding the staff, time, and financial resources to collaborate with a consulate. As the head of one of the largest legal aid groups in Chicago explained, "I think the challenge is that there is no funding for it. . . . The Mexican consulate doesn't provide any funding as far as printing out brochures or . . . helping organizations that might not have the capacity to travel . . . [or] reimburs[ing] them for mileage and things like that. It's one of those entirely volunteer operations, and that limits a little bit some of the groups that can participate."[88] This statement confirms the budgetary analysis we present in chapter 2: while an elite subset of organizations do receive modest support for outreach and referrals at a handful of consular offices, this help is insufficient given community need.

The consular ethos of neutrality has proved challenging time and again, even for legal service providers who are themselves constrained by legal mandates. Under the rubric of legal protection (a preordained activity for consulates), consular staff are usually comfortable only in pushing to implement *existing* law. In some cases, though, consuls act more boldly and are willing to act outside norms of neutrality. For example, in the Washington, DC, metro area, the consulate worked with the Legal Aid Justice Center to limit state and local collaboration with immigration enforcement. As one advocated noted: "The Mexican consulate here in Virginia actually got in a bit of a political dispute with some state and local legislatures who felt that it was entirely inappropriate for the Mexican consul to be sharing opinions on what they considered to be state and local issues."[89] Typically, as a staff member at the Legal Assistance Foundation in Chicago described, the overarching problem with consulates was that their actions were not institutionalized and were instead dependent on "what the individual who is leading the consulate wants to focus their energy [on]."[90]

This variability was compounded by the inconsistency of some consular practices. According to one advocate, consular staff would often refuse her clients a passport, only to relent when she intervened. This combination of rigidity (e.g., formalized protocols) and inconsistency (e.g., the personal preferences of the consul) could make it difficult to develop a close working relationship with communities, especially vulnerable ones that required flexibility, noted a Raleigh provider: "The consulate is quite formal and bureaucratic, so it's harder to schedule things . . . because we work with farmworkers. . . . [It is] a problem to go out in a suit to solve a farmworker problem, for example," adding that "because . . . they are who they are—it's harder for [the consulate] to be accessible [than] for other organizations."[91]

The inability to pivot in order to meet community needs is unsurprising for a centralized bureaucracy unaccustomed to community work. Therefore, partnerships with community organizations can be uneven and often disappointing. Describing an inability to reach consular staff, repeated attempts to schedule mobile consulate outreach to outlying farm labor camps, and a generally uninterested consular leadership, the Raleigh service provider explained: "They [the consulate] keep reminding us to do something in their waiting room, and that's just not where the farmworkers are. . . . These farmworkers are severely disadvantaged, they would like transportation, they're out in the sticks, they are the most disadvantaged, or among the most disadvantaged, of the Mexican immigrants who are here. But you're not going to see any of them if you just sit in the consulate."

This disconnect was compounded by the perennial problem of turnover, explained one San Francisco provider, who expressed frustration after long efforts to build a relationship with consular staff: "Once you lose contact with that person because they have changes in their staffing, it's really hard to establish that [connection again]."[92] Doing so took tremendous time on the part of local organizations, who "have to keep in touch to make sure that . . . [we] have someone from the inside able to answer questions who knows you and who knows of your work and who wants to help."[93]

In sum, legal service providers frequently voiced frustration over the excessive bureaucratic hurdles their clients faced when visiting a consulate to obtain documentation. While some very dedicated consuls were willing to risk diplomatic skirmishes with local US authorities, local aid providers frequently cited a disconnect between office bureaucrats who seemed apathetic about meeting their constituents in the community. This disconnect was particularly consequential in newer immigrant communities, where a civic advocacy infrastructure was lacking and there were fewer alternatives for migrant workers seeking help.

ASSESSING TRIPARTITE CO-ENFORCEMENT
AND CONSULAR ENGAGEMENT: VALUE ADDED,
PERSISTENT COSTS

Seen through the lens of these bureaucratic and technical collaborations, the consulate is a crucial partner in many areas. By leveraging its institutional resources to reach immigrants where nonprofits are typically more scarce, or by facilitating technocratic requirements (e.g., procuring documents), tripartite co-enforcement can be an important corrective to the standard claims-driven approach to holding employers accountable. Free from the surveillance requirements that often complicate federal agencies' access to vulnerable immigrant communities, the consular network can leverage homeland allegiance to allay the fears of some reluctant workers. Though community-based organizations often have tremendous access to such communities and a wealth of linguistic and cultural capital, they often lack the resources and legitimacy that consular offices enjoy. This is particularly the case with the Mexican consulate, whose fifty-two-office network in the United States represents the largest migrant flow in North America.

Yet as our interviews with both labor organizations and legal service providers illuminate, tripartite co-enforcement is often largely symbolic, and there are serious challenges to scaling up and sustaining these partnerships. Like any other major bureaucracy, consulates are complex organizations that often follow archaic rules and establish jurisdictional silos between and even within offices. The turnover of consular leadership is a constant source of frustration for community organizers, who may spend years developing working relationships, convincing consular leaders to step up to the plate, and then training consular staff to be functional partners, only to see them depart. Because of the nature of the consular system, officials are regularly reassigned after only a few years, career diplomats rarely stay in one place for a long time, and building grassroots trust and capacity is thus a never-ending challenge.

While the memoranda of understanding signed by US agencies and Mexico's SRE laid the groundwork for collaboration, workers' rights are only one of many concerns that consulates are asked to address. Equally pressing issues include providing legal counsel for incarcerated Mexican nationals, arranging the repatriation of corpses, securing educational access, facilitating the complicated bureaucratic dynamics of transnational families, and, recently, testing and vaccinating a low-wage worker population that is disproportionately vulnerable in the global COVID-19 pandemic.

Our research calls into question the efficacy and sustainability of relying on the sending state to act as a co-enforcer. While consulates are uniquely situated to wield influence and deploy resources, they are not necessarily the best case managers and certainly are not equipped to cultivate worker resistance, as critics we spoke with argued. From a purely organizational perspective, a consulate is set up to process at scale, much like a DMV. The consulates we observed rarely had in-house resources for service provision, relying almost entirely on referrals to other organizations in their network. Thus, we found that the most important function of consulates was not necessarily handling everyday cases directly but rather being sufficiently connected to community partners so that they could effectively guide individuals seeking redress to other sources of aid. With several exceptions, consular offices were neither equipped to follow up on cases nor adequately funded to ensure that a claim was submitted and pursued to the end. All of these limitations plagued worker centers and other advocates as well, who were themselves attempting to fill the gaps left by the paltry national level of union representation (6 percent) and an underfunded and claims-driven labor standards enforcement mechanism that focuses on reacting to labor violations as they occur but invests little in prevention.

Consular outreach was inconsistent and often met with skepticism. Advocates often felt that consular officials were simply pursuing their own self-interest and lacked a real vision for year-round programming that would serve the most vulnerable Mexican migrant worker populations in outlying areas. Advocate after advocate bemoaned uncoordinated events that they saw more as PR efforts, an unreasonable reliance on the volunteer labor of community collaborators, and even consular nepotism toward preferred legal service providers, a form of organizational gatekeeping that discounted the efforts of the pioneering community organizers who had begun demanding accountability decades ago.

For migrant-led labor organizations in particular, the challenges plaguing tripartite co-enforcement perhaps had less to do with the unique role of the sending state than with the distinction between promoting regulatory compliance and building worker power. And on that last metric—building worker power—consulates (and every other labor standards enforcement agency) fell and will continue to fall short. As one local organizer charged, the Mexican consulate is a *depoliticized space*, one that intentionally skirts around political entanglements and remains inactive on "issues that matter." To be sure, the central tension between service provision and organizing, which Fine (2006) details at length, is ever present in tripartite co-enforcement as well, with or without consular involvement. And as the next two chapters examine, demands for accountability far exceed the aspirations outlined in ministerial agreements.

In Mexico's case, civil society organizations—including the labor and legal groups mentioned above—have pushed for an agenda that goes beyond merely propping up a crumbling US labor regulation regime. Civil society organizations have also argued for a more expansive view of migrant worker needs and of the receiving *and* sending state's mandate to fulfill these social welfare protections. For groups in the United States, advocates have addressed a litany of demands to Mexico, which many see as responsible for the lack of economic opportunities driving nationals from their homeland. Many migrant advocates see their emigrant labor as the sole saving grace for transnational families and communities left behind who rely on remittances. Their concerns go beyond compliance with minimum-wage and health/safety laws (the primary focus of local co-enforcement efforts): they are calling for more comprehensive development policies that privilege Mexican workers over multinationals, for states and companies to be held accountable for deep-seated corruption, and for a greater willingness to confront the US government's neocolonial approach to border militarization, exploitative guest worker regimes, and skyrocketing deportation levels sending people to (and through) Mexico. Though seemingly unrelated, Mexico's complicity on all these fronts further stymies attempts at tripartite co-enforcement efforts, while also creating innovative openings for the advocacy we describe in the next two chapters.

4

Advocacy and Accountability in State–Civil Society Relations

While origin countries and their diasporic bureaucracies have the potential to control and exploit their emigrant populations, they can also serve as an important advocate. Historically, Mexico has a sordid track record of fanning the flames of antiunionism and fueling a race to the bottom in terms of labor export—failing to defend the rights of its workers abroad. Indeed, immigrant expectations for the sending state have been shaped by these histories and past experiences. However, as many localities in the United States have made a hard-right turn toward anti-immigrant policies, the consular network remains one of the few organizations that can meaningfully step in to redress migrant abuses. To be sure, many consuls cited the constraints of diplomatic neutrality when asked about the extent of their advocacy, but many of these diplomats also exercised a great deal of power when possible, remaining within their jurisdictional capacities but at times going straight up to the line of interventionism.

Despite its limitations, therefore, the sending state has the clear *potential* to be an important actor in facilitating immigrants' access to rights and resources at the workplace and beyond. Thus immigrant advocates have called on Mexico to be accountable and to utilize its power and capacity to address these diverse needs. Their pressure has led to key provisions in the binational accords and consular initiatives described in chapter 2. These commitments have been valuable, but true accountability depends on the extent to which the Mexican government successfully fulfills these promises throughout *all* aspects of immigrant life. Indeed, despite specific agreements focusing on labor standards enforcement efforts, immigrant workers themselves do not see their labor concerns as separate from their issues with the other institutions with which they must interact back home and in their new destination.

The domestic Mexican situation in fact shapes migrant expectations abroad. In Mexico, as in many other Latin American countries, a protracted history of colonial rule still restricts equal access to political institutions and basic freedoms. Rural and peri-urban communities are often overlooked, and class overly determines social location in a country famous for having some of the highest levels of income inequality in the region—where 1 percent of the wealthiest individuals have 21 percent of the income (Esquivel Hernandez 2015). These geographic and material disadvantages follow ethnic lines as well, as indigenous poverty rates are four times higher than those of other groups. Each of these structural factors has shaped access to education, jobs, and other basic services such as health care, social welfare supports, and legal protection (Fox 1998).

These factors and life experiences affect the subjective perceptions of Mexican immigrants living in the United States when they encounter consular institutions and attempt to access their rights and benefits (Martínez-Schuldt 2020). For example, as Mexican immigrant workers consider approaching a local consulate for help, they may also consider the Mexican policies that influenced their decision to leave home in the first place, as well as Mexico's uneven track record in supporting them abroad. This complicated and tense relationship between Mexicans living abroad and the institutions that represent them is mediated by diverse civil society organizations. Some of these organizations view Mexico as a trusted partner for immigrant worker rights, others as a government bureaucracy that must be held accountable.

In this chapter, we examine these diverse relationships that emerge beyond the well-defined realms of labor co-enforcement. We do so by focusing on alt-labor groups such as worker centers and the wide array of immigrant rights organizations that seek to expand the scope of sending-state accountability.

THE ROCKY EVOLUTION OF MEXICO'S
STATE-SOCIETY RELATIONS

The relationship between consular officials and Mexican immigrants has significantly shifted since the early days of direct consular interference in the unionization efforts of Mexican farmworkers. As historian Gilbert González (1999) documents, Mexican consulates in the 1930s frequently sided with California growers in opposition to the best interests of the Mexican workforce. In fact, consuls consistently steered Mexican workers away from radical leftist unions in favor of a more moderate labor agenda based on the Mexican state model, which aimed to cultivate loyalty and political dependency among migrants. In sum, the consuls promoted a paternalistic policy and supported the formation of Mexican unions instead of encouraging multiethnic organizing.

The Mexican government's paternalistic attitudes toward the diaspora in the 1930s were in line with the labor laws that emerged following the Mexican

Revolution (1910–20). Progressive federal labor laws enacted in Mexico's constitution offered crucial legitimacy for a budding social movement looking to challenge the state's conservative capitalist aspirations (Bensusán and Cook 2003). However, a democratic and independent labor movement never materialized (Bensusán 2000). While organized labor did benefit from tripartite labor conciliation systems and publicly financed social welfare programs under postrevolutionary authoritarianism, few independent unions flourished prior to 1985,[1] a date considered by many scholars to be the beginning of Mexico's long democratic transition.

The Partido Revolucionario Institucional / Institutional Revolutionary Party (PRI), the long-standing authoritarian party that inherited the ideals of the Mexican Revolution, all but abandoned its democratic impulses when it exerted control over Mexican labor unions. Every member of the Confederación de Trabajadores de México / Confederation of Mexican Workers was automatically enrolled in the PRI, and the party and the unions formed a natural alliance throughout the twentieth century (Roberts 2014). Even in the 1930s, Mexican presidential candidates would periodically visit Mexican expatriates in hopes of winning the hearts and minds of their relatives left behind. In subsequent decades, Mexican migrants would organize from California to Kansas City and Chicago to demand absentee voting rights without any success (Santamaría Gómez 2001). It was not until 1989 that migrant political rights took center stage, when Cuauhtémoc Cárdenas Solórzano of the Frente Democrático Nacional / National Democratic Front made a series of visits to the United States after narrowly losing his first bid for the Mexican presidency. In a speech in Chicago, Cárdenas Solórzano famously called for migrants to be included in the political arena, urging them to mobilize to demand the right to vote absentee (Cárdenas Solórzano 1989).

In the 1990s, many Mexican immigrant organizations demanded the passage of a constitutional amendment that would allow Mexicans abroad to participate in presidential elections. Key proponents included hometown associations and political committees such as the Coalición por los Derechos Políticos de los Mexicanos en el Exterior / Coalition for the Political Rights of Mexicans Abroad. In 1996, Mexico reformed Article 36 of its constitution to eliminate the territorial restriction to vote in an electoral district. Between 1996 and 2005, eighteen electoral reform initiatives were submitted with the support of activists, migrant organizations, political parties, and academics. This advocacy paved the way to amending the federal electoral law—the Código Federal de Instituciones y Procedimientos Electorales—in 2005 to grant absentee ballots for Mexicans living abroad. The first Consejo Consultivo del Instituto de los Mexicanos en el Exterior / Advisory Board of the Institute of Mexicans Abroad (CCIME) led the final push to pass this amendment, whose approval spurred multiple migrant-led organizations to lodge new demands, including improving the quality of consular services. The immigrant rights marches of 2006 in cities across the United States in fact coincided with "Get Out the Vote" mobilizations of Mexican expatriates to be included in

Mexico's electoral register. This ultimately contributed to the increase in absentee ballots in Mexico's 2006 presidential election. These organizations also united to leverage collective remittances to aid development in rural communities of origin via the now-defunct Tres por Uno (3 x 1) program, a federal matching-funds program aimed at leveraging family remittances to finance infrastructure, scholarships, and productive projects in rural Mexico (Bada 2010, 2011, 2014; Félix 2019; Pintor-Sandoval 2021).

Switching focus from the political to the labor arena, we should note that for all the conversations about how US labor and employment laws apply to immigrant workers, scholars often overlook the significance of Mexico's own tradition of relatively progressive *formal* labor regulation. In Mexico (as described in chapter 1), a tripartite system of labor enforcement was established in the 1930s to guarantee the labor protections offered by Article 123 of Mexico's constitution, which formally promised: "All persons have the right to socially useful and dignified work; to that end job creation and social organization for work will be promoted." The regulatory framework relies on labor conciliation and arbitration boards comprising labor, business, and government representatives at the federal, state, and local levels (Middlebrook 1995). This constitutional protection laid the groundwork for the emerging social movement rallying cry proclaiming the "right to stay home" (Bartra 2008) rather than be forced to migrate because of structural economic precarity.

These formal protections, however, are highly politicized. Mexican labor law grants the state unprecedented enforcement powers, with regulators having the ability to resolve both labor-management and intraunion conflicts. The state also keeps a tight grip over wages and strikes through its discretionary authority to interpret constitutional protections for labor rights and its ultimate control of tripartite labor boards and tribunals (Bensusán 2000; Bensusán and Cook 2003). These boards are composed in such a way as to prevent the creation of independent unions (which do not stand a chance at securing representation on them), and strike certification is rare, as represented unions tend to have fierce government loyalties. As a result, union members face an uphill battle to challenge existing practices or certify new union representation (De la Garza Toledo 2021).

Moreover, the low unionization rate of Mexico's labor force is compounded by the scale of its informal sector, which surpasses the size of the formal workforce. Today, Mexico has fifty-three million wage workers, but only about twenty-four million are defined as being in formal employment and by extension covered by one of the government-run social security funds and eligible for federal labor protection. In 2021, there were twenty-nine million informal workers. Furthermore, as in the United States, unionization rates in Mexico have fallen since the 1980s, and only about 4.4 million workers (14.5 percent) were unionized by 2018—with about half of these workers in the private sector (on par with the US workforce) (INEGI 2018, 2020, 2021).[2] The globalization of capital now guarantees a steady supply of precarious workers to multinational corporations, who decide where and when they should establish operations depending on flexibility, costs, and the labor regulation frameworks in the United States, Canada, and Mexico.

The significant size of the informal labor force (along with the woefully insufficient implementation of Mexico's labor reforms) is one of the leading causes of migration to the United States. In Hirschman's (1970) framework, the pattern of leaving low-wage informal employment in search of a higher-paying job in the United States is a classic example of an *exit* made necessary once the people's collective *voice* (e.g., popular protest) no longer has any chance of producing the desired change. Indeed, efforts to democratize labor unions and challenge labor law violations have mostly failed. Meanwhile, access to social security funds and other forms of social protection is severely limited. This is the predeparture context in which Mexican migrants have decided to head north over the last four decades.

CONFLICTED CONSULAR RELATIONSHIPS: BALANCING THE GOOD AND THE BAD

Across the board, union membership has fallen in the United States, especially in those industries in which Mexican immigrants are concentrated. While "alt-labor" groups have a limited capacity to bridge this gap, Mexican migrants have become a central target for outreach and have become critical leaders in corners of civil society often overlooked by labor scholars, including immigrant rights grassroots groups and hometown associations. Yet these organizations have also raised concerns of Mexican migrants that go far beyond the core issue of labor standards enforcement. They have urged the Mexican consular network to provide holistic support to migrant workers, especially those who are undocumented. In this regard, while alt-labor groups see the Mexican government—and the consular network as its representative abroad—as a necessary collaborator, they also push for increased accountability.

Worker centers emerged during the late 1970s and early 1980s in response to changes in manufacturing processes that increased the precarity of factory workers and drove down wages in service-sector jobs that attracted Latino immigrants. These organizations, many of which were connected to faith-based groups and labor unions, were frequently critical of existing organized labor institutions. Worker centers—many of which catered to immigrant workers—provided an alternative vehicle for collective action in the absence of an existing organizational infrastructure that addressed the needs of these low-wage workers (Gordon 2005; Fine 2006). In parallel fashion, the Mexican consular network was compelled to respond to the rapid growth of Mexican immigrant communities in new destinations. This was in large part a response to the demands of Mexican civil society organizations for better consular services to serve these new communities. For example, following more than a decade of advocate demands, a consulate office was established in Milwaukee (whose community previously had to travel hours to the nearest office in Chicago).[3] However, rural communities have continued to demand more frequent mobile consulate visits to regions located outside the metropolitan consulates.

The goals of many of these organizations go far beyond passively educating workers about their workplace rights and providing legal support for a select few to bring individual claims against their employers. Apart from basic access to documentation and other transactions that undocumented migrants need to navigate daily life, low-wage worker advocates have called for the Mexican government to offer a wide range of social services, including health services, workforce development, educational opportunities, affordable housing, financial counseling, and of course help navigating labor regulations. As described in chapter 2, Mexico has an obligation to offer basic legal protection to emigrants, but consuls on the ground have also stepped—sometimes reluctantly and in response to advocate demands—into a broader role: catering to a fledgling emigrant constituency (Sherman 1999; Iskander 2010; Délano 2011; Délano Alonso 2018; Félix 2019).

Unique Benefits of Consular Collaboration

Collaborating with a consulate is a peculiar affair. Part of the reason labor unions and legal aid organizations (like the ones we describe in chapter 3) work so well with the consular network is that they too tend to be hierarchically organized and follow formal rules and protocols; they are thus well set up to help migrants navigate bureaucracies with similar procedures. In turn, consular staff view these types of organizations as their "preferred partners" and refer community members to them. Meanwhile, more informal, movement-oriented advocacy organizations are often left out in the cold.[4]

Few organizational leaders whom we interviewed were exclusively laudatory or critical of the consular network. Rather, they tended to see it as a potentially useful but flawed ally. When it comes to supporting potential claimants, grassroots organizations inhabit a liminal space within the labor rights arena. They accompany workers through often confusing and daunting bureaucracies, but they do not always have the same direct access to US labor standards enforcement agencies staff that consular officials do. Therefore, many worker center leaders see special value in their relationship with local consulate offices, which can help their members secure necessary documents and help advocates gain access to agency personnel who could provide key updates throughout the life of a claim, which can drag on for years.

Community leaders also value consuls' unique access and connections when community members are detained or face deportation. Indeed, the ever-present shadow of immigration enforcement is a central concern for worker centers. Leaders often described how members came for help with a wide array of challenges and how it was often impossible to differentiate immigration enforcement from labor rights efforts. As one leader explained, "There's a false separation in the idea of labor and immigration as two discrete issues. Immigration is certainly about labor, and inherently about labor rights."[5] Thus the consulate was a useful partner. If a community member could not be located or needed documents quickly after being detained, consular staff could provide critical assistance.

A consulate office is also a one-stop shop, offering not just access to documentation but outreach more broadly. We have already examined how labor outreach is necessary for co-enforcement (chapter 3), and the consulate office can attract various community members who might not otherwise approach a grassroots group directly for help. Consular staff routinely partner with experts in occupational health and safety, financial literacy, tax return advice, literacy and education (through the Plazas Comunitarias), and basic preventive health care services (through the Ventanillas de Salud). Many representatives from the CCIME with whom we spoke had an especially long and productive history of working directly with consular staff. These representatives often benefited from the Mexican government's transversal coordination of migrant affairs, which included funds to send delegations to Mexico to discuss trade and commercial exchange opportunities with government officials from various ministries such as trade, tourism, and agriculture, among others.

Perhaps the benefit of the Mexican consular network to worker centers and other immigrant rights organizations that we found most surprising was the ability, via Labor Rights Week, to reach non-Mexican Latino immigrants. In this regard, several worker centers we spoke with singled out the Mexican consulate for praise in comparison to other Latin American consulates with large immigrant populations in metropolitan areas. For Mexican diplomats, embracing non-Mexican Latino immigrants can be an excellent opportunity to reframe Mexico's reputation, which has suffered after the well-documented mistreatment Central Americans have endured at the hands of criminals, the Mexican police, and Mexican immigration authorities while they transit through Mexico (O. Martínez 2013).

A common fear among workers in the community is that the Department of Labor (DOL) may report them to Immigration Customs Enforcement (ICE) if they attempt to access their rights. While organization staff expend considerable energy assuring workers that DOL will not report them, workers are often more comfortable approaching consular representatives than DOL staff. One worker center leader, however, described the consulate office as an option of last resort for precarious workers who lacked the ability to navigate the social service landscape: "If people have to choose between the consulate and an NGO like ours, they come first with us to ask for help. In general, we offer help to people with more education, with an ID or with papers."[6] Nonetheless, given their limited opportunities for seeking help outside of working hours, many co-nationals like the idea of going to a one-stop shop with a low bar to entry like the consulate office rather than appealing to the DOL or worker centers.

Yet we found that despite these benefits, many community organizations struggled to work with consular staff, and their leaders relayed to us a multifaceted set of criticisms from member experiences, which we discuss below.

Typical Complaints about Consular Collaboration

Organizations that focus on educating workers about their workplace rights and/or helping them file claims have found some concrete ways to collaborate with the Mexican government. On the whole, though, we found many community organizations to be highly critical of their broader interactions with consular staff. Leaders we spoke with were frustrated by what they viewed as empty promises of legal protection and the challenges posed by consular bureaucracy, staffing shortages, and lack of communication. Their members often came to them with complaints that consular staff were arrogant, bossy, and ill-tempered and exhibited a lack of compassion for the everyday troubles of low-wage workers. By and large, grassroots immigrant organizations had (perhaps outsized) expectations for the consular bureaucracy, hoping it would be an activist, critically reflexive office instead of merely providing services (Freire 2000). They felt consular bureaucrats should be more present in the community and should publicly advocate for workers, perhaps by visiting New York City construction sites to witness the dangerous conditions under which their co-nationals worked.[7]

One former CCIME member who led a farmworker organization in Orlando spoke favorably of the IME's programming, such as thematic *jornadas* and other cultural celebrations. Nonetheless, they too were frustrated with the perennially neutral stance of consuls, who refused to advocate for policies that would improve farmworker labor protections and who failed to involve farmworkers in their deliberations. Such leaders saw the consular network primarily as a service-oriented institution that maintained the status quo of farmworkers in Florida.[8] Indeed, the lack of earmarked consular funds for labor outreach (reflected in staffing shortages for community work) severely limits what a consulate office is actually able to do as a lateral partner. For example, some activists lamented that their local consulate did not even have the resources to provide chairs and tables for a soccer game at a public park.

Funding aside, other civil society actors complained of other shortcomings. For example, one CCIME member who led a group in New York City that had historically organized Mexican workers recounted how community members were frustrated at the rigidity of the process for obtaining a passport or a *matrícula* from the consulate. Members would often travel long distances to Manhattan, only to be turned away because of what they perceived as a trivial and arbitrary reason, such as their documents having "too many wrinkles." For some people, being asked to return with another (unwrinkled) document to prove national identity would be annoying but doable. But for many—such as those who arrived in the United States at an early age and quickly joined the labor force instead of pursuing a high school diploma—it might be impossible. For instance, a Florida worker center leader complained about the obsolete and inflexible consular bureaucracy not understanding that DACA youth working in the fields did not usually have the two pieces of Mexican-government-issued documentation required to access services, let alone one from the US government.

These daily communication challenges, and a fundamental mismatch between the urgency of community needs and the glacial pace of bureaucratic protocol, were the source of much of the rancor we encountered in Mexican immigrant civil society in the United States. CCIME representatives in New York City tried to address this service gap by inviting consular staff to explain the rationale behind their strict documentation procedures,[9] somewhat easing members' criticisms. This largely fruitful collaboration was followed by several improvements in the digitalization of birth certificates, which ultimately sped up the process. Thus the efforts of transnational grassroots advocates to engage the Mexican consular network through urban democracy could produce successes (Fung 2004). However, these close working relationships were rare and rather fleeting, especially because high turnover at consulate offices made retaining institutional memory challenging. Through persistence and dedication, some remarkable collaborative relationships were formed, but on the whole, new consular staff in particular struggled to easily reallocate resources to crucial emerging priorities, hampering cooperation.

And yet even those critical of the consular network could pinpoint circumstances where a consul was uniquely positioned to help. For example, in one high-profile case, a consul provided a labor leader reliable assistance throughout the effort to prosecute an employer accused of seven instances of modern slavery. During this emergency, sympathetic consular staff immediately helped generate identity documents for the young workers, none of whom had a single piece of documentation.[10] This consul also quickly mobilized local officials in the Mexican state of origin and obtained new birth certificates in order to issue them passports. These documents were critical for enabling the abused workers to stay in the United States and participate in the trial. In turn, the publicity around this case was a boon to the consular Departamento de Protección's reputation and legitimacy.

Consular staff could thus prove extremely useful in navigating government bureaucracies (in the United States or Mexico), but a second order of complaints involved how workers were treated at the consulate. Though consular staff we spoke with often pointed to cultural differences to explain unsatisfactory interactions between bureaucrats and lower-class Mexican workers, civil society leaders acknowledged the challenges workers faced in effectively navigating the consular bureaucracy but also blamed the issue squarely on consular staff's failure to effectively communicate with their co-nationals. The problem was thus two-fold, as one Omaha worker center staff member explained: on the one hand, the Mexican bureaucracy was famously inflexible; on the other, many workers admittedly struggled to conform to a rigid time frame and were unable to make the appropriate preparations (e.g., document gathering) in advance of their visit to the consulate office. He explained,

> All organizations have good and bad apples. Bad apples are the ones that treat people like . . . they were their domestic workers, and that creates bad publicity for consulates. However, I also think that even though consulates print flyers or do outreach to disseminate which documents are needed or how many copies they need, people always prepare things last minute. And when we arrive at the consulate, we want a photocopy, but we already know that they don't make photocopies there, so I also think that we need an education process to change that attitude [of the community].[11]

The best working relationships emerged in places where "humble" consular staff were able to build trust with local advocates, such as a day labor center in New York City that began working with the consulate to provide "Know Your Rights" and financial literacy workshops in the community. As one of its leaders noted:

> We began to establish a relationship when [the consular official], in his first visit, proposed an opportunity. He asked us to give him a chance to understand us and work together, because he had just arrived from Chicago. He had been working there, and he knew that the relationship between the community and the consulate here was not good, but they wanted to do something different. After this conversation, we decided to give them an opportunity to start offering workshops to our constituents.

Despite its promising start, this relationship, like so many others in this arena, fell apart when this consular official left: "When [he] left, we lost everything. We don't even know the new staff. We don't know how they work."[12] In many cases, frequent turnover prevents the establishment of lasting community relationships and limits the potential to provide outreach in communities beyond the consular offices. Most local efforts lack any permanent funding and are often carried out according to the whims and discretion of consular staff, leaving community leaders with few assurances that they will continue when new officials arrive.

This lack of sustained dynamism is most starkly evident in consuls' typical refusal to publicly support campaigns or join protests. One high-profile Miami worker center staff member explained the dilemma as follows: "[The] Mexican government can't engage 100 percent in political affairs in this country. They are here to represent the Mexican government, but they can't participate in a campaign to improve wages. They can't lobby the US government, and this perhaps puts some limits [on] our relationship with them. Our relationship with them is different than the one we have with grassroots [organizations] that are willing to join protests outside a grocery store on our behalf."[13] This neutral stance, however, is not always maintained in places where organized labor has a long history of consular collaboration. For example, the Chicago consulate regularly attends the public launches of one worker center's campaigns. The leader of this center surmised that consular officials did so in part to signal to Mexican American workers that they had the same rights as native-born workers.[14] However, a different worker center in Chicago expressed frustration that the centrally controlled consular bureaucracy lacked autonomy to engage locally. Even so, this group also acknowledged that the local consulate's Departamento de Protección did display some flexibility compared to other units that seemed more beholden to Mexico City authorities.[15]

Finally, very few advocates we spoke with viewed their relationship with consular staff as helpful in addressing the root causes of migration or in tackling labor rights violations in Mexico. One major exception was community leaders who could leverage their connections at the CCIME to engage in Mexican policy debates. But on the whole, critical efforts to promote, say, cross-border reforms to address migrant abuse (as we discuss in chapter 5) had not gained traction. In this regard, a staff member from a worker center in Omaha saw an event like Labor Rights Week as a missed opportunity to push for a transnational educational program that would train workers in occupational health and other important issues:

> I believe we are good at bringing people [together] and do presentations all week offering trainings along with the EEOC [Equal Employment Opportunity Commission], OSHA [Occupational Safety and Health Administration], and others; however, [where] is the follow-up we are giving to LRW [Labor Rights Week] or to any other event? It seems that action is dead from the start, and there's no process . . . that will have a bilateral advocacy in the problems that workers have every day. How is it that we can create a link between the LRW [and] the promotion, defense, and protection of labor rights in Mexico to push Mexico to respect their labor laws and promote [the idea] that an occupational health culture begins . . . in Mexico and not only when workers have arrived here?[16]

Not all consuls were as supportive of such transnational solidarity projects. And when they did engage advocates' demands, it was predominantly in response to acute emergencies, such as facilitating the return of migrants who were experiencing health crises, helping locate returned workers to transfer money owed to them by employers, or providing limited assistance to indigent workers left with no choice but to return.[17] However, such support often failed to satisfy. One San Jose advocate noted the irony of the consulate providing more aid to deceased co-nationals (via corpse repatriation) than to living ones, meager though the former assistance might be (Félix 2011).

BEYOND LABOR RIGHTS: DECENTERING IMMIGRANT NEEDS FROM THE WORKPLACE

Beyond just complaints and frustrations around the consular network's role as a solidaristic labor partner and as a resource for struggling (and even deceased) workers, grassroots immigrant rights organizations criticized the sending state for circumscribing the needs and issues of workers to the workplace. For many advocates, the rights of workers spilled into many other arenas of social life and social provision, far beyond the confines of labor standards enforcement. Immigrant-led organizations often felt that the consulate—as Mexico's representative in the United States—needed to be held accountable for attending to the full range of diaspora needs. This attention to the broader needs of immigrants is not unique to Mexican immigrant organizations and indeed can be traced back to a host of past immigrant associations.

The arrival of large numbers of new immigrants to the United States in the mid- to late nineteenth century led these newcomers to create nonprofit associations that would provide them with a communal identity and mutual aid. Immigrant nonprofit organizations formed along ethnic and religious lines to offer vital mechanisms for newcomers to integrate into their new society and cope with discriminatory workplace challenges (Bodnar 1985). These organizations were founded in a spirit of self-help, representation, and mutual support and instilled in immigrants a sense of pride and self-respect. Their ideals have shaped the scope of later organizations. For example, the mission statements of many immigrant rights organizations we interviewed incorporate a framework of economic, social, and cultural rights reminiscent of the International Covenant on Economic, Social, and Cultural Rights adopted by the UN General Assembly in 1976.[18]

Today immigrant rights organizations are key players in an expanding arena of social provision that depends on the third sector, which is largely privately funded and managed (Marwell 2010). The government is no longer the primary provider of state-sponsored social provision services in the United States. Devolution has decreased the total public dollars being spent on social service provision (Conlan 1998), and privatization has increased the amounts channeled through government service contracts to community-based groups, including immigrant service organizations.[19] Given this historical and economic context, the organizations included in our study often took a broad approach to the needs of immigrant workers.

While worker centers often collaborate with consular staff to improve access to documentation, educational workshops, and claims-making support, immigrant rights organizations also address multiple crises beyond labor issues: deportations, naturalization, legal services, domestic violence, lack of health care for the undocumented, and literacy challenges, among other pressing issues. In addition to cultivating good relations with lead consuls and their staff, immigrant rights organizations must cultivate collaborative relationships with an array of government bureaucracies and other nonprofit organizations. For example, in 2003, when the high-security *matrícula consular* document became available, the consulate became a critical resource for undocumented workers who were unable to obtain US identification documents. This new consular ID allowed them to fulfill an array of basic necessary functions, such as opening bank accounts, signing a rental lease, and buying car insurance.

The few dedicated labor hotlines described in chapter 3 have proved to be important community resources for Mexican and non-Mexican nationals alike. Yet paid consular staff are limited to helping Mexican nationals, which narrows community outreach potential. Further, community advocates have reported that workers whom they refer to these hotlines often complain that they cannot get through the understaffed lines.[20] Beyond referrals for labor issues, educational programming through the Plazas Comunitarias (Délano 2014) and health services through the Ventanillas de Salud (Osorio, Dávila, and Castañeda 2019) are common. These community partnerships have a broad reach across the Latino immigrant population and often advocate on fronts far beyond the stated consular directives.

In sum, community partnerships with consular programs play an important role in meeting the variety of needs of immigrant communities. However, challenges remain, such as reconciling clashing leadership and decision-making styles, expanding outreach targets (e.g., indigenous organizations and other non-Mexican Latinos), and more meaningfully addressing concerns in communities of origin. We discuss each of these dynamics below.

Uneven Encounters: Demanding Greater Equality and More Respect

Beyond labor regulation, the consular network engages in a variety of collaborations with community nonprofits for cultural, educational, health-related, and financial literacy programs, as well as for transnational community development in rural Mexico (Goldring 2002; Byrnes 2003; Boruchoff 2019). However, despite the various benefits of consular collaboration described in chapter 3—specifically for groups focused on workplace co-enforcement—these are often hierarchical relationships, with the consular network determining the agenda. Many immigrant rights organizations we analyzed sought greater equality and respect in their collaborations with consular officials (Fennema 2004).

Apart from issues of respect, there were practical concerns. Advocates bemoaned the glacial pace of the consular bureaucracy. Foreign nationals found such delays even more irksome, given that they saw themselves as having to endure consular mistreatment, classism, and racism as well. The solution for some migrants was to hire brokers who could more effectively navigate the myriad rights bureaucracies—including the consulate itself. Migrants who did not have the option to forgo a day of work to wait many hours on the phone to get a service appointment at a consulate could hire a service (a practice sometimes called *coyotaje*) to do this for them instead—a worthwhile investment. The use of these *aviadores* or *gestores* (as they are also sometimes called) is a familiar strategy in Mexico—across sectors and class strata—for dealing with a slow and complicated public bureaucracy (Spener 2011).

At the organizational level groups we interviewed often complained that consular officials played favorites. For example, organizations disputed who was allowed to provide notary services, who was given preferential legal referrals, and who received other consular stamps of approval.[21] The consular program's trusted referral lists were a critical resource for inquiring co-nationals, so organizations sought to expand the range of referral options offered to community members.

These referrals were not always for pro bono services, often including private attorneys as well.

Many groups reported a litany of complaints from their members, who contested the notion that the consulate was a viable community resource. For example, one Los Angeles leader explained, "Our members don't rely on the consulate. They rather rely on grassroots organizing to help them with their paperwork because they don't trust the consulate and feel like they are not going to help them."[22] Others, calling out the classism embedded in consular institutions and Mexico at large, lamented that any effective consular interaction required intervention from more savvy community advocates. One New York City leader explained that her organization was a necessary broker for many members attempting to navigate the consular bureaucracy: "When a member without any documentation calls the consulate, the answer is like, 'Mmm, there's little we can do.' They don't get as many options unless I call them."[23] This leader—an educated, middle-class woman from an established worker center—had a better chance of getting a prompt, effective response than an uneducated, undocumented worker.

Organization staff too voiced frustrations. One leader charged that the consulate lacked a sufficient media strategy to promote the hotline they helped staff in the community.[24] Others complained about patchy access to the consulate's community events, and many demanded less neutrality and more aggressive advocacy on the part of consular staff.

Yet these complaints also implicitly recognized the important role of the consular network and the potential benefits of consular collaboration. And while institutional gripes abounded, advocates would also laud the personal commitment of many of their consular colleagues. For example, the nonprofit that ran the New York City consulate's hotline had its central funding abruptly cut in 2012 following Mexico's presidential election (after which personnel assignments changed). In response, the consul in charge commissioned a report detailing how many callers from both the United States *and* Mexico the hotline was serving, along with client success stories. With these data in hand, dedicated consular officials presented the report to the Secretaría de Relaciones Exteriores / Ministry of Foreign Affairs in Mexico City, and according to the staff we interviewed, "They harassed the people in charge until we got the funding back." This did not go unnoticed by the consulate's partner organization: "So that was really impressive, and it shows us that they appreciated the services that we were providing, and that was great."[25] This advocacy cemented the organization's trust in the consulate.

On a broader scale, the varying local conditions for immigrant rights advocacy across the country go along with a variety of consular relationships. While metropolitan organizations tend to operate in a richer civil society system, immigrant rights organizations serving rural and suburban communities face additional challenges such as lack of access to public transportation and few alternative sources of support. These conditions elevate expectations for consular services, which can lead to frequent disappointments. For example, a Mexican hometown association from Zacatecas in the Los Angeles metropolitan area complained that consular invitations to participate in Labor Rights Week were not disseminated to other hometown associations further from the urban core of Los Angeles, blaming the local consulate's lack of media reach for publicizing these events.[26] A service-oriented organization in Los Angeles similarly voiced concern that the lack of coordination and information dissemination was failing to keep their clientele abreast of consular events.[27]

Community leaders also complained about the consulate's contradictory qualities: they always seemed to lack capacity, yet they made constant requests for collaboration. One Quaker-led immigrant organization in Miami complained that the local consulate never returned their phone calls, yet the consulate expected solidarity and mobilization during Labor Rights Week. Moreover, the representative we spoke to charged that the consulate neither disseminated its program information nor engaged with local worker-led nonprofits as Labor Rights Week partners. From this organization's perspective, the consulate was useful only in dire emergencies, such as with workers who had lost everything and whose only solution was to accept a voluntary repatriation paid for by the consulate.[28] Critics argue that this last-ditch consular "support mechanism" is in fact emblematic of a long history of viewing undocumented migrant workers as ultimately disposable (González 1999; Goodman 2020).

As we have repeatedly discussed, community frustration often emanated from a misunderstanding about the limits and possibilities of consular intervention. Organizations frequently questioned the consular network's central purpose. A grassroots immigrant organization in New York, for instance, became frustrated that instead of getting involved in social justice campaigns to improve labor rights, the local consulate focused on offering passport services and engaged only superficially with the labor and human rights of Mexican workers.[29] Another Mexican immigrant working for a suburban grassroots immigrant rights organization in Chicago described his frustration with this consulate in blunt terms:

> There are many bad habits, many abusers with bad habits there in the consulate. You have to clean and bring [in] new people. I am angry, enraged, and feel impotent. I feel angry when I see that citizens don't have what they deserve, no attention, no justice, nothing. The consulate can't help them with anything at all because they can't do anything. I have never heard a single person say: "The Labor Rights Week was very good." They don't even know that this thing exists. Every time I need them to support difficult cases that involve dead people or difficult legal cases, they never take such cases.[30]

Such frustrations seemed to undercut the consulate's purported mission to be a resource for (often precarious) emigrants. In this vein, another leader of an immigrant organization in San Diego lambasted consular efforts to protect vulnerable migrants in this border city: "We perfectly know everything that the consulate does not do and everything that they should do and don't do. And something that I can indeed tell you, with full knowledge of the facts, is that the consulate in San Diego is a white elephant, and I hope that Mexicans abroad unite to shape different ways of working in these institutions, because these are funded with taxpayers' pesos. And they are here like lazy people, without doing anything."[31]

Even when consular aid was offered in certain cases (such as arranging for documentation or securing legal counsel), some organizers saw this help as a waste of resources in the absence of a simultaneous political commitment to remedying deep inequities. Even organizations that exclusively focused on defending DACA recipients—arguably the most sympathetic immigrant group in the country at present—lamented the local consulate's lack of proactive engagement. For example, one group of mothers (of DACA-mented children) in San Diego expected bolder action from consular staff:

> It is not like consulates are very much siding with Mexicans abroad. I see actually the opposite. I don't see that they are sufficiently involved. I think that they are afraid of losing their diplomatic visas, losing their diplomatic immunity. I don't really know. But even if this is the case, I only know that they don't participate a lot in direct actions with the community. They don't go out there and try to find out who are the community leaders. I don't see a total support. I think that should be their job as representatives of this community.[32]

By and large, immigrant rights organizations conceded that basic consular assistance was helpful while pursuing strong labor cases, and sometimes even in extreme circumstances such as corpse repatriation (Félix 2011) and deportation defense (a service that officials proudly espoused during the Trump administration). For example, a janitorial watchdog group in Los Angeles serving immigrant workers praised the consulate there for helping it to identify members of a class action lawsuit who had already returned to Mexico.[33] Several organizations also noted the consulate's helpfulness in assisting with funeral expenses.[34]

However, not all organizations were as appreciative. One Dallas day labor center leader expressed a particularly cynical view of consular documentation fees: "The consulate doesn't offer them [its members] much assistance, because . . . they see [them as] . . . customers they can get money from."[35] While such perspectives could be seen as singular and misplaced, they do reflect the understandable ire of migrants who have fled poverty in Mexico, face workplace abuse in the United States, and then feel betrayed—or fleeced—by their government. For these migrants, the unavoidable consular bureaucracy can become a source of intense frustration, a frustration compounded by deep-seated race and class hierarchies.

Legacies with Indigenous Organizations

In Mexico, access to political institutions, services, and other basic freedoms varies depending on geographic location (urban vs. rural), social class (middle class vs. working poor), and ethnic group (indigenous vs. mestizo). Histories of class elitism and racism (which affect both indigenous people and Afro-Mexicans, among others) fuel skepticism toward government officials. The consular network's attempts to improve community relations often generate a "rational wariness" on the part of immigrant organizations, who are often reluctant to participate (Fox 2007).

Most poignantly, Mexican indigenous communities in the United States continue to experience high levels of marginalization and abandonment by the Mexican government. As migration origins have shifted south—away from traditional sending regions and toward communities in Oaxaca and Chiapas—organizations representing these migrants have demanded improved access to health services and linguistic support for monolingual speakers of indigenous languages (Fox and Rivera-Salgado 2004; Leco Tomás 2009). On the whole, the consular network's track record has been dismal on this front.

In Los Angeles, for example, Maya organizations we spoke with expressed dissatisfaction with the consular network's supposed advocacy role. Many attributed the root of consular disengagement to clear class differences: "[The consulate], they claim that they can't participate in political things because all our platforms and demands are political and they don't have time. They don't have the mechanism, and definitely they only side with the winners. They simply side with those who feel they are bourgeois, [well-funded organizations] that are pretending to help . . . but the working people, the honest people, they [the consulate] don't care about them."[36] An indigenous organization leader in Fresno further explained that distrust impeded deeper collaboration with the consular office, which, they pointed out, was run largely by mestizo bureaucrats. Even though both sides were trying to bridge the gap, they remained frustrated: "Supposedly, the consulate has a mission to protect Mexican citizens, but few Mexicans want to go there because the consulate doesn't treat them well. They are arrogant."[37]

This long-standing distrust is transnational. An indigenous Oaxaqueño organization spokesperson based in San Diego explained that they had been in constant conflict with local consular officials for two decades and had been unsuccessful in forging a healthy, fruitful relationship with them: "Sometimes they send me emails, but [then] sometimes one or two years go by and I don't hear anything from them. So it's difficult for us to know what are they really doing."[38] Part of the challenge was that this organization had adopted a holistic approach to labor advocacy that went far beyond the statutory protections embedded in the formal memoranda of understanding. More than simply processing bureaucratic claims, they had established autonomous spaces for their members, used radio programming for education and dissemination, and maintained relations with a variety of advocacy networks including unions and worker centers. Within this framework, consular engagement was less straightforward, and the ideal partnership would require far more than neutral engagement in processing claims.

These same communities were also skeptical that the Mexican government would significantly support immigration reform in the United States—a key topic of immigration advocacy over the last three decades. This went beyond complaints about consular neutrality; rather, many Maya hometown association leaders viewed Mexico's own domestic immigration policies as suspect. Indeed, they argued that the Mexican government had no legitimacy to negotiate an immigration reform for Mexicans in the United States given that Mexico "does the same thing to indigenous communities and immigrants from Central America."[39] The solidarity between Mexican and Central American populations and the ongoing crisis at Mexico's southern border fuel this critique. In this context, one San Diego–based organization has made the protection of Central American migrants in transit an important issue on its agenda.[40] And one Houston-based worker center organizes migrants from across Mexico and Central America, often attempting to collaborate with consular officials from governments across the region. As one leader put it: "Mexicans aren't blind to what's going on in their own country, [and they know] how Mexico has responded to [largely indigenous] Central American immigrants coming through Mexico."[41] These sentiments confirm that state-society relations in destination contexts cannot be understood in a domestic vacuum and require a cross-border lens.

Transnational Immigrant Advocacy

As for immigrant rights groups led by immigrants themselves, these are often compelled to adopt a transnational advocacy approach, which can include funding transnational programs serving immigrant families left behind in Mexico. In Salt Lake City, one organization used their consular relationship to focus exclusively on managing Tres por Uno projects. The group rationalized this approach as a way to "stop the labor exodus from Mexico while supporting productive investment of migrant workers in the US."[42] While such relatively newer immigrant organizations share the rosy view that increased development can stop the labor exodus from Mexico, there is little evidence of any causal relationship between Tres por Uno projects and low migration intensity indexes (Duquette-Rury 2019; Bada and Fox 2021).

Many transnationally focused immigrant rights groups have also worked to champion justice for guest workers. Several well-funded organizations led by US-based lawyers, for example, have hired full-time organizers to establish monitoring programs in Mexico (as we describe further in chapter 5).[43] Groups such as these have leveraged their robust networks of lawyers—often in conjunction with the Mexican Secretaría del Trabajo y Previsión Social / Ministry of Labor—to provide information and training sessions on the rights of H-2 guest workers. Key issues include combating visa fraud and recruitment abuses and training workers about their rights in their seasonal jobs. These highly professionalized organizations are media savvy and understand the pressure points that trigger the Mexican government's attention. As we discuss in the next chapter, they invoke not only domestic law but also bilateral accords such as the North American Free

Trade Agreement (NAFTA) to raise awareness around migrant workers' precarity—especially those temporary workers living in rural and suburban areas whom traditional Labor Rights Week programming can sometimes miss.[44] Relying on their capacity in both the United States and Mexico, these transnational organizations advocate a global justice framework that brings attention to the portability of rights for all workers, regardless of legal status, nationality, or consular jurisdiction. As one leader put it, "I think there's been a really good effort by the Mexican consulate to help with labor rights issues for their citizens in the United States. I think it's a good honest effort. I wish it applied equally to protecting migrant workers in Mexico."[45]

However, only a select group of organizations have the resources for this "grasstops" form of advocacy. Grasstops groups have a national profile (Betancur and Garcia 2011) and often are run by professional elites focused on policy advocacy (Ashar and Lai 2019). In contrast, hometown associations and other indigenous organizations in San Francisco and Fresno, for example, operate with mostly volunteer staff and largely focus their efforts on the needs of Mexican workers in their local communities. For example, hometown associations routinely mobilize their *paisanos* to respond when someone is jailed (triggering the possibility of consular advocacy) or needs help obtaining an emergency passport or a *matrícula* from the local consulate. Yet it can be challenging to obtain direct support from a consular official, especially in a large metropolitan area like Los Angeles, where consular staff do not have the capacity to make frequent visits to detained people. In some cases, the consular staff may call on a hometown association volunteer to help broker an intervention to stall deportation proceedings.[46] Official delegations from state governments in Mexico can also prove helpful following a migrant death or other emergency situations. For example, in San Francisco, Maya hometown associations have a close connection with the state government of Yucatán.[47]

All of these state-society relations are politically fraught. Although consular diplomats insist that they are nonpartisan and do not work for a political party, organizations understand that new elections bring certain political parties into power and new agendas to the consular network. For example, one Omaha group remembered that when the PAN (Partido Acción Nacional / National Action Party), whose candidate was Vicente Fox, won the presidency in 2000 after the seven-decade reign of the PRI, much of the long-standing consular programming was suspended.[48] Additionally, as migrant demography shifts, inevitable changes in consular jurisdictions can significantly interrupt trust-building efforts, especially affecting those small and informal groups that lack an office, are less established, and are less likely to be on a consul's radar. These common (and often well-founded, based on the experiences of our respondents) perceptions that the consulate is a highly partisan operation where only sympathizers of the incumbent party can have their voices heard prevents grassroots organizations with different or nonpartisan political agendas from pursuing transnational advocacy projects.

HOW PLACE MATTERS FOR SHAPING CONSULAR RELATIONSHIPS

Beyond uncovering these universal challenges to achieving broad-based consular collaboration, our interviews with immigrant labor advocates throughout the country reveal how the wide variety of local contexts can dramatically shape the collaborative landscape. This holds true even for federated organizations with a broad national presence across the United States and for consular programs that have been rolled out nationwide. Local demographic and political dynamics are certainly crucial, but we also found that the organizational infrastructure of each consular jurisdiction determined how state-society relationships evolved, as many other authors have confirmed in their analyses of domestic government coalitions (Bloemraad 2006a, 2006b; de Graauw 2016; Gleeson and Bada 2019). While a formal typology is beyond the scope of this analysis, we offer some important dynamics that emerged in more and less established destinations.

More Established Destinations

In large established metropolitan areas with a long history of immigration from Mexico, organizations that provide specialized services and focus on case management are far more common. In these places, organizational density also tends to be much higher, rendering the local consulate an insignificant actor. For example, the leader of a well-established worker center in San Jose, California, noted the limited value of the consulate there: "The consulate is a place where people go to find some information, but I need to say—without sounding pretentious—that our center offers lots of information. We have multiple workshops where our members can learn about labor rights, and we likely offer more workshops than the consulate because we focus a lot in education."[49] Similarly, a staff member of a garment worker center in Los Angeles offered the frank reflection that their organizers had not been in communication with the consulate for more than three years—with no adverse effect on their operations.[50] In San Francisco, arguably the city with one of the densest immigrant civil society landscapes (de Graauw 2016), the consular relationship was similarly nonexistent. One worker center leader claimed that the consulate did not really help them, even when one of their members died.[51]

The consulate is also seen as a relatively minor or ineffective player in major emerging destinations (Singer 2015) where organizations have made significant headway on the immigrant worker advocacy front and tend to lead far ahead of the consulate. For example, a worker center leader in Phoenix expressed frustration over the consulate's lack of involvement, saying that its members had therefore come to not count on consular aid: "It is very rare that they mention the consulate, and when they do, they sincerely say that the consulate couldn't help them or did not solve their problem. Other than that, the members do not mention the consulate."[52] Staff from an Alinsky-inspired organization in Phoenix expressed similar reservations about consular help: "They are usually not good. Long lines, long waits. For the most part, if our members enter the consulate, it's to get an ID. But actual services, we haven't had many of our members speak about that."[53] For some, the overwhelmed and understaffed consulate appointment system shaped their poor impression of the consulate, which was commonly associated with long lines and interminable waits. In sum, for those groups that had long-established trust and access to migrant communities, the consulate was not so much an active partner as yet another bureaucracy with which to contend.

Part of the challenge in establishing fruitful consular collaborations is the mismatch in organizational cultures between consulates and civil society organizations, as described by Gleeson (2012). In large metropolitan areas, consulates typically engage in co-enforcement efforts with ubiquitous US (and state and local) labor standard enforcement agencies. Like consulates, these agencies are highly formalized, with a clear leadership command and a narrow set of expectations for consular involvement. In contrast, worker centers and other immigrant rights organizations often have less formal communication styles, hampering the development of their relationships with local consulates. One Chicago worker center leader did not undervalue the benefits of consular-government agency cooperation, pointing to the importance of formal agreements ensuring that a consulate receive regular visits from the DOL and the Occupational Safety and Health Administration. The leader's worker center, however, did not have the capacity to staff repeated, all-day visits to the consulate office because of lack of funding; able to arrange only four consular visits a year, the organization felt left behind. This leader hoped to see consular attention more evenly split between government agencies and community organizations, each of which served a fundamentally different function. The modus operandi of government agencies, this same Chicago leader remarked sarcastically, was: "Bring me your claim, wait a year, and I will give you back $50." By contrast, his organization had a broader set of concerns, which could lead to contrasting expectations for partnerships: "For us, we care about organizing. Government agencies only care about offering a service."[54]

Indeed, many worker center leaders wanted consular staff to espouse the value of worker mobilization, rather than merely pursuing individual claims that did little to address the root causes of labor abuses. In contrast, consular staff saw themselves primarily as street bureaucrats charged with offering individual services to the Mexican diaspora. Consular staff were thus compelled to preserve their neutrality and were often judicious in supporting organizing campaigns. As a result, consular support was largely limited to referring workers to US labor agencies and community groups that could help them navigate those bureaucracies, rather than championing a specific group's cause.

Meanwhile, civil society groups faced myriad logistical challenges accessing and navigating the consulate office in these big cities. For example, visiting the local consulate can be tricky for groups located farther from consular offices, given transportation challenges, bureaucratic delays, and long wait times. As a result, one worker center in the Tristate area almost never referred out-of-state clients to the New York City consulate.[55] Groups serving non-Mexican Latinos—in New York City or Chicago for instance—were also limited in their ability to access the Mexican consulate on behalf of their members who were not Mexican nationals. In large global cities like Houston, Mexico was able to convene the entire Latin American consular corps. However, Mexico's consular network was by far the best resourced, as one Washington, DC, community leader acknowledged. Compared to the Salvadoran consular staff, they explained, Mexican officials "just have a lot more resources that they put on the ground here."[56] This imbalance affected the relationships that groups chose to pursue. In Miami, one worker center staffer explained how the center often opted to work with the Mexican consulate since it was better organized and resourced than the Guatemalan consulate.[57] The Mexican consulate there threw more support behind community events and select individual cases, another Miami organizer explained.[58] Nonetheless, even in these well-established immigrant destinations, non-Mexican Latinos likely struggled harder to reap the benefit of consular collaborations.

Newer and Outlying Destinations

While more established places are home to more varied civil society interests and a diverse Latino immigrant population, newer destinations tend to lack established groups and have a thinner history of consular collaboration. This was the case with one worker center in Salt Lake City (a minor emerging destination [Singer 2015]) that offered basic services such as English classes. As a city known for its refugee resettlement infrastructure, Salt Lake City has far fewer organizations focused on economic migrants. Though certainly aware of the local consulate, one worker center we talked to had yet to strike up a working relationship with it.[59]

In newer destinations like this, there are fewer groups with the capacity to specifically serve Mexican immigrants, so the Mexican-oriented groups that do exist must largely shoulder the burden themselves. Often, given the sparse consular presence for other Latin American countries, they end up serving these similarly situated migrants. In places like Atlanta, the Central American consulates have very limited resources, so the Mexican consulate operates as an important clearinghouse for many other Latino populations in the absence of other legal aid, social services, and general community support.[60]

Albeit stretched thin, consular involvement in these regions is still crucial. Community leaders we spoke with in these settings did not have the luxury of expending energy on well-founded consular criticisms. Rather, they were more likely to report appreciating consular help when it arrived. For example, a staff member from a worker center serving meatpacking workers in Omaha, Nebraska, praised the leadership role assumed by the Mexican government in offering a broad menu of services throughout the state. The consulates of Guatemala, Honduras, and El Salvador, meanwhile, also relied on the Mexican consulate for resources and the space to conduct outreach, which was limited to a few events throughout the year.[61]

The Mexican consulates' health services through the Ventanilla de Salud and Seguro Popular (a public health insurance program offering minimal coverage to migrants' families in Mexico) were especially popular in communities such as Raleigh and Salt Lake City, which lacked abundant alternatives for immigrant health care access. These consular outreach initiatives provided thousands of community members with information about low-cost health services in their region (R. Smith, Waisanen, and Barbosa 2019).[62] In other newer destinations like Atlanta, there were fewer organizations focused on immigrant workers relative to other metropolitan areas in our study. Instead, consulates often turned to employers' associations as outreach partners. These business associations tended to be especially active at safety fairs catering to workers and their family members, which also happened to be convenient recruiting opportunities. However, they focused much less on worker organizing and voice, placing more emphasis on industry leadership and skills training.

The consular network played an especially important role in the suburbs, where transportation woes combined with a paucity of services, language access, and cultural competence to erect formidable barriers for immigrants. For example, the leader of an organization serving low-wage immigrant workers in suburban Illinois saw consular collaboration as mutually beneficial:

> For us, the most important [thing] is that the consulate offers resources that we don't have and we offer them resources that they don't have, like having the possibility to do outreach to workers that live in the suburbs and to farmworkers who may believe in the benefits of organizing. The consulate can help us when someone is in jail or was caught driving without a license and will be deported. While we arrange for a last payroll payment, the consulate has diplomatic privileges and can visit the worker in jail and get a signature. If the consulate calls the EEOC to follow up on one of our cases, the agency picks up the phone faster. They also help us to mediate conflicts between worker centers and unions as a neutral party.[63]

Generally, the absence of other community resources and the more hostile local political environment tended to bring the benefits of the consulate into sharp relief for immigrant suburbanites and the organizations that served them.

AMPLIFYING IMMIGRANT VOICES: SEARCHING FOR BROADER ACCOUNTABILITY

By and large, immigrant advocates have managed to find a way into previously impenetrable diplomatic bureaucracies and are voicing their concerns more loudly than in the past. While we have presented many instances of frustration and criticism, we have also highlighted examples of varied community partnerships that leverage consular resources for community outreach. Yet these successes represent only a particular kind of community outreach dependent on centralized consular priorities and resources. Challenges still abound, especially in newer destinations and those farther from urban cores. It is therefore doubtful that even successful models can necessarily be scaled up universally. Limitations to consular outreach persist, and burned-out advocates are often wary of relying on shifting, unevenly applied government policies.

Budgetary constraints further limit the consular network's ability to fulfill its obligations under the Vienna Convention to fully represent the eleven million Mexican nationals living in the United States (half of whom are undocumented) (Israel and Batalova 2020). Consulates therefore rely on local organizations to expand their reach and more effectively liaise with US government bureaucracies. These efforts are no doubt hampered by class and racial biases among diplomatic bureaucrats and advocates that may not be easily addressed. However, it is clear that empowered and engaged immigration and labor activists are willing to make claims visible and attempt to shatter the social structures behind such divisions. Meanwhile, the services offered by consulate offices—however imperfect—play a critical role, especially in places with few other options.

In sum, immigrant advocates must navigate US and Mexican bureaucracies while also attempting to amplify migrant worker voices democratically. Both countries of origin and countries of reception typically follow a Westphalian framework that can leave little room for bottom-up, cross-border accountability politics. While many grassroots migrant worker advocates are actively holding consulates to account and collaborating to further migrant justice across an array of arenas in the United States, grasstops organizations are attempting to address these issues transnationally. Chapter 5 reviews several key stories of transnational labor advocacy that has been successful precisely because of the elite expertise and resources that advocates are able to deploy.

5

The Strategies of Transnational Labor Coalitions and Networks

Thus far, we have examined the genesis of the accords that laid the foundations for Mexico's outward turn toward engaging its emigrant workforce (chapter 2), the local dynamics of consulates and migrant civil society collaborating to implement labor co-enforcement goals in the United States (chapter 3), and the wide range of demands made by immigrant rights organizations and others to hold Mexico accountable in arenas extending far beyond US workplace regulation (chapter 4). In chapter 5, we examine how global civil society rooted in the United States *and* Mexico is leveraging international "soft law" to defend the rights of migrant workers prior to their departure and after they return. In particular, we consider the role of free trade agreements as a platform for advocates to double down on globally oriented demands.

As the last two chapters reveal, civil society in the host country confronts a number of locally determined challenges (de Graauw, Gleeson, and Bloemraad 2013). Civil society organizations operating in the sending state have also crafted strategies to advocate for their compatriots—including those who never leave, those who do, and those who leave and then return. These groups often mobilize transnational strategies in coalition with partners across the globe, encountering unique opportunities and challenges in each environment (Piper 2005; Greer, Ciupijus, and Lillie 2013; Gleeson and Bada 2019).

Often led by social movement lawyers with strategic transnational connections, many global civil society organizations have engaged both international instruments and regional agreements to shine a light on the conditions that drive migrants north, including the lack of pathways for democratic collective bargaining in Mexico and the rampant abuses facing temporary guest workers in the United States. Here, we document how strategic alliances came together to address key human rights issues shaping migrant experiences, such as femicide in communities of origin and at the border, gender discrimination in the workplace, rampant violence against migrants in transit, and the need for sustainable agricultural development to give people an option to remain in their homeland.

We consider how transnational campaigns have emerged across these various arenas, the power dynamics that have determined their success or sowed division, and the ability of these campaigns to craft a broader migrant worker rights agenda that holds states accountable on all fronts. Specifically, this chapter examines how advocates have leveraged the 1993 North American Agreement on Labor Cooperation (NAALC), also known as the labor side accords under the North American Free Trade Agreement (NAFTA) (Compa 2001; Kay 2011; Vega 2000). We focus on the strategies that Mexico-based transnational civil society advocates pursued to exercise pressure at the local, bilateral, regional, and international levels to bring visibility to migrant labor rights violations. While efforts in Canada are certainly relevant and long-standing, our fieldwork and archival inquiries focus on the US-Mexico aspects of these broader campaigns.

Elsewhere, we have analyzed the dual strategies pursued by two of the most high-profile transnational migrant rights groups: the Centro de los Derechos del Migrante / Migrant Rights Center (CDM) and Justice in Motion (formerly the Global Workers Justice Alliance), both of which maintain advocacy initiatives and programs in the United States and Mexico (Bada and Gleeson 2019, 2020). Both the CDM and Justice in Motion/Global Workers Justice Alliance were key actors in establishing a transnational coalition of advocates seeking to leverage the public petitions offered by the NAALC, the consular partnership program, and the joint ministerial declarations between the US Department of Labor and Mexico's Secretaría del Trabajo y Previsión Social / Ministry of Labor to demand restitution for labor violations in both countries. Here we investigate the work of other, less visible organizations that have also forged transnational coalitions to confront labor violations and the detrimental effects of free trade agreements in the region.

We find that in the North American region, tripartite systems constructed to defend migrant labor rights have created what Keck and Sikkink (1998) have called the "boomerang effect"—whereby international allies urge their own governments to pressure the offending state. These migrant rights activists have also deployed Hertel's (2006) "dual-target" campaign model for cross-border advocacy that targets both offending states (i.e., the sending and receiving states) simultaneously. In each case, transnational coalitions help amplify civil society's power to effect change in a context where advocates alone have insufficient power to hold state and market actors accountable. In the case of Mexican migrant workers in the United States, local actors have implicated both receiving and sending governments when pursuing restitution for those subjected to labor violations, regardless of jurisdiction. In doing so, they have forged new transnational labor advocacy networks and strategic (if sometimes tenuous) alliances between unions and NGOs. This chapter maps those networks in the United States and Mexico, outlines their strategies and challenges, and describes their victories and ongoing battles.

THE BILATERAL RIGHTS FRAMEWORK
FOR MEXICO-US MIGRANTS

Several international instruments guarantee the rights of all workers regardless of immigration status. The Migrant Workers (Supplementary Provisions) Convention 143 (1975) of the International Labour Organization (ILO) sets basic minimum protections. Building upon ILO Migration and Employment Conventions 47 (1949) and 143 (1975), the UN International Convention on the Protection of the Rights of All Migrant Workers and Members of Their Families includes protections for both documented and undocumented migrants. As we explore in chapter 2, the NAALC also recognizes basic principles across member states within the framework of NAFTA (1994) and in terms of labor regulation standards. Trade agreements between Latin American and Caribbean countries have also aimed to increase labor inspections (Dewan and Ronconi 2018). Similarly, the new generation of Free Trade Agreements signed by the European Union include sustainable development clauses promoting minimum labor standards and adhering to the Conventions of the ILO. In the global arena, in 2013 the United Nations convened another High-Level Dialogue on Migration and Development in which member states, including the United States and Mexico, collectively vowed to protect the rights of migrants irrespective of their legal status (Berg 2016).

The rights laid out by these international bodies are largely symbolic and unenforceable in national courts. For example, trade barrier regulations diminish the capacity of bodies like the European Union to uphold labor standards with partner states (Bronckers and Gruni 2019). At the national level, receiving countries such as the United States have codified labor and employment laws that formally extend many rights even to undocumented workers. Yet workers are reluctant to access these rights in practice, given widespread immigration enforcement concerns that deteriorate community trust. Similarly, in Mexico, the tight alliance between many nondemocratically elected unions (also known as *charro* unions) and government leaders renders collective bargaining agreements—dubbed as "protection contracts"—largely meaningless.[1]

In parallel to these formal mechanisms, migrant civil society actors have crafted local, regional, and bilateral strategies of their own to go beyond the (nonbinding, largely symbolic, and ineffective) international governance frameworks in place (Delgado Wise 2018).[2] They do so by leveraging this panoply of international governance frameworks (often labeled "soft law") alongside social movement campaigns that garner resources and power from global allies and migrant workers on the ground. This can be a solid investment of resources. Indeed, while mobilizing claims via national and international bureaucracies may be costly, unfeasible, or simply impractical for individual low-wage workers without access to legal representation, litigating such cases can bring much-needed visibility to transnational advocacy organizations calling for improved conditions.

The NAALC is a good example of how civil society has leveraged international governance frameworks. Despite its many flaws, it set a precedent in the hemisphere by incorporating labor standards into free trade negotiations, even if those standards were originally excluded from the binding elements of the agreement itself. Thus far, according to Robert Russo (2011, 38), the most promising result of the NAALC process has been the "greater cooperation and inclusiveness among various NGOs and civil society groups, including previously marginalized groups such as unofficial Mexican unions and Mexican migrant workers in the United States." The NAALC provides a framework of participatory democracy in which to experiment with a tripartite model of labor rights enforcement, wherein sending and receiving governments, civil society organizations, and employers work together (Amengual and Fine 2017; Ayres and Braithwaite 1992; Dias-Abey 2016). This model empowers advocates to work alongside regulators—and to call them out if necessary—to address employer impunity. Savvy migrant worker advocates stake out a middle ground on the world stage between deterrence and compliance, with the goal of making it increasingly difficult for employers to abuse workers without facing any consequences. Thus any assessment of the potential of tripartite co-enforcement regimes to enforce migrant worker rights must pay attention not only to the local context of implementation (as described in chapter 3) but also to the work of advocates in the sending state and those working transnationally across borders.

ISSUES FACING WORKERS AND TARGETED
OUTREACH CAMPAIGNS

Our interviews with Mexican civil society organizations reveal a network of advocates pushing for the effective co-enforcement of domestic labor laws as well as wider policy changes. For these advocates, a long list of issues are tied up with immigrant labor precarity: economic pressures in communities of origin, forced rural displacement, agricultural disinvestment, the militarization of Mexico's northern and southern borders, overdue compensation to former braceros, a guest worker labor recruitment industry ripe for abuse, Mexico's failure to support unionized guest workers toiling on Canadian farms, lack of internet access and digital fraud prevention tools in rural areas, unsatisfactory language interpretation services in courts, violence against women and femicide, union corruption, insufficient predeparture outreach to migrants, insufficient services for returned or deported migrants, and justice for the Central American, Haitian, and other migrant workers fleeing poverty and insecurity who require asylum and jobs in Mexico. These network coalitions typically leverage a human rights frame to support workers irrespective of legal status, ethnicity, or citizenship.

One of the most prominent rallying points for advocates is the rampant abuse in Mexico's temporary labor export programs. This has been widely documented in Canada (Basok 1999; Fuller and Vosko 2008; Goldring 2017) but often gets less attention in the United States given that guest workers there compose a far smaller proportion of the migrant workforce—an estimated 450,000 low-wage guest workers (Costa 2017) compared to 8 million undocumented workers (Passel and Cohn 2016), most in both groups hailing from Mexico. In the United States, Mexican guest workers with temporary visas are recruited to fill low-wage positions in agriculture, fishing industries, or seasonal and other service jobs (ILRWG 2013). These workers have limited access to other forms of community support, given that their stay in the destination country is often short and seasonal. While the NAALC obligates each nation to provide migrant workers with equal labor law rights, in practice the United States excludes legal guest workers from some of its labor provisions under the Migrant and Seasonal Agricultural Worker Protection Act. For example, the act allows domestic and undocumented workers to sue their employers in federal court and provides for actual or statutory damages. However, it also explicitly excludes H-2A workers from its coverage (Linares 2006; Russo 2011).

In Mexico, Article 28 of the federal labor law protects the labor rights of all temporary migrant workers and includes private recruitment fraud prevention mechanisms. However, the relatively small size of bilateral guest worker programs prevents adequate enforcement and inspections, as private recruiters operate in rural areas where workers have limited means of submitting complaints to labor regulators when violations occur. Moreover, since those workers are covered by special bilateral agreements negotiated between sending and receiving states, they have few opportunities for claims making and must seek help from diaspora-serving organizations and labor unions with cross-border operations in Mexico, Canada, and the United States (Dias-Abey 2016; Vosko 2019). Since 2005, however, a small but highly visible group of pioneering cross-border civil society advocacy organizations have successfully leveraged transnational labor advocacy tools on behalf of temporary migrant workers (H-2 visa holders), utilizing the NAALC framework to pursue an increased portability of labor rights for migrants, regardless of country of residence (Bada and Gleeson 2020, 2019; Caron 2005; Caron and Lyon, forthcoming).

Increasingly, immigrant advocates in Mexico and the United States have pointed to a range of workplace abuses endured by guest workers in North America (most of them from Mexico). In 2013, a Southern Poverty Law Center report described the guest worker program in the United States as "close to slavery" (SPLC 2013). The binational CDM, moreover, has issued reports on the challenges facing fair and carnival workers (American University Washington College of Law, Immigrant Justice Clinic and CDM 2013), agricultural workers (CDM 2020), and crab pickers (American University Washington College of Law, Immigrant Justice Clinic, CDM, and Georgetown University Law Center, Federal Legislation Clinic 2020). They have also documented fraud in labor recruitment practices (CDM 2019b, 2019c), including in the TN (Trade NAFTA) visa program created by NAFTA for professionals (CDM 2019a), as well as in other specialized temporary foreign worker programs such as the J-1 summer work travel exchange (ILRWG 2019) and the Au Pair program (ILRWG 2018). While each of these temporary foreign worker programs composes a relatively small part of the immigrant work-force, each represents a paradigm of state-sanctioned labor exploitation for a sub-set of workers whose authorization to live and reside in the United States is tied to a specific employer and work contract. This restriction, by design, limits their occupational mobility and keeps them from earning a wage premium relative to their unauthorized counterparts (Costa 2020).

TRANSNATIONAL STRATEGIES TO CONFRONT GUEST WORKER ABUSE

Transnational advocacy groups anchored in the United States, such as the CDM and Justice in Motion, have led the charge in filing petitions and complaints on behalf of guest workers during their stay and after their return to Mexico. However, Mexico-based immigrant worker rights advocates have also sought to raise awareness around temporary migrant workers whose rights are frequently abused *prior* to their journey. Mexican federal labor laws protect workers from fraudulent contracts and scams, but the lack of reporting among rural and illiterate work-ers encourages impunity. Some campaigns run by local advocates have brought national visibility to the large-scale, fraudulent recruitment practices of private contractors by targeting federal bureaucracies such as the National Commission of Human Rights, the Secretaría del Trabajo y Previsión Social, and the Secretaría de Relaciones Exteriores / Ministry of Foreign Affairs. Lacking resources and politi-cal will, these central offices (located in Mexico City) are not always well versed in the intricate details of temporary contracts (usually carried out in rural areas) or familiar with the alphabet soup of temporary work visas (the H-2A agricultural and H-2B nonagricultural visas most common among them), which in any case represent a very small part of Mexico's emigrant labor force. Consequently, advo-cates frequently use media campaigns to push for greater oversight and account-ability on the part of government offices that facilitate these arrangements.[3] In these cases, close and frequent communication with counterpart organizations based in the United States helps Mexican advocates understand the labor stan-dards enforcement agencies operating across federal, state, and local jurisdictions throughout the United States and sets the stage for high-profile bilateral cam-paigns and litigation strategies.

While it does not coordinate its export labor efforts to the same extent as coun-tries like the Philippines (Guevarra 2009; Rodriguez 2010), the current Mexi-can government does play a central role in arranging visa approvals, regulating recruitment practices, and facilitating repeat applications for seasonal workers, who in some cases have been returning to the same job site for decades in Canada and the United States. However, there is a darker history to Mexico's export labor. Ample historical research has documented Mexico's coercive practices during the Bracero Programs (the United States' longest-lasting, wide-scale guest worker programs that operated from 1942 to 1964) (e.g., García y Griego 1988; Calavita 1992). More recently, scholars and advocates have documented evidence of consulates blacklisting workers labeled as prounion (Vosko 2016, 2018), even in the oft-hailed Seasonal Agricultural Worker Program / Programa de Trabajadores Agrícolas Temporales in Canada, where union representation is far higher than in the United States (UFCW Canadá and Alianza de Trabajadores Agrícolas 2020).

Apart from governmental processes, labor brokers and recruiters are key actors in facilitating immigrant labor networks on the whole, and especially guest worker programs the world over (Martin 2017). Individuals, subcontractors, and related agencies typically charge steep fees to desperate workers, who often accumulate debt that can take years to pay off—debt that then shapes what migrants are willing to endure on the job. Mexico has been called out for turning a blind eye to these exploitative practices abroad and at home, for example when indigenous migrant workers travel to other parts of the country to work on farms in conditions of forced labor (Moloney 2017). Additionally, fraud in international recruitment is notoriously rampant, bordering on trafficking by some accounts (Fernandez 2013). According to one estimate, between 2005 and 2018 at least ten thousand Mexican workers were victims of recruitment fraud. This translates into millions of US dollars lost to ghost recruiters who disappear after charging exorbitant fees for nonexistent jobs in the United States (CDM 2019c).

Transnational advocacy groups have worked together to bring visibility to these abuses and other violations of migrant worker rights. They have not only called on the Mexican government to do more but also urged state governments to use the penal code to actually enforce the labor protections already on the books. As a direct result of this advocacy, several Mexican states have begun to classify recruitment fraud as a criminal activity. Advocates also have succeeded in increasing federal protections against fraudulent international recruitment. Amid these efforts, RADAR, a new transnational labor advocacy program, was established by the Mexico-based human rights organization Proyecto de Derechos Económicos, Sociales y Culturales (ProDESC), with additional support from the AFL-CIO Solidarity International in Mexico City and the CDM. The RADAR program seeks to eradicate labor rights violations committed against migrant workers during the recruitment process for temporary employment (ProDESC n.d.). It focuses on joint responsibility among recruiters, employers, and other actors within supply chains and provides a bilateral framework for addressing broader workplace abuses that often go ignored. The RADAR program is the culmination of almost two decades of strategic communication around building shared strategies among Mexican advocates, US labor unions, and other human rights NGOs.

BUILDING TRANSNATIONAL NETWORKS

The Emergence of Transnational Networks

Inclusive and loosely structured transnational immigrant rights networks benefit from open boundaries that enable the rapid mobilization of participants and the free exchange of ideas (Massa and O'Mahony 2021). Transnational labor advocates with "big tent" agendas (rather than those focused on singular issues) provide a broader platform for participation and do the important coalitional work of connecting different migrant rights struggles. However, this work requires frequent communication and compromise that is unlikely to persist past specific campaigns. Indeed, collective practices designed to foster engaged democratic participation are difficult to sustain in the long term (Polletta 2012; Whyte and Whyte 1991).

Transnational migrant labor advocacy in Mexico emerged amid the long transition from Mexico's one-party rule (which lasted from 1929 to 2000), a transition that was hoped would increase opportunities for meaningful citizen engagement. Mexico-US binational coalition building arose as advocates in both countries deepened their interest in cross-border organizing strategies, especially in the wake of NAFTA. To be sure, the creation of the Red Mexicana de Acción Frente al Libre Comercio / Mexican Action Network Confronting Free Trade (RMALC) in 1991—a coalition that sought not only to oppose NAFTA but also to discuss alternatives to neoliberalism and strategies to strengthen democracy—paved the way for increased cross-border organizing. This coalition worked across multiple sectors beyond free trade, including sustainable agricultural development, human rights protections (particularly in light of rising femicide and gender inequality), Mexico's own framework for labor rights (for migrants and nonmigrants), and environmental justice. Previously, ties between cross-border social constituencies were concentrated primarily in the border region and were limited to labor issues in maquiladoras, undocumented migrant border crossings, and environmental concerns. During the 1980s, however, Mexico's economic dependency on the United States was growing steadily, and national policies were increasingly crafted on a broader scale to attract the attention of US political and economic elites. By the early 1990s, trade unionists in both countries realized that they were confronting similar issues: antiunion policies, privatization, and deteriorating living conditions and job security for workers. Years of local, regional, and national campaigns to challenge such conditions broke down long-standing divides between sectors (Brooks and Fox 2002b, 2002a).

As the public debate around NAFTA and the structural economic changes occurring in the two countries intensified, the boundaries between international and domestic policy issues blurred. Domestic civil society actors across Mexico and the United States struggled to mitigate the impacts of free trade and soon realized that a cross-border strategy was necessary. This shift reinvigorated the internationalist wings of the labor movement (Hathaway 2000) but also tested the typically protectionist tendencies of the AFL-CIO, which had previously failed to take the concerns of Mexican labor leaders seriously (Moody 1995). The irony is that NAFTA itself (and the global governance institutions it created) has helped increase North American labor solidarity by providing mechanisms with which to demand accountability. This newfound solidarity has changed the purely domestic identity of labor unions, whose members now fear job-outsourcing and the influx of new migrant workers who might undercut their wages, forcing unionists to reimagine alternative strategies that include advocating for improved labor conditions in sending states. It has also led to strategic alliances between labor organizations (who have been quickly losing membership [Nolan García 2011]) and NGOs, for whom labor rights have been but one of a long litany of demands against governments and employers (von Bülow 2010).

The first coordinated binational efforts between unions and NGOs occurred in the 1980s and dealt with the maquiladora and agricultural sectors. Founded in 1989, the multisectoral Coalition for Justice in the Maquiladoras brought together religious, environmental, labor, community, and women's rights organizers active around binational integration issues related to improving the working conditions and living standards of workers employed in Mexico's maquiladora industry (Williams 2002; Hennessy and Ojeda 2005). A similar long-running organizing campaign emerged around farmworkers in the Midwest who supplied vegetables for Campbell's Soup, headquartered in New Jersey (Corporate Campaign, Inc. n.d.). In this case, the midwestern AFL-CIO affiliate the Farm Labor Organizing Committee partnered with an agricultural worker union in Sinaloa, Mexico, affiliated with the Confederación de Trabajadores de México / Confederation of Mexican Workers to combat the Campbell Soup Company's efforts to divide unions in the United States and Mexico (Barger and Reza 1994).

These two pioneering efforts paved the way for subsequent cross-border labor organizing campaigns against violations of freedom-of-association laws, even if the resulting claims filed through the NAFTA labor side agreements yielded few tangible results affecting government policies or private employers. The continued relationship between organized labor and NGOs interested in worker rights would eventually open the door to sustained cross-border networks. Those coalitions became denser and inspired new strategies to strengthen labor regulation in Mexico and the United States. Mexico-based advocates impressively crowd-sourced coalitional resources to increase momentum, which they could then mobilize within different international, national, and domestic jurisdictions to make worker rights more portable.[4] In 2005, the Global Workers Justice Alliance (now Justice in Motion) introduced the concept of portable rights to the United Nations in Geneva, and several migrant rights organizations subsequently adopted this advocacy platform (Caron 2005; Caron and Lyon, forthcoming). One important site for this advocacy exchange was the 2010 Peoples' Global Action for Development,

Migration, and Human Rights, an event that coincided with the Global Forum on Migration and Development taking place in Puerto Vallarta, Mexico. These simultaneous events offered an opportunity to develop a claims-making agenda with a strong transnational justice and human rights framework that could incorporate a diverse group of labor rights advocates throughout the North American corridor and Central America.

Sectoral Dynamics

The transnational networks that have emerged around migrant worker rights in North America span a number of "issue areas," much like the varied domestic immigrant advocacy landscape described in chapter 4. While a complete accounting is beyond the scope of this chapter, it is instructive to examine how distinct sectors have approached migrant worker rights, often with different end goals and cross-border strategies in mind. Adopting distinct discursive frames (Benford and Snow 2000), they reveal a diverse set of transnational labor advocacy strategies.

Workers' Rights across Borders.   Communications between Mexican and US labor unions predate NAFTA (Kay 2011), though NAFTA did reinvigorate the AFL-CIO's alliances with Mexico's labor movement. In 1997, the AFL-CIO established a solidarity center in Mexico City to support the democratization of Mexico's labor unions and the elimination of protection contracts awarded to *charro* unions. While their main objective was to support Mexico's unions in attaining collective bargaining rights, the AFL-CIO and its international affiliates have also created alliances with local NGOs and other labor allies working to protect migrant rights, especially Mexican guest workers in Canada and the United States.

Perhaps one of the most well-known examples of cross-border alliances between the two countries is the Frente Auténtico del Trabajo / Authentic Labor Front (FAT), a Mexican labor organization founded in 1960 that encompasses cooperatives, unions, tenant organizations, *ejidatarios* (common-land shareholders), and training centers. This national umbrella organization cites plurality, democracy, and social struggle as its main principles. The FAT "distinguished [itself] from most Mexican unions by its early and continuing conviction that profound political change is needed for workers to be able to achieve their goals" (Hathaway 2000, 428). The organization was a leader in organizing maquiladora workers, frequently collaborating with the US-based United Electrical, Radio and Machine Workers of America (UE) in coordinating "worker to worker" tours and hosting worker trainings and exchanges (Hathaway 2000). In one of those FAT-UE exchanges, Mexican artist Daniel Manrique created, in 1999, *Manos Solidarias*, the mural that is on the cover of this book and is located outside of the UE headquarters in Chicago, while a US-based artist created a painting for Mexico City's FAT offices (Duncan 2008; Stone 2019).

In addition to its organizing work, the FAT joined petitions filed with the NAALC in solidarity with temporary migrant workers. FAT coalitions would eventually submit several petitions to the United States' National Administrative Office to denounce Mexico's failure to uphold the freedom of association. For more than two decades, FAT officials testified before the ILO on the violation of freedom of association in Mexico, and as a result of these efforts, the Mexican Congress eventually passed a constitutional amendment to guarantee secret ballots in union elections in 2017. These changes took effect just after the election of Andrés Manuel López Obrador, whose party—Movimiento Regeneración Nacional—controlled both parliamentary chambers and would go on to pass a list of long-desired labor reforms. This boon to union democracy affirmed the ILO Right to Organise and Collective Bargaining Convention, 1949 (No. 98), but it should be noted that prolabor policy changes also risked a backlash from *charro* unions. Further challenges remained. For example, many progressive labor leaders denounced key omissions that allowed subcontracting to proliferate and that failed to strengthen mechanisms to investigate violations and assess sanctions. In the border region, maquiladora leaders refused to comply with López Obrador's minimum-wage increases, and today the violent repression of progressive labor leaders persists (Bacon 2019).

Binational labor advocates have also focused their organizational efforts on former braceros. RMALC sought to help the thousands of Mexican braceros who had had about 10 percent of their wages withheld by the Mexican government in a forced saving scheme that lacked accountability (Durand 2007). The Mexican government was supposed to function as the guarantor of its citizens' rights (and money) in guest worker programs, but these savings often disappeared, and the Mexican government has claimed it has no record of these transactions. Several grassroots organizations created cross-border coalitions around this issue in the late 1990s. Activist researchers from RMALC sent students to Chicago to conduct archival research to support recuperative litigation, with some success. By 2006, the Mexican government had agreed to compensate—up to $3,500 USD—all those who could demonstrate participation in the program (Martin 2003). After a long campaign to disseminate information among potential beneficiaries, 250,000 former braceros and relatives of late braceros had registered for compensation by 2006. The resulting demand ($875 million) far exceeded the fund established by the Mexican government (a mere $27 million), and as a result the garnished wages remain a central issue for Mexico-based organizers today. These "illicit" deductions were just one among many abuses braceros endured in the United States under the watch of the consular network (Gordon 2006).

Agriculture/Land.   Beyond the worker coalitions that NAFTA's labor side accords have propelled, widening free trade has led to an exodus of Mexicans, the undisputed result of reduced agricultural employment demand in the rural countryside, where farmers have struggled to compete with big agribusiness and subsidized US farmers (Audley et al. 2004). This exodus not only was an unintended consequence of the marketized race to the bottom but also revealed one of NAFTA's core premises to be faulty: that trade liberalization would stem, and even reverse, the flow of migrants. This highly politicized promise foreclosed any provisions for the free flow of labor, provisions that were incorporated into the European Union and later the Schengen Area. In fact, NAFTA was negotiated during the same era as the (still-ongoing) southern border buildup and militarization, which only succeeded in funneling migrants to more dangerous crossing points, leading to an increase in border deaths (Nevins 2002), many of them involving people from crop-producing indigenous regions (Nevins 2007).

Indeed, NAFTA's impact on agricultural regions was severe, especially for small-scale, peasant producers. Mexico's agricultural census found that the number of jobs in agriculture dropped 20 percent between 1991 and 2007. By 2019, the agricultural share was less than 15 percent of total Mexican employment, according to the National Survey of Occupation and Employment (Bada and Fox 2021). But this decline does not represent the full story, as many peasants have fought back. The sustained level of protest among the peasantry since NAFTA has shown the resiliency of *campesino* identity and their resistance to displacement (Fox 1994). For example, Mexicans were able to diversify their income sources by pushing for government subsidies to blunt the impact of opening trade, and at the same time rural communities began accessing urban employment opportunities as well (Hoogesteger and Rivara 2021; Torres-Mazuera 2013).

To be sure, the impact of trade liberalization has been significant. However, despite dire predictions, the rural economy has not been obliterated by NAFTA, and rural livelihoods are not sustained solely by family remittances sent by migrant workers in the United States. While many rural Mexicans have indeed chosen to exit and migrate north, others have stayed and made their voices heard. Famously, the Zapatistas have offered sustained resistance to globalization, and other rural social actors have engaged in protests such as the 2002–3 El Campo no Aguanta Más (The Countryside Won't Take It Any More) movement (Rubio 2004), or the more transnational mobilization of farmworkers who conducted an unprecedented strike across Baja California's strawberry farms (Bacon 2015; Garrapa 2019). The latter managed to build international solidarity and launch boycotts against Driscoll, a multinational distributor. The long-standing Driscoll campaign is an especially trenchant example of the post-NAFTA advocacy landscape. As photojournalist David Bacon explains, transnational labor solidarity is gradually emerging because employers in places like Washington and Baja California "aren't just connected by a common distributor, Driscoll's, but by the workforce that picks the berries. Agricultural labor in virtually all the berry fields on the Pacific Coast comes from the stream of indigenous migrants from southern Mexico."

Organizations interested in fostering bottom-up transnational worker solidarity have often leveraged the fact that Mexican agricultural workers are likely to work in the United States at some point in their lives. As an organizer from the Labor Council for Latin American Advancement (LCLAA) explained to us in 2015: "The same workers end up working in Washington State. These are the same people, same family members. It's interesting to see also the communication that's happening with the *campesinos* in Washington with the *campesinos* in San Quintín and vice versa, going back and forth because they are all from the same community."[5] These campaigns have normalized migrant labor as central to agricultural production and land stewardship, while also supporting Mexicans' "right to stay home" (Bacon 2014; Bada and Fox 2021) rather than be forced to migrate by economic concerns.

In sum, the transnational migrant labor demands emerging from Mexico are inextricably linked to peasant movements demanding land reform, as described below through a discussion of the challenges facing workers without access to the *ejido* system of community-based properties created through agrarian reform. These campaigns have highlighted the impact of free trade on commodity supply chains and stressed that labor solidarity across borders is necessary as bilateral policies continue to affect the lives and working conditions of workers in both Mexico and the United States.

Human Rights.   Human rights campaigns typically make demands irrespective of workers' legal status, ethnicity, or citizenship. Unions and their allies have come together to demand migrant worker rights within the framework of labor protections afforded by domestic statutes and international norms, and peasant movements have anchored their claims as part of their right to the land. Meanwhile, human rights advocates broadly view migrant worker struggles as untethered from national territory or specific legal frameworks. This universalistic approach to labor rights has alienated some advocates but has also created innovative strategies for connecting disparate struggles.

The human rights frame for transnational migrant labor advocacy has been adopted by a wide range of organizational types. As a member of a border network established in the 1990s in El Paso, Texas, explained:

> There has been a qualitative change in Mexico in the last few years, where migration has been contextualized with a human rights framework. And I believe that this is the best opportunity that we have and it should not be seen as a challenge. We need to recognize that what connects the migratory phenomenon in the United States and Mexico is the phenomenon of the obligation to respect human rights. I believe this has been a great opportunity in international fora, to make an impact in the United Nations committees to push for a human rights agenda.[6]

In this vein, advocates have litigated on behalf of indigenous communities throughout Latin America at the Tribunal Internacional de Conciencia de los Pueblos en Movimiento. The tribunal was inspired by the 1966 Russell-Sartre Tribunal (International War Crimes Tribunal), in which Mexico and other Latin American states have frequently been placed on trial, most recently in the 2011

San Fernando massacre in the Mexican state of Tamaulipas, where 193 bodies were found in mass graves. While these victims were determined to be Mexican nationals, the horrific discovery came less than a year after seventy-two travelers (mostly migrants from Central America and South America) were similarly abducted from buses and killed also in the municipality of San Fernando in Tamaulipas, as part of a vicious cartel feud. These abuses are unfortunately "nothing new," and, as Delgadillo, García, and Córdova Alcaraz (2019) argue, "have been an intrinsic element of the treacherous migratory route through Mexico."

While the human rights abuses of the failed drug wars—in which Mexican authorities have repeatedly been implicated—may seem unrelated to the concerns of migrant workers, they are in fact deeply connected. Indeed, the same forces that displace migrants (by creating a context of violence and economic insecurity) also draw them north (WOLA 2020; Bada and Feldmann 2017). This is true both for migrants transiting through Mexico and for Mexican nationals, whose demands for better working conditions are often met with repression, inaction, or violence. The 2014 disappearance of forty-three students from Ayotzinapa Rural Teachers' College exemplified this perilous situation, as the military most likely helped facilitate their capture, torture, and killing—or at best looked the other way (Raphael 2021). They had been en route to a protest in Mexico City calling for the repeal of neoliberal educational reforms and showing support for striking teachers (A.R.E. Editorial Collective 2015; Bracho 2020).

Immigrant Families, Children, and Women's Rights.   A fourth sector of civil society active in transnational migrant advocacy circles is focused on the rights of families and children, many of whom rely on the livelihoods of migrant workers. These are universal concerns that often garner bipartisan support and can soften the push toward increased border militarization and punitive enforcement measures. Shining a light on children and family rights also undercuts the bombastic, stereotyping rhetoric that typically brands migrants as criminals and threats to society (Pallares and Flores-González 2011; American Immigration Council 2017). For labor advocates, focusing on immigrant families can also shift the discussion away from migrants "stealing jobs" to their "providing for families," a preferred frame (Lederer 2019; Glynn 2021).

Civil society groups on each side of the border have approached the issue of family well-being in distinct ways. For example, US advocates have long called for the end of "baby jails" and family detention practices that were seared into the public imaginary during the Trump administration, though the foundations of this practice were established under the Obama administration (Miroff 2020). Indeed, the closest the United States has come to mass legalization arguably is the 2012 Deferred Action for Childhood Arrivals (DACA) Program, which was struck down by various lower courts but continues to exist precariously on a temporary stay for existing beneficiaries as of or before July 16, 2021 (CLINIC 2022). A later Obama-era executive action—the 2014 Deferred Action for Parents of Americans and Lawful Permanent Residents (DAPA)—was struck down altogether (Capps et al. 2016).

One of the most profound, visually striking protests over the way that borders fracture families is the annual Abrazos, No Muros gathering. This moving event allows separated families to come together for three minutes along the banks of the Rio Bravo thanks to a painstakingly negotiated local agreement with the US Border Patrol in the El Paso–Ciudad Juárez border region (Ramos Pacheco and Corchado 2021). Border activists have also joined forces with Mexican organizations to demand better public policies that respect the human rights of migrants.[7] However, a legalization program for undocumented workers in the United States remains an elusive goal, as does a more humane management of border crossings. Moreover, the border buildup ebbs and flows according to presidential administrations and in response to periodic calls for "national security," most profoundly after 9/11 (Andreas and Biersteker 2003; Rodriguez 2008). In fact, one could argue that this push toward national security (and the subsequent further militarization of the border), combined with the incessant criminalization of immigrants, has amplified advocates' focus on family as they seek to construct a counternarrative in the United States.

Meanwhile, immigrant rights groups have increased the visibility of Mexico as a transit country, which has infused public policy debates with a gendered perspective on migrant rights. For example, the CDM, which has offices in Oaxaca, Maryland, and Mexico City, has worked with researchers and policy makers to emphasize that many of the most precarious migrant guest workers are women and that their precarity has ripple effects on their transnational families in and outside the United States (Costa and Martin 2018). Mexico is also home to transnational advocates specializing in women's and family rights such as the Instituto para las Mujeres en la Migración, a large legal service and advocacy organization with diverse international and domestic funding sources.[8] This organization was established during the peak of Mexico's deportation of Central Americans to their countries of origin.[9] While such groups share many of the same concerns as their US counterparts regarding the deleterious effect of immigration and labor policies on families and children, rather than focusing solely on US abuses and calls to halt deportations, much of their advocacy has also targeted the Mexican state's responsibility to integrate children who are effectively deported from the United States alongside their parents. The Instituto para las Mujeres en la Migración and its broad range of advocates have similarly decried Mexico's failure to address the needs of accompanied minors entering the country from the southern border (Asylum Access México et al. 2021; IMUMI n.d.).

The Creation of Cross-sector Networks

The organizational landscape of civil society groups working transnationally comprises Mexico-based groups seeking international linkages and US-based groups joining their partners in Mexico. These networks have been buttressed by forums designed to bring interested groups together across sectors (though grass-roots organizations can often be excluded). For example, the Comité Fronterizo de Obrer@s (CFO) emerged in the late 1970s to address labor exploitation in the maquiladora border region along three states: Coahuila, Tamaulipas, and Chihuahua. Its work intensified during the free trade agreements era, during which time it transformed into a registered worker center.[10] With funding from the Philadelphia-based American Friends Service Committee, the CFO participated in the 1995 UN Conference on Women in Beijing and the World Summit on Social Development in Copenhagen. These opportunities expanded their networks with US-based organizations, and the CFO went on to collaborate with a Washington, DC–based law school to file claims first via the ILO and later under the NAFTA labor side accords.

The FAT, described earlier in this chapter, has also embraced international networking in its struggle to democratize Mexican labor unions since the 1960s. This network of independent labor unions has a Catholic background and would later be inspired by liberation theology to support the Chilean workers denouncing the military overthrow of Salvador Allende in the 1970s. The FAT developed alliances with the United Farm Workers union during the Cesar Chavez era and had strong contacts with Quebec's National Union Confederation. These transnational contacts led to a 1991 meeting in Zacatecas with like-minded Canadian and Mexican NGOs and unions, as well as with US-based NGOs and the UE. The collaboration between FAT and the UE would lead to a strategic alliance formed to take on General Electric and Honeywell factories in Chihuahua and demand collective bargaining rights. Together, they would file a petition under NAFTA's labor side accords in 1994, with the support of the US Teamsters union (Hathaway 2000).

After this initial trinational 1991 meeting, the FAT would also become a key player in the founding of RMALC, a leading transnational network that included "several FAT unions, unions from various universities, environmentalists, women's groups, academics, the National Association of Democratic Lawyers, and labor representatives from two political parties, the PRD and the PRT, as well as peasant organizations and other NGOs" (Hathaway 2000, 173). The FAT's participation in RMALC led to its increased presence in the international arena, as they participated in the 2001 World Social Forum of Porto Alegre and met with the Argentine Confederación General del Trabajo and with unions from Uruguay.[11]

RMALC was instrumental in the negotiation of NAFTA's parallel environmental and labor agreements, but the network has since transformed its mission, privileging action research for social change to support various social movements. Because of the loose coalitional structure it has maintained for more than three decades, RMALC benefits from open boundaries that enable the rapid mobilization of participants and exchange of ideas (Massa and O'Mahony 2021). This strategic network activates when its members launch specific projects. For example,

RMALC offered support when the Brazilian Movimiento de los Afectados por Represas sought to consolidate in 1991 and when the Mexican Red de Afectados por la Minería attempted the same in 2008. When Mexican president Vincente Fox announced the Plan Puebla Panama, a trans-Isthmus megaproject including new superhighways along the Pacific and Gulf Coasts that would connect southern Mexico to the north and also to Central America, RMALC denounced the potential displacement it would cause. They convened a meeting in Tapachula, Chiapas, with many NGOs from Central America discussing how to resist the Plan and the maquila-based development model that has consistently failed to respect labor rights. RMALC members were the natural allies of Central American NGOs because they had already gained policy expertise from the NAFTA negotiations. As a founding RMALC member explained: "It was our turn, as RMALC, to be an important part of this organizing process because we already had networks with lots of organizations in Central America. We knew that free trade agreements had been discussed for the Northern Triangle. When CAFTA [Central American Free Trade Agreement] came, we invited NGOs to Mexico to discuss resistance plans, and this process led to the Mesoamerican Social Forum in 2000 and later to the Mesoamerican Project in 2008 that now includes Colombia as well."[12] In other words, just as the FAT was organizing binationally with an eye north to its North American neighbors, it was also cementing its role (through RMALC) as a leading labor leader in Latin America as a whole.

The ability to unite across sectors can grant transnational campaigns enormous power. Forging these alliances, however, comes with a number of challenges, which we describe next.

DIVERSE ORGANIZATIONAL MISSIONS AND COALITIONAL TOOL KITS

Organizational missions that span multiple transnational labor advocacy divides—that is, across sectors and geographical borders—vary substantially and give rise to unique coalitional tool kits. While the sectoral frames described above reveal the central foci of each respective social movement, we have also identified distinct organizational missions within each sector. The power and benefits of coalitions notwithstanding, these missions can often clash, exposing major power and resource inequities.

Highlighting the Crisis of Migrants in Transit

Labor organizations working across borders generally agree on the centrality of respecting workers' rights regardless of nationality. Yet each group has also developed particular priorities, often determined by uneven resource distribution. A veteran advocate who began working in transborder coalitions during NAFTA and who had been a labor organizer for the CFO explained that her organization aspired but was not able to open a shelter in Piedras Negras for deported Guatemalans who had been attacked by the Mexican police and/or the US Border Patrol. Despite resource constraints, the CFO managed to expand into a labor organization in the border region with offices in the Mexican states of Coahuila, Tamaulipas, and Chihuahua while maintaining connections with like-minded organizations in Canada such as the Toronto-based Red de Solidaridad de la Maquila, a NAFTA-era organization. The CFO's evolution reflects the tension that border advocates constantly face in addressing the needs of transit migrants in crisis as well as broader coalitional goals across the region.

On the international front, border advocacy groups such as the CFO have strategically deployed their coalition networks with unions in Canada, the United States, and Europe to advocate against protection contracts with the ILO. While they recognize that the ILO takes many years to issue (usually nonbinding) recommendations against Mexico, the organization values the opportunity to tap into the ILO's resources and create connections within the international arena. They must take care, however, to remain autonomous and maintain egalitarian decision-making with unions in the United States, even as they work to support their domestic agenda (which also includes offering leadership opportunities and services to women workers and laborers in maquiladoras across the border region):

> We are doing lots of follow-up to the implementation of the amendments to the [Mexican] federal labor law. And with other unions such as the Steel Workers in the US, they have been supporting a campaign that we have in Ciudad Acuña, and we value these relationships because they are based on mutual respect and autonomy. We do not depend on any organization of any type. We work on a level playing field, as equals. A labor union can be very powerful, but they don't have the authority to tell us what to do. If we want to invite a union to request their support to go against an employer, we don't accept relations of subordination.[13]

Despite decades of divisive tactics, organized labor today largely views supporting Mexican workers as beneficial to US labor as well. For example, the AFL-CIO Solidarity Center in Mexico City believes that protection contracts are responsible for the substantial minimum-wage disparities between Mexico and the United States and has thus invested resources in challenging them. In Mexico, the minimum wage is established by a national governmental commission with union representation that has historically sided with government officials and employers to attract foreign investment by offering cheap labor. In seeking to address these disparities, the AFL-CIO has mainly targeted *charro* labor unions affiliated with the government-backed Confederación de Trabajadores de México for outreach. These are the unions often preferred by US and European automakers, who pay lower wages in Mexico for the same job performed at their plants elsewhere in the world.

More broadly, organizing opportunities in Mexico have expanded. When the Solidarity Center was established in Mexico City in 1997, advocates worried about the feasibility of supporting a temporary workforce liable to migrate north. But the arrival of workers from Central America has turned Mexico into an important labor education target and organizing hub as those workers move into formal sectors. In contrast, according to the AFL-CIO Solidarity Center, the large unions in Mexico that represent sectors such as pilots, teachers, or telecommunication workers are simply not too invested in organizing campaigns involving migrant workers.[14]

Within this context, the AFL-CIO has increased its Mexican networks by working with community-based groups that offer training and capacity-building workshops. For example, they have collaborations with ProDESC, the CDM, Justice in Motion, the CFO, the Centro de Apoyo al Trabajador in Puebla, the Red de Solidaridad de la Maquila, and several other union federations. As we saw in chapter 2, the AFL-CIO has also promoted training opportunities for US-based union leaders to learn more about the status of labor rights in Mexico. Meanwhile, the FAT has evolved over the last sixty years into a social movement network that includes worker cooperatives, tenant rights organizations, and a group of autonomous labor unions created by workers that support labor and human rights—with a growing focus on women's rights perspectives. The FAT is officially independent from the government, political parties, churches, and employers. While the AFL-CIO has reached south to expand its outreach efforts, the FAT has looked north, collaborating in campaigns to train undocumented workers in union organizing in Chicago and Milwaukee.

Widely recognized as one of main organizers of the peasant social movement El Campo No Aguanta Más (The Countryside Can't Take It Anymore), the Asociación Nacional de Empresas Comercializadoras de Productores del Campo / National Association of Marketing Companies of Rural Producers (ANEC) was founded in the 1990s and now includes more than sixty thousand small and medium agricultural producers. In ANEC's view, Mexico's neoliberal model has devalued the peasant economy, with the government repeatedly attempting to reduce the size of the rural population without offering any real alternatives to rural employment.[15] ANEC's main focus is supporting economic projects that diversify and expand the regional markets of small producers and that empower *ejidatarios* and their families to stay home. For ANEC, the right to stay home is a core advocacy goal. While they recognize that US agricultural subsidies have pushed thousands of peasants to migrate to the United States, the lack of parallel agriculture subsidies to small *ejido* landholders in Mexico has caused others to leave the countryside and become salaried factory workers. These workers are often incorporated into government-backed *charro* unions—an important link to US-Mexico solidarity, as it is in the interest of both Mexican and US workers to have access to greater workplace democracy free from intervention by political and economic elites.

In a country where 25 percent of the national population is still classified as living in rural areas, Mexico's agricultural workers without access to *ejido* properties have been another target of coalition building. These workers are forced to labor for minimum wage as *jornaleros* (day laborers), facing abuses and labor violations due to the lack of effective labor regulation in the agricultural industries. Since the mid-1990s, ANEC has fostered connections with hometown associations and US-based nonprofits working with small family farms in the Midwest to raise awareness around corn-dumping practices and production disparities exacerbated by differences in governmental corn production subsidies. In the last twenty years, they have also strengthened their relations with organizations in Canada, the United States, and Central and South America and have supported labor rights campaigns to respect the labor rights of all migrants, regardless of immigration status. They have also maintained a constant presence in international coalitions as a way of highlighting regional food sovereignty issues.

Contextualizing the Migrant Worker

While organized labor advocates on both sides of the border have focused on the labor extraction process that individuals confront before, after, and following migration, other groups have contextualized these struggles more broadly within the structural and direct violence that has long affected migrant workers across an array of social institutions. As a result, there is a range of diverse migrant worker advocacy strategies that often differ across sectors and borders. Especially in this capacious framework, Mexico must be understood as a sending state, a transit country, *and* an ultimate destination for precarious migrants.

The ecosystem of immigrant rights NGOs in Mexico is comparatively smaller than in the United States. While most immigrant rights organizations we interviewed emerged in the 1990s, several pioneering organizations also sprang up in the aftermath of the Central American wars in the 1980s, when Mexico became an important country of reception for Guatemalans and other refugees fleeing violence. These organizations, like the Mexico City–based Sin Fronteras, advocate for migrant rights along the southern border and bring visibility to the abuses committed by Mexican authorities upon Central American migrants in transit. As one of the older NGOs with extensive expertise in immigrant human rights, Sin Fronteras is the leader of multiple networks and coalitions in the region that seek to provide direct service to migrants while also pushing for policy change across the Americas. For example, Sin Fronteras is the leader of an action plan for the Brazil Declaration, a 2014 cooperation agreement supported by the United Nations High Commissioner for Refugees to strengthen the international protection of refugees displaced and stateless persons in Latin America and the Caribbean.[16] Though not legally binding, this instrument offers a blueprint for member states to respect basic international asylum protocols (UNHCR 2014).

Adopting a similar human rights frame, ProDESC is a transnational feminist human rights organization that has successfully utilized the environmental and labor side accords of NAFTA to secure restitution for peasant communities exploited by Canadian mining corporations, *ejidatarios* in Coahuila, and temporary migrant workers enduring labor violations. They have a distinctively intersectional approach to human rights defense and offer legal and capacity-building services to individuals and grassroots organizations. In the last two decades, ProDESC has nurtured a network of transnational labor advocacy organizations focused on migrant rights, including the AFL-CIO Solidarity Center, the National Workers Alliance of New Orleans, the National Domestic Worker Alliance, the National Day Laborer Organizing Network, and several legal service organizations and law schools across the United States.

Also focused on migrant justice litigation, the organization Prevención, Capacitación y Defensa del Migrante (PRECADEM) deploys a restorative justice framework and participates in both formal litigation strategies and international citizen tribunals on behalf of migrants in transit and other individuals who have been forcibly displaced (Fundación para la Justicia y el Estado Democrático de Derecho 2018). Reflecting on their decision to participate in the Tribunal Internacional de Conciencia de los Pueblos en Movimiento, PRECADEM staff explained that this was a strategic way to collect testimonial data that could eventually be used in a formal international tribunal, as such citizen tribunals were "an open microphone in a global effort to offer voice to those who are never heard, to victims, to marginalized, to the vulnerable, to the invisible."[17] While the road to justice is long and uncertain, advocates see these exercises as an important tool for demanding accountability for the many instances of state violence (Delgadillo, García, and Córdova Alcaraz 2019).

Beyond the dense network of Mexico-based civil society groups, US-based NGOs play a central role in defending migrant workers and erecting a legal scaffolding supporting migrant rights. In September 2005, after offering a series of training workshops on US labor law to Mexico's consular corps, a US-trained attorney established the CDM in Zacatecas, Mexico. Its focus is to improve the working conditions of low-wage migrant workers in the United States. By setting its headquarters in Mexico, CDM pursued an innovative transnational approach: in providing migrant workers with training, legal services, and advocacy opportunities in their communities of origin, it could help workers safely and effectively claim their rights under US law. Ultimately, when security conditions became untenable from drug cartel violence in Zacatecas, it moved its base to Mexico City and opened up outreach and policy offices in Juxtlahuaca, Oaxaca, and Baltimore, Maryland.

In 2008, the Global Workers Justice Alliance, now Justice in Motion, an established immigrant worker advocacy organization based in New York City and founded in 2005, would also set up a satellite office in southern Mexico to document abuses experienced by H-2A and H-2B low-wage guest workers and to redouble efforts to recover their back wages. Unlike CDM, Justice in Motion does not maintain a physical office in Mexico, opting instead to support (with its limited budget) local organizers, whom they rely on to train and equip a small group of grassroots advocacy organizations. By late 2016, Justice in Motion had developed an active Defenders Network to promote a portable rights model, with forty immigrant advocacy NGOs operating in Mexico, Guatemala, Honduras, El Salvador, and Nicaragua. Justice in Motion also supports cross-border humanitarian immigration work and family law, asylum, and unaccompanied minor cases, among other issues (Dias-Abey 2016).

In sum, groups operating in Mexico have utilized dense cross-border networks to achieve their aims throughout Mexico, Canada, the United States, and Central America, despite their often differing points of entry to migrant worker advocacy. These efforts culminated in the Regional Initiative on Labor Mobility (INILAB) (CDM 2018). INILAB forged a network of twelve organizations from Canada to Central America with ties to United Food and Commercial Workers of America (UFCW), an international union with operations in the United States, Canada, and Mexico City. UFCW, in turn, has worked to support immigrant workers in the United States, as well as seasonal agricultural workers in Canada, and has explored opportunities for launching a campaign aimed at Walmart workers in Mexico (Galvez, Godoy, and Meneima 2019).

Like INILAB, El Colectivo Migraciones para las Américas / Migration Collective for the Americas (COMPA), formerly known as Colectivo PND-Migración, is a group of 128 organizations and networks scattered across eleven countries in North and Central America. The impetus for this collective began in 2013, when the recently inaugurated government of Enrique Peña Nieto convened a series of citizen forums with civil society organizations in Mexico, the United States, and Europe to discuss how immigration would factor into Mexico's national development plan. After eight public consultation meetings held in Tijuana, Mexico City, Guadalajara, Tijuana, Tapachula, Chicago, Los Angeles, and Zurich, many participants took advantage of the repeated gatherings to form a monitoring network that would hold the government accountable.[18] Ultimately, COMPA has focused on the security of migrant workers, decrying the abuses of immigration authorities and urging the federal Mexican government to effectively implement and enforce the Programa Especial de Migración 2014–2018 / Special Migration Plan 2014–2018, a dedicated section in the country's National Development Plan created in April 2014 that was heralded as ushering in a new era in Mexico's migration management. Among the many lofty objectives of this plan, the federal government committed to respecting migrant rights by harmonizing all internal laws and international treaties to establish a nondiscriminatory framework for human rights, legal protection, and the prevention of rights violations (Secretaría de Gobernación 2014).

Some of these networks activate and deactivate depending on their level of funding, the cost-effective calculations of their social accountability goals, or whether member organizations choose to pivot once campaign goals have been achieved. One such campaign, Jornaleros SAFE, was an ambitious research network project financed by the Centro Independiente de Trabajadores Agricolas, the Dimensión Pastoral de la Movilidad Humana, the Global Workers Justice Alliance, United Farm Workers, and Catholic Relief Services. This project focused on the challenges facing temporary migrant workers and internal agricultural migrants, targeting both the Mexican and US governments. It produced important research reports, though the collaboration formally ended when funding ceased, leaving unfinished the important work of on-the-ground outreach.[19]

Varying Tool Kits for Transnational Advocacy

The tool kits utilized by advocates vary depending on the resources at their disposal, their organizational capacities, and campaign goals. Coordinating legal petitions in bilateral jurisdictions takes time and many witnesses willing to share their experiences and expertise around submitting claims—which may or may not bring restitution and will certainly prove costly. Consequently, some organizations may opt to focus their efforts instead on high-level changes to trade agreements or to domestic policies that shape labor recruitment practices. For the vast majority of advocates, the choice to devise and pursue a legal strategy to target a Mexican or US court or an international body is taken with care, and the deliberations usually involve how to maximize an issue's visibility.

For groups such as the FAT involved in direct organizing, capacity building and inclusive worker training are key. In 1992, the FAT inaugurated the Strategic Organizational Alliance, aimed at organizing Mexican workers whose employers also had factories in the United States. The goal was to highlight wage differentials and make workers aware that US factories interested in moving to Mexico were trying to cut labor costs.[20] This focus has also shaped labor organizing on the ground in the United States, with advocates seeking to challenge the often xenophobic and protectionist tendencies of rank-and-file workers nervous about seeing their jobs shipped abroad (AFL-CIO 2020).

For organizations with robust access to lawyers, supranational mechanisms such as the NAALC are important tools that allow them to submit multiple and frequent petitions on behalf of workers. Yet these efforts also require on-the-ground coordination, especially in rural communities like San Luis Potosí and Oaxaca, which send a large number of guest workers and are hotbeds of recruitment fraud. The CDM has incubated a group focusing on these efforts called the Centro de Defensa del Migrante, as has Justice in Motion through its defender network. These strategies employ local grassroots organizing tactics along with high-level policy advocacy; the goal is both to strengthen their legal case and to build legitimacy in communities of origin that may be wary of outside influence.[21]

For ProDESC, an important strategy has been to create equitable and respectful binational collaborations with short-, medium-, and long-term goals. To this end, it has convened bilateral meetings with Mexican and US organizations to outline commonalities and differences, share resources, and create mutually beneficial common work plans. In 2007 in Mexico City, ProDESC convened its first meeting to discuss binational labor justice in collaboration with the CDM and a group of thirty organizations, fifteen from Mexico and fifteen representing the United States. With funding from the Ford Foundation, this collaborative project would produce an essential bilingual manual of binational labor justice that explains the main legal mechanisms for enforcing labor rights in Mexico and the United States (ProDESC and CDM 2010).

Along the border, maquiladora organizers have gathered *testimonios* of wage violations perpetrated by corrupt union leaders. These narratives have been critical to litigation brought before Mexico's labor courts and the ILO, the NAALC, and the Interamerican Commission on Human Rights. By contrast, other border activists focused on family reunification have championed a watchdog mechanism that would allow for a more collaborative relationship with enforcement authorities when voicing community complaints. Such collaboration, these activists argue, is necessary, even if fraught. In El Paso, for example, the US Border Patrol is seen as both a reviled arm of the immigration enforcement apparatus and an inevitable presence in a community. Indeed, many officers are from immigrant families themselves. However, an event like Abrazos, No Muros can occur only by the establishment of a (fragile) foundation of trust. This cooperative focus places activist organizations in a delicate position vis-à-vis government surveillance, as well as opening them up to endless critiques from leftist advocates who decry these strategies as a form of theater, stunts merely serving to soften the image of the federal government.

While our focus here has largely been on US- and Mexico-based organizations, Canadian organizations are members of these collaborations as well and have been involved in training and educating workers navigating the Seasonal Agricultural Worker Program (and the many associated abuses and fraudulent schemes). UFCW (an international union with a strong presence among the Canadian agricultural workforce) initiated a bilateral strategy in 2007 by inviting Mexican legislators from the three main political parties (PRI, PAN, and PRD [Partido Revolucionario Democrático / Party of the Democratic Revolution]) to witness the conditions of Mexican workers in Canada. Once back in Congress, these legislators held discussions about modifying the Seasonal Agricultural Worker Program.[22] UFCW also established an office in Mexico and began collecting testimonies from workers who had been forced to bribe Mexican authorities in order to get their names on recruitment lists. For UFCW, generating local publicity around such cases was vital in the "mobilization of shame" that could pressure decision makers. This campaign was run in parallel with the co-enforcement efforts taking place in the United States (as described in chapter 3). UFCW had supported the Consular Partnership program since its inception, and their US organizers also coordinated with their Canadian counterparts. Eventually, UFCW was successful in holding accountable fraudulent recruiters preying upon desperate workers seeking entry into the Seasonal Agricultural Worker Program. It also established cooperation agreements with Estado de México, Michoacán, Guanajuato, Guerrero, and Oaxaca to promote predeparture training for workers. The union would also later denounce corruption in the state of Guanajuato, singling out officials in Mexico's Ministry of Labor who were illegally demanding kickbacks from migrant workers. The campaign won restitution for Mexican guest workers who had experienced retaliation after they exposed these rampant violations (Galvez, Godoy, and Meneima 2019).

In sum, grassroots organizations are the linchpins of a transnational advocacy strategy that actually results in domestic policy change. These cross-border networks must mobilize workers on the ground to maintain legitimacy and execute educational campaigns aimed at abuse prevention. Meanwhile, they are also raising awareness about the portability of worker rights while generating solidarity among Mexican and US workers. Educating workers about the role of free trade agreements in driving labor precarity and highlighting multinational corporations' labor practices that create a "race to the bottom" in each country's labor arena is crucial. Yet this process is long and slow, and achieving justice and restitution requires constant organizing and deliberation.

COALITIONAL FRICTIONS

The work of any social movement is riddled with coalitional challenges, and immigrant worker rights advocacy is no exception. While there are myriad opportunities for disagreements that can threaten the sustainability of these networks, two are worth highlighting here: capacity and funding disparities; and organizing challenges and unevenly distributed power.

Capacity and Funding Disparities

Expanding networks in Mexico and the United States face funding imbalances, which affect their negotiating power vis-à-vis regional governments. In 1980, Mexico had only six human rights organizations; by 2010, there were more than 1,100, some of them advocating on behalf of transit migrants from El Salvador, Guatemala, and Honduras fleeing poverty, unemployment, and unfettered violence perpetrated by state and nonstate actors (París-Pombo 2017). Many of these organizations are relatively new and are hard-pressed to find enough funding for programs to prevent abuses, provide legal protection, organize migrants, effect policy changes in migration management, and improve migrants' access to labor rights (Rojas Wiesner 2022).

Furthermore, Mexico's civil society infrastructure is spread thin, with 3.6 civil society organizations per 10,000 inhabitants compared to 65.1 per 10,000 inhabitants in the United States (Layton 2011). Many organizations in Mexico struggle to obtain funding in a country where social inequality has depressed levels of social capital and trust. Case studies of social capital in Mexico help explain the lack of a robust and formal civil society capable of demanding better services from the government or of creating efficient alternative models to solve community problems beyond the local level (Cleary and Stokes 2006; Layton and Moreno 2010). For example, one Mexico City–based organization offering legal services mostly to Haitian and Central Americans estimates that their budget represents just 10 percent of the local Human Rights Commission's annual funding. Their meager resources allow them to have only one lawyer per country of origin, despite the enormous need for representation.[23]

Furthermore, regional differences in organizational density have emerged, as Mexican NGOs are frequently dependent on private domestic and foreign donors to operate, exacerbating existing hierarchies of power and influence between Mexican and US labor advocates. The funding that Mexican civil society organizations receive from foreign sources is minuscule, as only 6.4 percent of their resources come from foreign donors, 75 percent from private domestic donors, and the rest from the government (Chávez Becker, González Ulloa, and Venegas Maldonado 2016). Difficulties in finding sustainable sources of funding, coupled with low density and a disproportionate concentration of organizations in a few states, limit their ability to effectively fulfill their mission. For example, Mexico City, the Estado de México, and the state of Oaxaca are home to 36 percent of the nonprofit organizations in Mexico (CEMEFI 2019). The unequal distribution of resources among existing networks of transnational advocates in the North American region—which Anner and Evans (2004) dub "the double divide" across borders *and* sectors—also makes it difficult to coordinate successful campaigns that can challenge the power and influence of agribusiness and international labor recruiters and enact meaningful migrant worker rights reforms.

Key issues facing migrant workers currently include wage theft, occupational safety and health protections, criminal international recruiters, and growing security concerns that often target migrants in transit and return migrants. Advocacy funding disparity is thus consequential given that immigrants commonly face labor and employment law violations and struggle to access social protections in host countries, especially in communities where watchdog civil society groups do not have a presence. Groups may also fear establishing a presence in such areas because of insecurity. On the whole, a thin and scarcely funded civil society infrastructure in the sending state forces migrants (and return migrants) to rely on complex government bureaucracies to claim rights as the only avenue for redress, and the weak enforcement system has allowed abuse to flourish (Gunningham, Thornton, and Kagan 2005).

While funding from international donors to Mexico-based organizations is rather small, many of the organizations interviewed frequently rely on international and US-based donors such as the AFL-CIO Solidarity Center, Catholic

Relief Services, the Ford Foundation, the MacArthur Foundation, and OXFAM, to name a few with transnational labor advocacy agendas and active programming in Mexico. These sources of support are critical, though often fickle and fleeting. Member-based organizations such as unions, worker defense networks, and worker centers rely on voluntary member contributions, ad hoc organizing funds, or union fees to support transnational organizing efforts. Many of these Mexico-based organizations also depend on Mexican government subsidies and domestic private donors to offer direct services, including access to labor litigation in US courts.[24] Some networks have diversified their donor base and increased direct services, but this can siphon resources away from their organizing efforts around demanding state accountability.

The organizations that value their independence from the Mexican government have decided to base their fundraising exclusively on international donations or private donations. Yet relying on international donations can also be fraught, as many international organizations seek out successful Mexican organizations to offer financing in exchange for their participation in preexisting projects that are not necessarily jointly envisioned. An organization with a history of successful collaborations with US NGOs complained that these organizations use Mexican groups to implement and execute broader projects with little interest in garnering local feedback. In general, Mexican organizations mentioned that it is difficult to obtain international funding because the same groups are competing for the same donors.[25]

Organizing Challenges and Uneven Power

Organizations must constantly adjust their agendas to align with their funders' priorities. The Mexican organizations we observed noted that certain US-based organizations have a utilitarian view of partnerships and are not interested in establishing equitable collaborations through sustained dialogue and common agendas. Similarly, many organizations complained of being prevented from lodging direct complaints in international organizations such as the ILO. For example, border groups were entirely dependent on a labor union to lodge complaints at the ILO, and this was a major obstacle for using this international mechanism to bring visibility to worker abuses.

Organizations struggle both to hold states accountable and to effectively rally workers. They must constantly battle the state's refusals to accept responsibility for being the main perpetrators of violations. In the view of one labor organizer, it is very difficult to launch organizing worker campaigns in Central America and defend the rights of migrants in transit when *all* governments in the region deny their involvement in abusing human and labor rights.[26] Finding avenues to let migrants in transit secure access to unionized jobs in Mexico is also a difficult project for a union. Despite the challenging environment, independent labor unions in Mexico strive to defend the labor rights of Central Americans trying to find temporary work in Mexican factories, even when they know that their ultimate goal is to cross into the United States.[27] Uneven attention is also a factor; in comparison to the disproportionate attention paid to migrant workers in the United States, migrant workers in Canada still receive relatively little attention from Mexican organizations. This imbalance creates additional competition for resources among advocates.[28]

Transnational organizations must also balance their legal work with their collective organizing and outreach among workers. These efforts are all the more vital because of the government's outreach failures. According to the NAALC framework, the Mexican Ministry of Labor is in charge of educating workers about fraud prevention in international recruitment, though the government does not have the political will or adequate funding to implement a national campaign aimed at eradicating such fraud.[29] As a result, it lacks the internal capacity to design its own educational programming, having to piggyback instead on the training workshops that international coalitions have produced. Even when transnational coalitions manage to mount preventive campaigns to educate workers through interactive phone apps and websites, the vast majority of rural workers do not have access to this information because they lack internet or smartphones.[30]

Worker outreach is further impeded by the unsafe conditions organizers face in areas where organized crime operates with impunity. Moreover, opportunities for legal redress are uneven. Thanks to tireless advocacy, the states with the highest levels of insecurity have modified their penal codes to classify recruitment fraud as a criminal activity. But while trainings offered in the states of Michoacán and Zacatecas may eventually allow access to claims making in the municipal prosecutor's office, the same training will prove less valuable in states where fraud recruitment is not a punishable crime.[31]

Finally, transnational advocates focusing on organizing and educating local workers in guest worker programs are increasingly coming to terms with the reality that any such program will primarily fulfill the needs of sovereign countries and the employers who request them. This realization, one organizer explained, ultimately presents a conflict: whether to continue monitoring employers within a guest worker framework that does not ultimately address the race to the bottom in the labor practices of these industries.[32]

LOOKING TO THE FUTURE

The sustained effort of transnational advocates to bring awareness to labor violations since the enactment of NAFTA in 1994 paved the way for a new era marked by an increased recognition of labor rights for all workers in international trade agreements. This change has offered new possibilities for the bilateral enforcement of labor rights. The 2020 United States Mexico Canada Agreement inaugurated the direct use of trade agreements to respect labor rights in the region. The parallel agreements on labor established by NAFTA became integrated into chapter 23 and its annex 23A on worker representation in collective bargaining in Mexico and are now part of the agreement. The forty-five public communications (petitions) lodged by the National Administrative Offices between 1994 and June of 2020 to bring attention to labor rights abuses—including violations of collective bargaining rights and failures to guarantee basic labor protections for guest workers—had a limited but symbolic effect in a few arenas such as collective bargaining rights and the prevention and deterrence of recruitment fraud around Mexican temporary guest worker visas.

While the public submissions system remains in place, the new chapter on labor makes the labor provisions of the United States Mexico Canada Agreement fully enforceable and subject to dispute resolution. It also requires parties to adopt and maintain core ILO labor standards, including freedom of association and the right to strike. These reforms, however, will still rely on the capacity of labor advocates to lead the charge in making sure they are enforced. Nonetheless, the new language is heartening for advocates. In Article 23.8, the agreement includes migrant rights and recognizes their portability: "The parties recognize the vulnerability of migrant workers with respect to labor protections. Accordingly, in implementing Article 23.3 (Labor Rights), each Party shall ensure that migrant workers are protected under its labor laws, whether they are nationals or non-nationals of the Party" (USTR 2020). In 2020, UFCW Canada signed a new agreement with the Confederación Autónoma de Trabajadores y Empleados de México that aims to strengthen the protections of Mexican migrant workers while in Canada. It also seeks to coordinate communication and training approaches focused on labor, health, and safety rights to better protect migrant workers in that country.

Low-wage Mexican workers in the formal economy continue to face multiple hurdles in claiming their labor rights. Currently, the tripartite conciliation and arbitration boards take anywhere between two to ten years to resolve worker claims, and few even reach labor courts. In 2018, Mexico introduced an important amendment to its labor laws that may provide faster access to claims-making procedures and may democratize collective bargaining, among other major changes. The new legislation establishes that by 2022, salaried workers will have access to local and federal labor courts to resolve labor disputes that cannot reach an amicable resolution after negotiations in conciliation and arbitration boards. Most importantly, the labor courts will now depend on the judicial instead of the executive branch. The new law also guarantees collective bargaining rights by allowing workers to choose union leaders in a secret ballot procedure, and all collective bargaining agreements will be filed and deposited in a national registry (Straulino-Rodriguez and Delsol Espada 2019). In Mexico, the gradual democratization of labor practices, combined with the election of a president at the head of a center-left coalition, led to substantial increases in the national minimum wage: a 16 percent rise in 2019 and 20 percent in 2020.

While the ambitious framework of the Programa Especial de Migración 2014–2018 has yet to be implemented across Mexico's federal government, the high concentration of advocates in Mexico City has led to increased demands for better services and protections for all migrants. Mexico City's 2011 Law of Interculturality, Migrant Attention, and Human Mobility and Mexico City's 2017 Constitution ratified the decriminalization of migrants and offered equal access to basic social services. Both instruments recognized migrants, refugees, and their families as persons with portable rights, regardless of immigration status. While the necessary bylaws that will regulate the delivery of basic services to migrants and refugees have yet to be discussed in Mexico City and elsewhere in the country, transnational advocates do have a few benchmarks by which to measure how well these commitments are being met.

Finally, though many of the international jurisdictions put in place to enforce labor rights are nonbinding and minimally effective in remedying conditions on the ground, the trilateral adjudication process inaugurated by NAFTA did pave the way for increased strategic cooperation among transnational advocates. These actors are ready to take advantage of political opportunities to embed multilayered coalitions—comprising worker centers, labor unions, academia, legal service organizations, transnational migrant organizations, and human rights organizations—in the regional governance regulatory framework of labor enforcement initiated by NAFTA. Over the last two decades, transnational labor coalitions have multiplied and have built on the early gains of anti-NAFTA activists. The outcomes of these post-NAFTA coalitions may seem rather modest and the changes minimal at best; however, assessing change always depends on one's frame of reference and geographic location. While preventing fraud in international recruitment may seem meaningless for empowered migrant workers in Chicago, this issue looms very large for displaced peasants in rural Oaxaca.

Conclusion

Scaling Migrant Worker Rights

The roots of this book extend back over a decade to when we were each engaged in simultaneous research on the organizational lives of Mexican immigrant workers in the United States. As sociologists working in interdisciplinary spaces, both of us became interested in how the Mexican state had emerged as a critical interlocutor in the conversations around workplace precarity (Gleeson, as a labor scholar obsessed with how bureaucracies function, and Bada, as an expert in Mexico's politics and transnational civil society). We each viewed the question of why and how the consular network had taken up the task of labor rights outreach and co-enforcement through our own lens.

What emerged—through the work of over sixteen research assistants, 206 interviews in twenty cities, and countless hours sorting through media and government archives—is a story that disrupts how we think migrant policies are created and implemented, why coalitions emerge and retreat, and the centrality of national borders—but also bilateral relations—in enforcing domestic rights.

EPISTEMOLOGY OF THE SENDING STATE

From the beginning, the central approach of this research was *triangulation*. Rather than focus on the sending state as an autonomous actor, we attempted to understand both the multiple *relationships* Mexico maintained with other states and civil society organizations and the diverse *advocacy strategies* that shaped these relationships and Mexican policy. We knew that the letter of the law—as inscribed in the labor side accords of the North American Free Trade Agreement (NAFTA), the various labor codes in the United States, and the constitutional assurances Mexico extended to its emigrants and, more recently, to all migrants—was largely aspirational and often disregarded. Our first step was to understand each of these legal arenas and the bureaucracies that had emerged to implement them.

To gain an understanding of how US labor standards affected Mexican immigrant workers, nearly half of whom were unauthorized, we started by talking with US labor agency staff themselves about their outreach strategies. We spoke with a range of US labor regulation actors operating across the span of a decade and three presidential administrations during which time a deterrence-oriented model of labor enforcement has persisted (Piore and Schrank 2018). We knew that the well-meaning "Don't ask, don't tell" approach of labor agencies when it comes to immigration status (Gleeson 2014) was not enough to dissolve community anxiety in an era of intensified immigration enforcement (both through the spectacle of devastating large-scale raids and through the far more effective but lower-profile audits honed during the Obama administration) (Griffith and Gleeson 2019). We spoke with representatives from each of the major US labor standards enforcement agencies (the Department of Labor [DOL]'s Wage and Hour Division, Occupational Safety and Health Administration, and Bureau of International Labor Affairs), the Equal Employment Opportunity Commission, and the National Labor Relations Board. We also spoke with seven Community Outreach and Resource Planning Specialist (CORPS) staffers, whose job it is to create and maintain consular relationships.

We fielded a survey with all representatives of the Mexican consular network and followed up with interviews with consuls in the Departamento de Protección (and sometimes other departments as well, such as Comunidades) in each of the fifteen cities that formed the pioneer cohort of the Semana de Derechos Laborales / Labor Rights Week. We then spoke with key Mexican officials at the Secretaría de Relaciones Exteriores / Ministry of Foreign Affairs (SRE) and the Secretaría del Trabajo y Previsión Social / Ministry of Labor, two federal bureaucracies that have proven critical to negotiating and fulfilling Mexico's obligations to its emigrants. We treated enforcement and consular agencies as complex bureaucracies in which the left hand does not always know what the right hand is doing, officials have an enormous amount of discretion, and the implementation of national directives is subject to local capacity and preferences. All told, we spent at least fifteen years following and attending consular events in Chicago, New York City, and Northern California. We paired these longitudinal observations with recurrent (and often unsuccessful) formal requests to interview key foreign affairs personnel, as well as data requests to Mexico's Instituto Nacional de Transparencia, Acceso a la Información y Protección de Datos Personales (INAI). We also did a deep dive into the various social media (Facebook, Twitter) and news (print, radio, community TV) outreach related to labor rights that consular officials have cultivated over the years. These data formed the basis of chapter 2.

But the data that have perhaps most shaped our story here are the 176 conversations we had with civil society organizations across the United States, which gave us their sometimes brutally honest take on the binational effort to improve Mexican immigrant worker conditions. These organizations (which include traditional labor unions, legal service providers, and an array of alt-labor groups, including worker centers and immigrant rights organizations) helped bring into stark relief the challenges Mexicans living in the US contend with when they interface with their local consulate. Our empirical goal was saturation in each project city, which we selected to represent traditional immigrant-receiving places whose consulates have been active on the labor rights front and new and emerging destinations (Atlanta, Austin, Chicago, Fresno, Houston, Los Angeles, Miami, Nashville, New York, Omaha, Orlando, Phoenix, Raleigh, Sacramento, Salt Lake City, San Diego, San Francisco/Oakland, San Jose, Tucson, and Washington, DC). Many of the groups in our study were part of federated organizations (e.g., labor unions), and we aimed to speak with their national leadership as well as with staff at sister chapters in other cities. Each city where we sampled respondents had a distinct infrastructure for immigrant labor advocacies. In some, unions were major players; in others, faith-based organizations took the lead in offering legal assistance. Throughout these cities, the advocacy goals often differed substantially, as did the local demography and political landscape of immigration policies. Insights from these national and local groups form the basis of chapters 3 and 4.

Finally, we spoke with twenty-two transnational NGOs operating in Mexico, which provided a critical perspective on the range of issues for which the sending state should be held accountable, as described in chapter 5. Beyond the consular network in the United States (and Canada), these organizations and the coalitional networks they have forged have leveraged bilateral and regional instruments to realize a migrant worker rights agenda that goes far beyond domestic co-enforcement models.

KEY PATTERNS IN STATE-CIVIL SOCIETY RELATIONS

The Invisible Labor of Demanding Accountability

Bilateral agreements do not simply arise through fully formed executive decrees. We uncovered hidden—and often conflicting—evidence regarding what led to the grand proclamations and policy shifts that dominated the news archives. The 2004 joint ministerial negotiations, the 2008 memoranda of understanding between Mexico's SRE and the US DOL, and the 2014 recommitment to enforcing immigrant worker rights were all preceded by loud and carefully coordinated calls for accountability from civil society on both sides of the Río Bravo. Thus we find that the official origin story of what became the Semana de Derechos Laborales gives outsized credit to bilateral diplomacy and overlooks the long haul of state accountability politics driven by civil society, whose efforts predate the joint ministerial negotiations and stretch as far back as the consular-appointed honorary commissions in the Midwest (Valdés 2000) and the independent *mutualistas* in the

Southwest, both in the 1920s (Pycior 2014). As Natasha Iskander (2010, 253) aptly describes, the state and migrants have redefined their goals and learned from each other transnationally through a long-running dance of state-society relations.

Such efforts to hold the sending state accountable can be traced back to the braceros' struggles to recover their meager savings from Mexican banks, as discussed in chapter 5. There are, to be sure, many instrumental reasons why the US DOL facilitated a partnership with Mexico's SRE, whose consular network could be used to conduct outreach within the largest immigrant group in the United States and a labor force overwhelmingly concentrated in low-wage jobs ripe for abuse. Similarly, the Mexican government (as Alexandra Délano Alonso chronicles) has over the years committed to a new path of engagement with its diaspora that has led to modest improvements on the issues of collective family remittances, absentee voting, and trade relations (Délano 2011; Délano Alonso 2018).[1]

Yet all along the way, the Mexican government has had to be coaxed into spending precious political capital on promoting immigrant labor rights and comprehensive immigration reform. Indeed, former Mexican president Felipe Calderón (2006–12), following the failure of his predecessor to make substantial advances on immigration policy, explicitly sought to *desmigratizar* the bilateral agenda[2]— that is, to remove immigration from it as a central issue (Durand 2013). However, pressure to keep immigration issues front and center in bilateral diplomatic negotiations came from multiple sources, including a new institution, the Consejo Consultivo del Instituto de los Mexicanos en el Exterior / Advisory Board of the Institute of Mexicans Abroad (CCIME), which was made up of many key Mexican labor leaders across the United States. Several union officials we spoke with claimed that they had single-handedly convinced the SRE to invest in what would become the Labor Rights Week, their preferred advocacy model of local engagement and one clearly inspired by the Semana Binacional de Salud / Binational Health Week.

Similarly, US labor agency officials in cities known for their collaborative partnerships (e.g., Chicago, Houston, Los Angeles, New York City) would all take credit for piloting the Ventanilla Laboral / Labor Rights Window. But whatever the origin (and there were likely many), it was clear that the Mexican government, and its US counterparts, would soon claim this national collaboration as their own; moreover, Mexico promoted a narrative that these partnerships were benevolent government creations that would help hold the US regulatory apparatus and unscrupulous employers accountable—thus downplaying its own regulatory failures vis-à-vis its foreign nationals. In turn, the long historical arc of Mexican migrant self-representation—in which migrants developed a "voice after exit" in order to gain visibility as political actors (Hirschman 1970; Fox 2007; Duquette-Rury 2019; Iskander 2010; Pycior 2014; Bada 2014; Valdés 2000)—was commonly downplayed by government bureaucrats.

But in fact, it was the demands of advocates themselves—sometimes outside formal channels, sometimes overly critical, and almost always rooted in a condemnation of the Mexican government's historic abuse and abrogation of duty toward its diaspora—that (at least partially) propelled government bureaucrats to begin to embrace a bilateral commitment to upholding immigrant worker rights. Advocacy claims would take many forms, including invitations to consular officials to speak with workers (who in turn demanded greater involvement), formal proposals by labor leaders via the CCIME, and denunciatory petitions by transnational advocates to the National Administrative Office of the North American Agreement on Labor Cooperation (NAALC), the 1993 labor side agreement negotiated as part of NAFTA. Establishing state accountability is a drawn-out, nonlinear process in which allies sometimes coordinate their efforts and sometimes do not. In short, there was a series of simultaneous efforts—of varied intensities—to pull the Mexican state into a more engaged modality for the legal protection of Mexican citizens living abroad. Some advocates focused on the co-enforcement of migrant worker rights on the books in the United States (chapter 3), while many others took a more inclusive approach encompassing economic, social, and cultural rights in the receiving country (chapter 4) and back in Mexico (chapter 5).

Moreover, state targets often varied. In local communities, these could include the consul in charge of the Departamento de Protección, but most often the advocacy target was a low-level functionary who, day in and day out, heard the complaints of workers struggling to navigate the behemoth consular bureaucracy. During Labor Rights Week, the consular network would host labor allies (public officials and private civil society actors) to conduct outreach and "Know Your Rights" workshops to their captive audiences of migrants (as described in chapter 3). The consulate office also provided a podium for higher-ups from the embassy who came to share their vision for diaspora engagement with community leaders. In places like Chicago—home to a seasoned corps of progressive labor advocates—these ambassadors and ministers rarely escaped without receiving an earful from their skeptical constituents (as told in chapter 4). Beyond the formal petitions lodged to specific National Administrative Offices by coalitions of well-funded advocates based in the United States, Mexican civil society (based largely in the capital city) and allied labor federations continuously pressed the Mexican government on migrants' *portable rights* and ultimately their *right to stay home* (as outlined in chapter 5). Each of these forms of migrant *voice* ensured that the formal declarations, memoranda, and agreements would have some enforcement bite and, at the very least, not become *letra muerta.*

The Possibilities and Limits of Tripartite Co-enforcement

Our research revisits tripartite co-enforcement and situates the role of the sending state in the coproduction of labor regulation. The SRE and its various bureaucracies and mechanisms for diaspora management offer a menu of supporting services for vulnerable migrants through the claims process. Despite its drawbacks, the Mexican consular network espouses an ideal version of immigrant rights claims making in which rights mobilization is not exclusively tied to deportation prevention, services are delivered in a claimant's language and according to the claimant's cultural sensibility, and a single ally can help manage a case and follow up with relevant bureaucrats directly as a claim inevitably drags on. The ultimate goal of the annual Labor Rights Week is to leverage the collaborative synergy of consular partners to educate workers about their rights, introduce each relevant agency in a neutral and safe space, and, in the best-case scenario, bring these resources directly into the community.

Yet we find that despite all their benefits, consulate offices are imperfect brokers. Labor regulation is only one of many priorities that consular Departments of Protection must juggle, and consular officials (who do not tend to stay long in a given post) bring with them their own agenda and list of programmatic priorities. Charismatic leaders often seek to leave a bold legacy, but their favored projects can vary substantially, from prison advocacy for Mexican inmates on death row to culture and art exhibits, fellowships for Deferred Action for Childhood Arrivals (DACA) students, and subnational trade missions. In the day-to-day operations of any Mexican consulate office, the issue of labor rights always has stiff competition. What is more, labor rights advocacy is a perennially underfunded priority, and the sheer magnitude of consular responsibilities and tasks can quickly overwhelm the best intents for outreach and direct service. This research thus highlights the need for greater institutional analysis of how priorities are set and executed within the consular network offices.

The collaborative nature of co-enforcement means that civil society/worker advocates must now coordinate with US labor agencies and Mexican diplomats, who sometimes—but not always—work in concert with each other. Harkening back to Piore and Shrank (2018), labor regulation is largely dependent on street-level bureaucrats who exercise an enormous amount of discretion (Lipsky 1980). And while this situation would ideally create an all-hands-on-deck approach that was mutually beneficial to all parties, what we find is that consular officials can sometimes cut out civil society advocates who are deemed too demanding, needy, or intent on the consulate sharing their labor organizing goals. They opt instead for direct partnerships with US regulators, whose directives are narrower in scope and less contentious and who are generally easier to work with. Consular officials are often civil service diplomats with narrow training, meager net salaries, and their own goals for promotion in the uncertain and highly political bureaucracy in which they are embedded. Therefore, while the sending state provides another important opportunity for supporting claims making and collaborating with local community partners (Gleeson 2016), it suffers from many of the same constraints as US labor regulators. This suggests that the work of an expanding set of actors engaged in reactive claims making will never be a sufficient substitute for meaningful strategic enforcement and broader efforts to shift labor power, as we explain in the first chapter (Piore and Schrank 2018; Goldman 2018).

How Place Matters

Any study of enforcement, civil society advocacy, and the role of the sending state must be locally grounded. Our research reveals the importance of place for understanding the devolution of enforcement patterns, as well as the factors shaping policy implementation (whether at the supranational, bilateral, or national level) (Varsanyi 2010). In the case of labor standards enforcement, certain state and local policies determine which enforcement agencies are relevant partners for co-enforcement. Labor and social movement actors simultaneously partner with and push against regulators, so local context also determines which ones they specifically target for accountability (Fine and Gordon 2010). For immigrant workers, labor policy inevitably clashes with federal immigration enforcement policy, and indeed, across the country various communities can skew either "pro rule of law" or "immigrant friendly." Yet even in communities defined as "sanctuaries," federal immigration enforcement is ubiquitous. On the flip side, in rural and other new destination contexts where immigrant reception is more circumspect and sometimes outright hostile, such as in Raleigh, North Carolina, immigrant advocates have worked tirelessly to create important openings for change.

Within this varied context the Mexican government implements its mandate to provide legal protection for its citizens living abroad. Industry differences across regions shape the priorities and statutory contexts for labor rights, as well as the outreach programming and coalition partnerships that are formed. For example, the concerns of agricultural workers in California's Central Valley have led other activists to focus on the labor conditions for construction workers in the booming residential construction markets of places like Houston, Atlanta, and Dallas. However, while California's Labor Commission and Agricultural Labor Relations Board provide some oversight over the agricultural industry there (collective bargaining rights that are otherwise absent from federal protections), in Texas and Georgia the dearth of state oversight leaves federal agencies as the main regulatory actor and contact point with foreign consulates. And even within states, regional differences can matter greatly, as central city populations are far better served than more isolated rural and suburban communities distant from the general consulate offices located in the urban metropolis. While mobile consulate mechanisms—sporadically coordinated and notoriously understaffed—meet part of this rural demand, they do little to extend the lasting collaborative potential of the consular network in newer destinations.

Demography also plays an important role in differentiating the strategies of each of the fifty-two consular offices. Places with large and long-established Mexican immigrant populations have offices with more resources and personnel, and in turn more capacity to respond to community needs. However, these traditional and historic immigrant destinations are also home to dense concentrations of civil society groups, which can sometimes render the local consulate a less relevant actor. Nonetheless, in hyperdiverse global cities like Houston, Los Angeles, and New York City, the Mexican consulate can take on the role of "elder brother," leading the consulate corps from Latin America in service and cultural programming for the Latino immigrant population as a whole. In places like California and Texas—home to ten and eleven offices respectively—cooperation between offices can also multiply capacity. Yet in cities with more recent indigenous migrant populations, such as Orlando, Miami, and Raleigh, local consulates have struggled to bridge the linguistic gap for non-Spanish-speaking migrants and to combat the classism and endemic racism of some diplomatic personnel.

Local consular priorities also vary according to the leadership of each consular office, whose aims often end up competing with those of labor rights advocates. The Departamento de Protección, for example, has no specific mandate or budget to handle workplace concerns, and thus its ability to funnel resources to labor outreach is highly variable across offices and changing presidential administrations. In this regard, immigrant civil society becomes a critical resource for orienting new staff (who may have scant knowledge of local labor issues and the regulatory bureaucracies that workers must navigate). A select group of these NGOs may even become consulate contractors to litigate high-impact labor/immigration cases (e.g., *abogados consultores*), or partners in staffing hotlines (e.g., the Catholic nonprofit in New York that staffs the LABORAL line or the collection of groups that help run the EMPLEO hotline in Southern California). These collaborations have provided the model for other consular collaborations, such as the EMPLEO-Pinoy partnership between the Consulate of the Philippines, state and federal agencies, and advocates in seven Southern California counties (including the Filipino Worker Center) (Constante 2015). Another place-based challenge is the lack of public transparency and social oversight in the provision of contracts to local law firms, which can create a climate in which conspiracy theories and allegations of fraud proliferate.

The Need for Portable Rights

For advocates working from within Mexico and across North America and beyond, the local labor standards enforcement bureaucracy is not their biggest target. Nor is the consular network. Many US-based organizations with satellite offices in Mexico (Mexico City in particular) have led strategically assembled legal teams to defend the rights of guest workers in the United States by calling on the protections afforded by the NAALC. Petitions are carefully curated by alt-labor groups that focus on specific industries and sympathetic workers who are willing to testify in long and protracted battles with limited odds of success. These efforts have created very narrow material wins for some groups of affected workers and have succeeded in putting both governments on notice. While not a complete deterrent, the high cost of this litigation sends a message to employers and labor recruiters looking to improve their bottom line by exploiting low-paid migrant workers.

Navigating international law arenas without the help of experts with law degrees is a nonstarter for the average person. For a returned worker awaiting restitution, winning or losing a wage theft case can have long-lasting effects and may affect reinstatement or trigger blacklisting in the next hiring season. The small group of dedicated pro bono lawyers mounting international class-action lawsuits to demand decent work conditions for temporary guest workers is part of a larger strategy to shift industry norms. These transnational legal advocates carefully court funders and supporters to change on-the-ground reality: the international temporary foreign worker recruitment system is rife with abuse, and the meager enforcement mechanisms in place are in desperate need of an overhaul.

These citizen petitions result from the work of well-funded (primarily US) philanthropy organizations, activist lawyers, on-the-ground organizers in rural areas (including in countries of origin), a credible class of plaintiffs, and a strong coalition focused on garnering broad public support. The campaigns are not easy to execute, sometimes requiring decades of building trust, often among strange bedfellows. Moreover, the ability to maintain a presence in migrant communities is hampered by security concerns, which have led some transnational NGOs to abandon their original outposts to protect their staff's safety. Even in Mexico City, where violence is moderate compared to outlying communities, local organization offices have had to reinforce their security protocols.

Keck and Sikkink's boomerang effect model suggests that advocates in the Global South need their Global North counterparts to effect change. However, we find significant regional divides between US-based organizations and groups rooted in Mexico. *Los norteamericanos*, as US and Canadian groups are often called, tend to garner disproportionate attention, with a focus on demands for legalization and calls to end employer impunity for workplace violations. Mexico-based groups, meanwhile, have focused increasingly on the "right to stay home" by reclaiming food sovereignty and calling attention to the needs of returning migrants seeking to reintegrate (or integrate for the first time) into the Mexican economy, social institutions, and educational and health care systems. While US-based immigrant advocates have fought tirelessly to reunite families who have been torn apart by detention and deportation—calling for visas that would make a path to legalization possible—a return to the United States is not always the biggest priority for Mexican civil society. As Mexico has gradually transformed into a country of transit, expulsion, and destination, immigrant advocates have grappled with the urgent needs stemming from a chaotic border where both governments collude to trample on migrant rights on both sides of the border.

Rather than viewing their country as simply the David to the US Goliath, Mexican advocates have repeatedly called on Mexico to account for its role in the abuse of migrants at its southern border. As a major transit country that is now forced to contend with the aftereffects of Central America's brutal civil wars of the 1980s, Mexico has time and again feigned innocence as it denounces the United States for human rights abuses. Meanwhile, it willingly implements the "Remain in Mexico" policy of the US and expels destitute migrants from its own border communities without due process. After Mexico offered refuge to twenty-four Afghan journalists in the wake of the chaotic US military withdrawal from Afghanistan in 2021, Mexico's foreign minister and head of the consular network Marcelo Ebrard explained, "Maybe society in the United States is not aware of the Mexican tradition in terms of refugees." When he was pressed on the irony of making this statement while his country was simultaneously "stemming the tide of Central American migrants," the foreign minister responded that it was wholly consistent with Mexico's "push to make clear the difference between economic migrants and the people who are looking for refuge and asylum" (B. Smith 2021). Indeed, this illusory migrant-refugee binary, Rebecca Hamlin argues, is generated and fortified by the need to uphold state sovereignty around who has the right to entry (Hamlin 2021; FitzGerald and Arar 2018).[3] In the aftermath of this episode, Ebrard made public promises to process the asylum requests of thirteen thousand Haitian immigrants (teleSUR 2021). However, journalists continue to report on how the Instituto Nacional de Migración / National Immigration Institute has carried out ongoing deportations of migrants back to Port-au-Prince from Mexico (*El Sol de México* 2021).

As the region revisits possibilities for immigration reform, transnational advocates denounce any new proposals for guest worker programs that, harkening back to the Bracero Program, create cycles of debt and indenture (Gordon 2006). These programs inherently weaken labor protections and fuel an underground labor brokerage economy in which migrant workers are the least likely to benefit while a small group of growers reap significant profits. Moreover, though the Mexican government can indeed be a valuable resource for funneling restitution back to returned migrants (if and when they win their labor claims), Mexico has notoriously blocked any reforms that would create real improvements for the emigrant labor force. In 2014, after being held accountable for violations under the bilateral labor side accords, Mexico—via its National Administrative Office—was forced to institute changes to ensure that H-2A workers would receive information and resources prior to departing north. The long-lasting institutionalization of these supports remains uncertain.

The consular network represents a space where Mexican migrants can find refuge from endemic immigration enforcement and where they can demand linguistic and culturally appropriate support for navigating US laws and bureaucracies. Mexican immigrants on the whole, however, do not trust the Mexican government any more than Mexicans in Mexico trust their government. The opaque and antidemocratic institutions that Mexicans must navigate to exercise their full citizenship rights generate a rational sense of caution and wariness (Fox 2007). After the ousting of the Salinas de Gortari administration in 1994 marked the end of an era of neoliberal antagonism toward migrants, governments inaugurated a rapprochement that included more forceful demands to defend migrant rights in the United States and Mexico. This shift, however, must be understood not only in terms of the dispositions of government leaders but also within the context of migrant advocates demanding change, budget transparency, and social accountability. This push now includes extending domestic rights and, increasingly, making rights *portable* (Caron and Lyon, forthcoming).

Immigrant Civil Society Is Not a Monolith

The literature on state-society relations has previously focused on efforts to hold governments accountable to promote rural democratization (Fox 2007), political migrant engagement (Félix 2019), and the use of collective remittances for rural development (Goldring 2003; Duquette-Rury 2019; Bada 2014; Iskander 2010; Byrnes 2003). In our book, chapters 3 and 4 reveal the ever-shifting nature and complexity of these relations, which are defined by competing agendas and demands. For civil society groups involved in the relatively straightforward task of labor co-enforcement, there are well-defined ways in which the consular network can partner with labor organizations and legal service providers to educate workers about their rights. Labor Rights Week has created a template for turning the physical consulate office into a space for labor education and for training consular staff to field community queries about state and federal protections. In practical terms, local consulates are also able to leverage their diplomatic standing to interface with federal regulators and follow up with claims or cases in ways that civil society advocates rarely can. And for returned migrants, consular staff become a critical resource for tracking down claimants who are owed restitution.

Yet beyond the labor advocates and lawyers engaged in the formal bureaucracy of labor standards enforcement, the consular network—as an emissary of the sending state—can be a more complicated partner. There are ideological divides even within the labor movement over the extent of consular collaboration, with some wanting to work within the existing system to mobilize workers' demands and others more critical of the formal bureaucracy and its enablers—including the Mexican state and its representatives. More importantly, immigrant advocates vary in terms of what demands they make of Mexico: whether to focus on the challenges of immigrant life in the United States, the events that led to their decision to leave home, or both. The endemic corruption in Mexican governance, the farce of postrevolution labor protections (in a country where over half the population is in the informal labor market and fails to qualify in any way), and the deep-seated frustrations that immigrants relive with every visit to the overburdened and understaffed consular office color the relationship between Mexico's government and many immigrant advocates. Moreover, the official consular directive to stay "neutral" in the host country means that paradoxically, the same diplomatic standing that gives consulates an opening to advocate for their citizens abroad also renders them formally unable to visibly advocate for them in most struggles for basic justice. Consulates therefore must balance this diplomatic stance with the immediate need to offer meaningful and direct advocacy to show their constituents that they truly care about their emigrants.

All this explains why civil society groups may opt to work from within or from outside the system. While the Chicago consulate has a long history of offering up its building for labor union events, some advocates have far more experience picketing outside that space, denouncing Mexican government impunity and the failure to respect the rights of braceros and electrical, mining, or newspaper labor unions, for example. The situation is even more complicated for other groups. For example, hometown associations often work with the consulate to funnel remittance dollars back to their communities of origin, often to fund development projects that should in theory be the responsibility of any functioning state rather than that of migrants (Bada 2016). These same organizations, however, have also forcefully lobbied for additional rights for expatriates, including the right to vote, the right to be elected to political office, the right to extend Mexican nationality by *jus sanguinis* indefinitely, and the right to gain representation in the now largely defunct CCIME. While some activist leaders have leveraged their consular access narrowly for personal gain, they have also crucially pressured Mexico not only on perennial issues such as trade, development, education, and access to health care but also when individual emergencies arise and a direct consular connection is needed to cut through red tape. These connections, however, are tenuous, requiring constant rebuilding as career diplomats are (regularly) reassigned and rotated.

EPILOGUE: IMMIGRANT WORKER RIGHTS AMID PANDEMICS AND POLITICAL CRISIS

The fieldwork for this book spanned over a decade, drawing to a close prior to the COVID-19 pandemic, which was deadliest for low-wage migrant workers in the United States, the largest plurality of whom are Mexican. In the United States, the migrant workforce accounted for more than 16 percent of the health care sector in 2020 (BBVA Foundation and Ministry of the Interior 2021), while two-thirds of hired farmworkers were born in Mexico (Ornelas et al. 2021). By May of 2020, the SRE reported that 959 Mexicans had died of COVID-19 in the United States, 67 percent of them in the state of New York. The news prompted a Mexican senator to issue a resolution *encouraging* the consular network to cover the corpse repatriation of all those who had died of COVID-19 in the United States. This led to the return of 245 ash-filled urns, which were transported in a military plane from New York City to Mexico City in July 2020. As the fatalities mounted, however, the SRE discontinued tabulating the death count and instead issued a special how-to guide for handling corpse or ashes repatriation in times of COVID-19 (Redacción Animal Político 2020; Zepeda 2020).

This tragic scenario brings into sharp relief the ways in which diasporic bureaucracies become relevant, even in the afterlife. The necropolitics of counting and honoring the victims, however, should not overshadow the various inequities laid bare by the pandemic, including severe economic inequality, housing instability, barriers to health care access, and lack of social provision more broadly. During this crisis, the meager infusions of cash assistance provided by the US federal government excluded the most vulnerable immigrants, rental aid was difficult to access, and many immigrants feared making use of eviction moratorium protections (Cruz Guevarra, Bandlamudi, and Montecillo 2021). Mexico also failed its most vulnerable. While access to vaccines was essentially universal in the United States, in Mexico migrants from Central America and elsewhere were largely excluded in the early months of vaccine availability. The Center for Justice and International Law filed a report to the UN Special Rapporteur on the Human Rights of Migrants denouncing the lack of access to health care for migrants in transit with COVID-19. Pressure from local advocates mounted at the local level until Mexico's federal government, as well as some state health departments, agreed to offer limited access to vaccines for migrants (Cervantes 2021; CEJIL 2020; ZonaDocs—Periodismo en Resistencia 2021).

Consular assistance played an important role during the pandemic, especially in aiding travelers and visitors stranded outside their home country (IOM Research n.d.). In the United States, Mexican consular offices worked to direct food-insecure families to area food banks. In San Jose, these efforts were carried out in conjunction with the Ventanilla de Asesoría Financiera and the Mission Asset Fund (Consulado General de México en San José 2021). In Salt Lake City, consular officials circulated resource guides promoting safety measures and pointing to health care and other resources (Consulado General de México en Salt Lake City 2021). The Chicago consulate (which as of this writing covers counties in both Illinois and Indiana) created a guide specific to resources in the state of Indiana, encouraging migrants to also call the Centro de Información y Asistencia a Mexicanos / Center for Assistance and Information to Mexicans for navigational help (Consulado General de México en Chicago 2021). And in Miami, consular outreach included support from the Ventanilla de Salud, the Ventanilla de Orientación Educativa, and the Ventanilla de Atención Integral para la Mujer (with a nod to the rise in domestic violence during the shutdown) (Consulado General de México en Miami 2021). The New York consular office advertised a variety of state-run and philanthropic relief funds for restaurant and gig workers in New York City. Indeed, we identified at least two dozen such announcements by different Mexican consular offices across the country.[4]

Yet ultimately these resource and referral sheets reflected very little direct investment in relief efforts by Mexico, which is understandable given the country's limited response to the pandemic as a whole. Mexico's central-left government inherited an underfunded patchwork of health care systems that quickly buckled under pressure, and the government increased health-related expenditures during the pandemic only slightly. By and large, the thorniest challenge for workers involved deciding whether to ignore the government's stay-at-home orders given the limited COVID-19 financial support available to citizens and businesses. They had little choice. The economic shock caused by the pandemic in Mexico forced workers to ignore stay-at-home orders in the absence of robust emergency relief (even well into one of the largest case surges of the winter that caused oxygen shortages followed by a significant rise in deaths in January of 2021). Amid this nationwide predicament, migrants in transit through Mexico—given their segmented incorporation into Mexico's labor market—had fragmented access (at best) to housing, health care, and other basic necessities (Zapata and Prieto Rosas 2020).

Today, undocumented Mexican immigrants continue to battle not only the health and economic impacts of the pandemic but also the ongoing effects of being concentrated in jobs that often lack health insurance (Duncan and Horton 2020), the exclusions for undocumented residents under the Affordable Care Act (US Centers for Medicare and Medicaid Services n.d.), and very uneven Medicaid access (Kaiser Family Foundation 2021). Under the Trump administration, changes to Public Charge rules created enormous confusion and made it difficult to convince even qualified immigrants to access the state and federal aid for which they were eligible (National Low Income Housing Coalition n.d.).

In sum, the COVID-19 pandemic has reaffirmed that an inquiry into the sending state's role in managing and engaging its diaspora must also consider the need for global coordination to ensure the dignity of work and basic social protections. This inquiry, however, cannot take place without a serious critique of capitalism and the centrality of free trade in bilateral negotiations, most recently evident in the United States-Mexico-Canada Agreement (USMCA). Transnational civil society has played a key role in broadening the labor protections under discussion in such negotiations (as well as those in other regional instruments such as the Central American Free Trade Agreement). A year into the USMCA, advocates have noted an improvement over NAFTA in terms of protections afforded to workers, though they have highlighted the continued need for real compliance mechanisms (as they did in their first petition under the USMCA in March 2021, which also alleged US violations of gender-based discrimination protections). The CDM used this initial petition as a point of departure to call on Mexico to pressure the United States into compliance, a reversal of the typical boomerang effect that tends to focus on leveraging the power of the "Global North." The need for bilateral cooperation was the running theme in these testimonies, which called on both governments to take charge of their responsibilities toward labor migrants. In addition to demanding concrete changes in the United States, these advocates expected the Mexican government to address the abuses that would-be migrants face when being recruited from their own homeland (Peña 2021; CDM 2021).

DIRECTIONS FOR FUTURE RESEARCH

Our research suggests that the sending state should continue to be seen as both a coalition partner and an accountability target. While the United States is a prime immigrant destination, its relationship with Mexico is unique. Mexico does not replicate its vast bureaucratic presence in the United States in any other country, nor does any other country come close to replicating this consular presence in the United States. Further research, therefore, is needed to continue to hone the comparative scope conditions of these findings, and many scholars have already begun to conduct it (Iskander 2010; Margheritis 2016; Okano-Heijmans and Price 2019; Pedroza et al. 2016). Further, with fifty-two offices (fifty-seven including those in Canada), the Mexican consular network is not so much one central system as a collection of local outposts with rotating leaders who must respond to local norms and customs. Additional locally grounded research will continue to be important as new and emerging destinations evolve into well-established immigrant communities. And as Mexican migrants continue to move into diverse Latino metropolitan areas, it will be important to consider the role that pan-ethnic civil society plays in urging the entire Latin American consular network toward a more active negotiating stance with horizontal resource-sharing mechanisms (Délano Alonso 2018). The study of the Mexican state and its consular network (and the foreign ministry as a whole) as a complex institution (rather than a single bureaucracy) will continue to benefit from institutional ethnographies and an organizational approach that can disentangle the competing interests and power dynamics from within. As an example of this complexity, the various Ventanillas—some of them more aspirational than functional—often have very different directives and targets. Even with regard to labor rights, the legalistic instincts of Protección look very different from the outreach and prevention-oriented approach of Comunidades. The consuls in charge of each of these directorates wield a great deal of power, and more work is needed to understand their role in mediating rules from the central offices in Mexico City. Moreover, as we've seen with the implementation of the bilateral memoranda of understanding, and in light of the petitions to the National Administrative Office, the foreign ministry has increasingly coordinated with a range of domestic offices like the Secretaría del Trabajo y Previsión Social, the Secretaría de Desarrollo Social, the Secretaría de Hacienda y Crédito Público, and the Secretaría de la Función Pública, to name a few. Some of these ministries have offered transversal services to migrants and returnees, but resources to reintegrate Mexican migrants as binational citizens with full rights lack institutionalization and are still exceedingly opaque.

Similarly, US domestic agencies such as the DOL are complex entities that have to navigate different statutory obligations at home (such as the Wage and Hour Division and the Occupational Safety and Health Administration) as well as international engagements (such as the International Bureau of Labor Affairs—the unit responsible for coordinating the formal bilateral accords and collaborative outreach efforts). Indeed, beyond the DOL, the wide array of other federal and state labor regulators all have somewhat distinct relationships with the consular network. More research is needed to understand what drives these dynamics, especially as each agency (within and far beyond the labor regulation sphere) continues to contend with the pall that immigration enforcement (much of it concentrated in the workplace) casts over immigrants' claims to their rights.

The Mexican consular network needs to be understood as working within not only the broader bureaucratic arena of labor standards enforcement and immigration "management" but also the wide array of other social outreach and co-enforcement entities described above. Indeed, the aspirational CORPS system established by the DOL (not currently located in all offices) situates the consular network in this broader ecology. To what extent destination states coordinate with sending states as bilateral partners with unique diplomatic power or as community-based entities with privileged access to migrant populations reveals the complexity of the destination state's migrant integration apparatus. In the United States, this coordination is largely ad hoc—with the exception of refugee resettlement—in contrast to more robust systems of cooperation in Canada (Bloemraad 2006a, 2006b). These factors have a significant effect not only on individual immigrant trajectories but also on how bilateral migration management relationships evolve. Comparative work with other major Mexican immigrant destinations (most notably Canada) should continue, especially as US immigration proposals (even those championed by many left-of-center immigration policy circles) are likely to resemble Canada's Temporary Foreign Worker and points-based programs (Chishti, Gelatt, and Meissner 2021).

All told, our research reveals that the need for subnational comparative fieldwork will continue, as will the need to continue systematic reviews of government archives. Much of this research relied on public records requests from INAI. While intended to increase transparency with the broader public, the INAI system (and the parallel FOIA—Freedom of Information Act—system in the United States) requires additional systematization to fully clarify the patterns of investment to implement bilateral accords via the consular network and how they vary across regions. Similarly, it is clear that some data were lost to the public in the wake of the Trump administration, leaving some important holes in our knowledge of how the DOL and other sister agencies were conducting outreach and engaging in co-enforcement with the sending state and other partners. Indeed, some web archives simply disappeared. Further, this labor rights fieldwork involves chasing moving targets that will require periodic review as administrations shift (every six years in Mexico), as laws change (such as the much-anticipated immigration reform Biden has promised but has yet to realize as of this writing), and as bilateral agreements emerge and fall away. Moreover, to the extent that state and local governments will continue to be critical partners for worker struggles, the consular network will need to remain relevant in jurisdictions where their lateral federal partners are not the main attraction for claims making.

Finally, labor and migration scholars will need to continue to skate the fine line between seeing national governments as relevant actors for managing their vulnerable migrants abroad and paying attention to the broader forces shaping the precarity of global labor in an era of advanced capitalism. While nation-states are not the sole architects of capitalist economies, these logics permeate the governance of borders and the bodies that move across them. The neoliberal consensus is also relevant for how we understand the prospects for organized labor, which has—not always but increasingly—embraced migrant members, and for global civil society, which often experiences cleavages depending on the willingness to accept neoliberal narratives and solutions. Neoliberalism has also shaped how emigrants are viewed by the sending state, as either human beings entitled to full rights or export commodities to be managed.

As the frontal attack on labor unions continues unabated and unionization campaigns become increasingly difficult to win in both Mexico and the United States, labor advocates may turn to each other more frequently, emphasizing commonalities and de-emphasizing differences. The common goal of retrofitting a regulatory framework aimed at reducing unfair competitive national advantages that exploit wage differentials among the most vulnerable workers is a perennial aspiration. US advocates may continue to increase pressure on the DOL to improve enforcement mechanisms for all workers regardless of legal status, while Mexican advocates may continue demanding that the Mexican government uphold the constitutional right to dignified social work. Accomplishing such reforms would allow people to stay home and defend the rights of those who were forced to cross a border to find higher-paying jobs.

1. INTRODUCTION

1. Throughout this book, we use a variety of terms including *sending/receiving states*, *origin/destination countries*, and *country of origin/destination*. We are aware of the scholarly and political debate around these terms. Most significantly, colleagues have argued against the term *sending state* because it pigeonholes a particular country into one role and accords it a (circumscribed) agency as "sending" migrants, often ignoring and even reifying global power differentials. However, we argue that alternatives like *origin country* are not neutral terms either. Both accept the nation-state/country construct uncritically, ignoring the ways in which countries have often arbitrarily drawn borders around ethnic communities, leaving us with origins on one side and destinations on another. For the purposes of this inquiry, we have chosen to accept these constructs rather than attempt to coin new and potentially equally fraught terms. Often we refer to sending states to emphasize the positionality of Mexico's Secretaría de Relaciones Exteriores / Ministry of Foreign Affairs and its explicit directive to manage and engage with its diaspora. We also adopt the term *transit country* when appropriate to refer to Mexico's simultaneous position as a country of origin, destination, and transit of migrants, some of whom continue on to other parts of North America.

2. The impact of this expanded political influence of emigrants on Mexican politics is undeniable. The stakes of expatriate voting were highest during the 2006 election, in which Felipe Calderón was elected by a razor-thin margin of less than a quarter-million votes. In the 2006 election, 32,621 Mexican expatriate citizens voted in the presidential race and 40,876 registered to vote. In the 2018 presidential election, 181,873 Mexican citizens living abroad registered to vote, and a vast majority (65 percent) of the absentee electorate favored Andrés Manuel López Obrador, the left-leaning presidential winner.

3. On the whole, undocumented migrants are often concentrated in industries where wage and hour violations, racial discrimination, sexual harassment, and barriers to collective organizing are rampant (Bernhardt, Spiller, and Theodore 2013).

4. This definition is inspired by the republican tripartite model outlined in Ian Ayres and John Braithwaite's (1992, 56–60) *Responsive Regulation*, under which public interest groups get access to the same information as the regulator, a seat at the negotiating table with the employment firm and enforcement agency, and the same standing as the regulator to sue or prosecute under the regulatory statutes. When successfully implemented, co-enforcement is beneficial for migrant and other workers alike, as well as for industry and the government.

5. While studies analyzing the outcomes of these new state-society partnerships are limited, critics have pointed to the unequal power among participants and the highly local nature of these initiatives (Oswalt and Rosado Marzán 2018).

6. Article 123 of Mexico's constitution states that "every person has the right to dignified and socially useful employment. To attain that goal, the state will promote, according to existing laws, employment creation and the social organization of work" (our translation).

7. Since 1917, Mexico's liberal constitution and federal labor legislation have placed clear limits on the rights of foreigners and immigrants, curtailing their full freedom of expression and limiting their access to the domestic labor market, among other restrictions (Yankelevich 2019). Because of entrenched and widespread impunity in its judicial system, Mexico is among the worst offenders in allowing human trafficking within its borders and abetting the smuggling of its own citizens to the United States (Rojas Wiesner 2022).

8. Some labor scholars estimate that 37 percent of undocumented immigrant workers are victims of minimum-wage violations, compared with 24 percent for immigrants with work authorization and 16 percent for US-born workers. More than a quarter of all low-wage workers in the country's largest cities are paid less than the legally mandated minimum wage, and overtime violations are rampant (Bernhardt, Milkman, and Theodore 2009).

9. Some cities such as Seattle have implemented harsh penalties for minimum-wage violations and/or have instituted wage theft prevention initiatives in conjunction with worker advocates (Galvin 2016; Theodore 2020).

10. These cities represent a range of economic, demographic, and political contexts. In each case, local labor markets both incorporate and displace immigrant labor (Simsek-Caglar and Schiller 2018) as urban regeneration, real estate development, and capital accumulation have occurred in large part on the backs of low-wage and immigrant labor forces. Our sample includes cities whose overall foreign-born populations are significantly above the national average (13.5 percent), such as Miami, Chicago, and Dallas, and also newer immigrant destinations (including Omaha, Raleigh, and Orlando). In the majority of the cities in our sample (11), Mexicans make up more than a quarter of the total immigrant population.

2. THE MEXICAN CONSULATE NETWORK AS AN ADVOCACY INSTITUTION

1. Using family remittances as leverage to demand more consular services represents just one perspective. Alternative arguments utilized by Mexican migrant civil society

groups fully rest on citizenship claims as the basis of demanding more consular services, regardless of economic contributions to family remittances.

2. For example, consular staff need to be constantly retrained on local minimum-wage standards and other state labor protections every time they get reassigned to a different consular jurisdiction within the United States.

3. Section b of article 36 states, "If he so requests, the competent authorities of the receiving State shall, without delay, inform the consular post of the sending State if, within its consular district, a national of that State is arrested or committed to prison or to custody pending trial or is detained in any other manner." Section c states that "consular officers shall have the right to visit a national of the sending State who is in prison, custody or detention, to converse and correspond with him and to arrange for his legal representation" (United Nations 1967).

4. Both California and New York have strengthened their protections against employer retaliation on the basis of immigration, though enforcement remains challenging (Costa 2018; Litrownik and Kessler 2020).

5. Eduardo Medina Mora, Mexico's ambassador to the United States, speech to local civil society organizations at the Mexican consulate in Chicago. Translation by the authors, May 29, 2014.

6. Interview, Mexican embassy, Washington, DC, November 8, 2012.

7. According to Keck and Sikkink (1998), the boomerang effect consists of local NGOs bypassing their government and directly searching out powerful international allies to try to bring pressure on their state government from outside. This effect usually occurs when channels between the state and its domestic actors are blocked, as is the case mostly in nondemocratic societies.

8. The term *charro union* harkens back to the government-backed railroad unions in the 1940s led by Jesús Díaz de León, who iconically wore a charro suit, which became a symbol for party-controlled union corruption (Rubio Campos 2017; Martín 2017).

9. Interview, Frente Auténtico del Trabajo, Mexico City, June 26. 2018.

10. Interview, Mexican embassy, Washington, DC, November 8, 2012.

11. Interview, STPS, Mexico City, August 31, 2015.

12. Interview, STPS, Washington, DC, May 15, 2015.

13. Interview, IME and DGPME, Mexico City, September 19, 2014.

14. Interview, IME, Mexico City, September 19, 2014.

15. Interview, IME, Mexico City, September 19, 2014.

16. Interview, IME, Mexico City, September 19, 2014.

17. In 2002, President Vicente Fox appointed as the IME's first executive director Cándido Morales, a migrant leader from California affiliated with the California Human Development Corporation (CHDC).

18. Interview, Illinois Coalition for Immigrant and Refugee Rights, Chicago, June 24, 2013.

19. Interview, Illinois Coalition for Immigrant and Refugee Rights, Chicago, June 24, 2013.

20. We thank Benjamin Davis from the United Steelworkers (USW) for sharing a copy of the agenda with us.

21. See Gleeson and Bada (2019) for additional detail on interagency coordination.

22. Interview, Mexican embassy, Washington, DC, February 23, 2015.

23. Interview, Mexican embassy, Washington, DC, February 23, 2015.

24. Interview, SRE, Mexico City, October 15, 2014.

25. Interview, Mexican embassy, Washington, DC, February 23, 2015.

26. Interview, DOL, Washington, DC, January 25, 2013.

27. Interview, SRE, Mexico City, October 15, 2014.

28. Interview, DOL, Washington, DC, January 25, 2013.

29. Interview, DOL, Washington, DC, January 25, 2013, and interview, DOL-ILAB, Washington, DC, October 14, 2014.

30. Interview, DOL, Washington, DC, January 25, 2013.

31. Interview, DOL-ILAB, Washington, DC, October 14, 2014.

32. Interview, SRE, Mexico City, October 15, 2014.

33. Interview, STPS, Washington, DC, May 15, 2015.

34. Interview, SRE, Mexico City, October 15, 2014.

35. Interview, IME, Mexico City, September 19, 2014.

36. Authors' field notes, Trinational Solidarity Conference, UE Hall, Chicago, October 18, 2017.

37. The precarious position of some Mexican consular personnel sometimes creates headlines. In January of 2021, the consulates of Chicago, New York, Los Angeles, Denver, Las Vegas, Tucson, Houston, San Antonio, Dallas, Indianapolis, San Francisco, and Presidio (TX) made news when the National Committee of Local Consular Employees went to the press to denounce the dismissal of at least fifty local employees in the middle of a pandemic. They also brought awareness to the low wages and labor insecurity of local personnel working at consular offices (Ocampo and Reveles 2021).

38. Interview, Mexican consulate, Sacramento, CA, July 7, 2021.

39. For the events of one such consulate, see Casa ALBA Melanie (n.d.).

40. Authors' field notes, June 2, 2021, and Cámara de Diputados (2018).

41. Interview, Mexican embassy, Washington, DC, October 18, 2012.

42. Interview, Mexican embassy, Washington, DC, February 23, 2015.

43. Request to the Instituto Nacional de Transparencia, Acceso a la Información y Protección de Datos Personales / National Institute of Transparency, Information Access and Private Data Protection (INAI) for total number of calls from CIAM.

44. Interview, Mexican embassy, Washington, DC, November 8, 2012.

45. Interview, Mexican embassy, Washington, DC, February 23, 2015.

46. Interview, SRE, Mexico City, October 15, 2014.

47. Interview, Mexican embassy, Washington, DC, October 18, 2012.

48. Interview, Mexican embassy, Washington, DC, October 18, 2012.

49. Interview, IME, Mexico City, September 19, 2014.

50. Interview, Mexican embassy, Washington, DC, November 8, 2012.

51. Interview, Mexican embassy, Washington, DC, November 8, 2012.

52. Request to INAI for event statistics summary for the Semana de Derechos Laborales.

53. Interview, SRE, Mexico City, October 15, 2014.

54. Interview, SRE, Mexico City, October 15, 2014.

55. Interview, SRE, Mexico City, October 15, 2014.

56. For the most recent analysis of Tres por Uno, see Duquette-Rury (2019). Natasha Iskander (2010, 253), in her pioneering work on the program, claims that the state and migrants redefined their goals and learned from each other transnationally through a long-running dance of state-society relations.

3. THE SENDING STATE AND CO-ENFORCEMENT

1. According to Martínez-Schuldt (2020, 1036), "Specifically, a 10-percent increase in the number of local immigrant advocacy or related organizations coincides with a 7-percent decline in administrative cases. Though my analysis does not consider the efficacy of approaches to rights protection, my results do suggest that the concentration of local organizations may lessen the burden consulate offices face in the realm of rights protections."

2. Chapter 5 highlights transborder efforts to leverage soft-law instruments, including the roundly critiqued new governance model of corporate good behavior.

3. Bloemraad, de Graauw, and Gleeson (2020, 293–94) define an immigrant organization as a "civil society or nonprofit organization that serves or advocates on behalf of one or more immigrant communities, promotes their cultural heritage, or engages in transnational relations with countries or regions of origin [de Graauw, Gleeson, and Bloemraad 2013]. Such organizations may include second- or later-generation individuals of a particular cultural, ethnic, religious, or national-origin background, and even some citizens without immigrant origins. However, a substantial part of the organization's interests or activities should involve issues that tend to distinguish immigrants from native-born citizens, such as legal status barriers, linguistic or cultural obstacles to service, or concern over economic or political development in the country of origin."

4. Interview, SEIU, Chicago, December 4, 2014.

5. Interview, SEIU, San Jose, CA, January 30, 2015.

6. Interview, AFL-CIO, Houston, Harris County, TX, August 8, 2014.

7. Interview, UFCW, Chicago, December 11, 2012.

8. Interview, UFCW, San Jose, CA, April 14, 2014.

9. Interview, UFCW, Chicago, April 25, 2013.

10. Interview, UFCW, Chicago, April 25, 2013.

11. Interview, AFL-CIO, Houston, Harris County, TX, August 8, 2014.

12. Indeed, while the two national federations worked out their differences, at the local level central labor councils across the country signed solidarity charters with their longtime allies in breakaway unions (McNeill 2007).

13. Interview, Teamsters, Chicago, February 28, 2013.

14. Interview, AFL-CIO, Houston, Harris County, TX, August 8, 2014.

15. Interview, UFCW, Chicago, April 25, 2013.

16. Interview, Teamsters, Chicago, February 28, 2013.

17. Interview, UFCW, Phoenix, AZ, March 21, 2014.

18. Interview, SEIU, Chicago, December 4, 2014.

19. Interview, UFCW, Washington, DC, October 17, 2014.

20. Interview, UFCW, Oakland, CA, November 6, 2012.

21. Interview, UFCW, Washington, DC, October 17, 2014.

22. Interview, UFCW, Washington, DC, October 17, 2014.

23. Interview, UFCW, Phoenix, AZ, March 21, 2014.

24. Interview, Santa Clara and San Benito Counties Building and Construction Trades Council, San Jose, CA, February 14, 2014.

25. Interview, UFCW, San Jose, CA, April 14, 2014.

26. Interview, AFL-CIO, Houston, Harris County, TX, August 8, 2014.

27. Interview, UFCW, Phoenix, March 21, 2014.

28. Interview, SEIU, San Jose, CA, January 30, 2015.

29. Interview, Santa Clara and San Benito Counties Building and Construction Trades Council, San Jose, CA, February 14, 2014.

30. Interview, Department of Labor Wage and Hour Division, November 21, 2014.

31. Interview, UFCW, Washington, DC, October 17, 2014.

32. Interview, Roofers Union, San Jose, CA, March 18, 2015.

33. Interview, UFCW, Oakland, CA, November 6, 2012.

34. Interview, SEIU, San Jose, CA, January 30, 2015.

35. Interview, Teamsters, Chicago, February 28, 2013.

36. Interview, SEIU, San Jose, CA, January 30, 2015.

37. Interview, SEIU, San Jose, CA, January 30, 2015.

38. Interview, Teamsters, Chicago, February 28, 2013.

39. Interview, SEIU, San Jose, CA, January 30, 2015.

40. Interview, UFCW, Oakland, CA, November 6, 2012.

41. Interview, Community Justice Project, Reading, PA, July 29, 2015.

42. Interview, Center for Workers' Rights, Sacramento, CA, January 16, 2015.

43. Interview, Legal Aid of North Carolina, Raleigh, March 21, 2014.

44. Interview, Southern Poverty Law Center, Atlanta, GA, September 25, 2014.

45. Interview, California Rural Legal Assistance, Fresno, November 18, 2014.

46. Interview, Utah Legal Services, Salt Lake City, UT, August 6, 2014.

47. Interview, Catholic Migration Services, New York City, June 5, 2015.

48. Interview, Catholic Migration Services, New York City, June 5, 2015.

49. Interview, Services, Immigrant Rights, and Education Network, San Jose, CA, April 14, 2014.

50. Interview, Wage Justice Center, Los Angeles, November 11, 2013.

51. Interview, Center for Workers' Rights, Sacramento, CA, January 16, 2015.

52. Interview, Instituto Laboral de la Raza, San Francisco, April 30, 2014.

53. Interview, Instituto Laboral de la Raza, San Francisco, April 30, 2014.

54. Interview, Worksafe, Sacramento, CA, January 5, 2014.

55. Interview, Farmworker and Landscaper Advocacy Project, Chicago, February 7, 2013.

56. Interview, Legal Aid Society-Employment Law Center, Fresno, CA, December 3, 2014.

57. Interview, Santa Clara University, Alexander Law Center, San Jose, CA, June 16, 2014.

58. Interview, Farmworker and Landscaper Advocacy Project, Chicago, February 7, 2013.

59. Interview, Equal Justice Center, Dallas, TX, July 28, 2014.

60. Interview, Equal Justice Center, Dallas, TX, July 28, 2014.

61. Interview, Catholic Migration Services, New York City, June 5, 2015.

62. Interview, Catholic Migration Services, New York City, June 5, 2015.

63. Interview, Catholic Migration Services, New York City, June 5, 2015.

64. Interview, Community Legal Services of Philadelphia, July 23, 2015.

65. Interview, California Rural Legal Assistance, San Francisco, December 17, 2013.

66. Interview, Legal Aid Society, San Francisco, October 2, 2013.

67. Interview, Legal Aid Society-Employment Law Center, Fresno, CA, December 3, 2014.

68. Interview, Legal Aid Society-Employment Law Center, Fresno, CA, December 3, 2014.

69. Interview, La Raza Centro Legal, San Francisco, November 19, 2013.

70. Interview, Center for Workers' Rights, Sacramento, CA, January 16, 2015.

71. Interview, Golden Gate University School of Law, Women's Employment Rights Clinic, San Francisco, October 2, 2013.

72. Interview, Farmworker and Landscaper Advocacy Project, Chicago, February 7, 2013.

73. Interview, University of Arizona James E. Rogers College of Law: Immigration Law Clinic, Tucson, March 28, 2014.

74. Interview, Legal Aid Society, San Francisco, October 2, 2013.

75. Interview, Legal Aid Justice Center, Washington, DC, August 4, 2014.

76. Interview, Bet Tzedek Legal Services, Los Angeles, November 7, 2013.

77. According to Pew, DAPA would have legalized an estimated 3.2 unauthorized Mexican immigrants (two-thirds of those eligible) had it not been later struck down in the courts. Mexico is the country of origin with the most potential DAPA beneficiaries, with 44 percent of unauthorized Mexicans eligible to apply, compared with 24 percent for other nationalities (López and Krogstad 2017).

78. Public Talk, Mexican Consulate, Undersecretary for North America, Ministry of Foreign Affairs, Chicago, October 17, 2013.

79. Interview, Legal Aid Justice Center, Washington DC, August 4, 2014.

80. Interview, Community Justice Project, Reading, PA, July 29, 2015.

81. Interview, Legal Assistance Foundation, Chicago, April 1, 2014.

82. Interview, Mano a Mano Family Resource Center, Chicago, January 31, 2013.

83. Interview, Catholic Migration Services, New York City, June 5, 2015.

84. Interview, Farmworker and Landscaper Advocacy Project, Chicago, February 7, 2013.

85. Interview, Equal Rights Advocates, San Francisco, April 21, 2014.

86. Interview, Farmworker and Landscaper Advocacy Project, Chicago, February 7, 2013.

87. Interview, Catholic Migration Services, New York City, June 5, 2015.

88. Interview, Legal Assistance Foundation, Chicago, April 1, 2014.

89. Interview, Legal Aid Justice Center, Washington, DC, August 4, 2014.

90. Interview, Legal Assistance Foundation, Chicago, April 1, 2014.

91. Interview, North Carolina Justice Center, Raleigh, March 25, 2014.

92. Interview, Golden Gate University School of Law, Women's Employment Rights Clinic, San Francisco, October 2, 2013.

93. Interview, Golden Gate University School of Law, Women's Employment Rights Clinic, San Francisco, October 2, 2013.

4. ADVOCACY AND ACCOUNTABILITY IN STATE–CIVIL SOCIETY RELATIONS

1. In September of 1985, a strong earthquake hit Mexico City. The solidarity movement that ensued rallied multiple groups interested in encouraging a more democratic society. One of the most iconic organizing campaigns in the aftermath of the earthquake was led by a seamstress, Alejandra Martínez, who made it to the ruins of the factory to help her coworkers and would later establish the Sindicato Nacional de Trabajadoras de la Industria de la Costura, Confección, Vestido, Similares y Conexos "19 de Septiembre" (teleSUR 2017).

2. "The number of wage and salary workers belonging to unions . . . [is] at 14.3 million in 2020 . . . . In 2020, 7.2 million employees in the public sector and 7.1 million workers in the private sector belonged to unions" (BLS-DOL 2021).

3. Community meeting with Undersecretary for North America, Mexican Ministry of Foreign Affairs, at the Mexican consulate in Chicago, October 17, 2013.

4. Interview, Chicago Workers' Collaborative, Chicago, March 13, 2013.

5. Interview, ARISE, Chicago, April 25, 2014.

6. Interview, New Immigrant Community Empowerment, New York, December 8, 2014.

7. Interview, New Immigrant Community Empowerment, New York, December 8, 2014.

8. Interview, Asociación Campesina de Florida, Orlando, February 14, 2014.

9. Interview, La Union, New York, April 4, 2015.

10. Interview, Coalition of Immokalee Workers, Miami, October 27, 2014.

11. Interview, Heartland Workers Center, Omaha, NE, October 6, 2014.

12. Interview, Jornaleros Unidos, New York, March 19, 2015.

13. Interview, Coalition of Immokalee Workers, Miami, October 27, 2014.

14. Interview, ARISE, Chicago, April 25, 2014.

15. Interview, Chicago Workers' Collaborative, Chicago, March 13, 2013.

16. Interview, Heartland Workers Center, Omaha, NE, October 6, 2014.

17. Interview, Day Worker Center of Mountain View, San Jose, CA, January 31, 2014.

18. This covenant clearly asserts the right to work in favorable conditions, which include freedom of association and the right to strike. These latter two rights are often considered politicized domains in which consular staff rarely involve themselves.

19. These financial entanglements often limited the types of policy advocacy in which groups could engage and steered the focus of their service provision. For example, education- and health-related causes capture the lion's share of private philanthropic donations (Guthrie 2010).

20. Interview, Catholic Migration Services, New York, June 5, 2015.

21. Interview, American Friends Service Committee, Miami, November 13, 2014.

22. Interview, CARECEN Day Labor Center, Los Angeles, December 13, 2013.

23. Interview, New Immigrant Community Empowerment, New York, December 8, 2014.

24. Interview, Catholic Migration Services, New York, June 5, 2015.

25. Interview, Catholic Migration Services, New York, June 5, 2015.

26. Interview, Federación de Zacatecanos del Sur de California, Los Angeles, May 6, 2014.

27. Interview, Hermandad Mexicana, Los Angeles, May 7, 2014.

28. Interview, American Friends Service Committee, Miami, November 13, 2014.

29. Interview, El Centro del Inmigrante, New York, March 26, 2015.

30. Interview, immigrant rights organization, Chicago, February 19, 2013.

31. Interview, Centro Internacional de Derechos Humanos Todo por Ellos, San Diego, CA, May 7, 2014.

32. Interview, DREAMers' MOMs, San Diego, CA, May 9, 2014.

33. Interview, Maintenance Cooperation Trust Fund, Los Angeles, November 13, 2013.

34. Interview, Pueblo Sin Fronteras, Dallas, TX, July 28, 2014.

35. Interview, Pueblo Sin Fronteras, Dallas, TX, July 28, 2014.

36. Interview, EcoMaya, Los Angeles, May 9, 2014.

37. Interview, Frente Indígena de Organizaciones Binacionales, Fresno, CA, January 14, 2015.

38. Interview, Coalición de Comunidades Indígenas de Oaxaca, San Diego, CA, April 25, 2014.

39. Interview, Asociación MAYAB, San Francisco, April 30, 2014.

40. Interview, Angeles sin Fronteras, San Diego, CA, May 10, 2014.

41. Interview, Fe y Justicia Worker Center, Houston, TX, September 23, 2014.

42. Interview, Centro de la Familia de Utah, Salt Lake City, July 28, 2014.

43. Interview, Global Workers Justice Alliance, New York, October 14, 2016.

44. Interview, Centro de los Derechos del Migrante, Washington, DC, August 14, 2014.

45. Interview, Global Workers Justice Alliance, New York, June 11, 2015.

46. Interview, Casa Colima, Los Angeles, May 7, 2014.

47. Interview, Asociación MAYAB, San Francisco, April 29, 2014.

48. Interview, St. Mary's Cathedral: Immigration Program, Omaha, NE, October 14, 2014.

49. Interview, Day Worker Center of Mountain View, San Jose, CA, January 31, 2014.

50. Interview, Garment Worker Center, Los Angeles, November 13, 2013.

51. Interview, San Francisco Day Labor Program, San Francisco, April 30, 2014.

52. Interview, Arizona Worker Rights Center, Phoenix, June 16, 2014.

53. Interview, Living United for Change in Arizona (LUCHA), Phoenix, July 31, 2014.

54. Interview, Centro de Trabajadores Unidos: Immigrant Workers Project, Chicago, March 14, 2013.

55. Interview, New Immigrant Community Empowerment, New York, December 15, 2014.

56. Interview, CASA de Maryland, Washington, DC, October 6, 2014.

57. Interview, We Count!, Miami, April 18, 2014.

58. Interview, American Friends Service Committee, Miami, November 13, 2014.

59. Interview, English Skills Learning Center, Salt Lake City, UT, November 13, 2014.

60. Interview, Georgia Latino Alliance for Human Rights, Atlanta, GA, September 25, 2014.

61. Interview, Heartland Workers Center, Omaha, NE, October 6, 2014.

62. Interview, El Pueblo, Raleigh, NC, June 20, 2014; interview, Comunidades Unidas, Salt Lake City, UT, January 21, 2015.

63. Interview, Farmworker and Landscaper Advocacy Project, Chicago, February 7. 2013.

5. THE STRATEGIES OF TRANSNATIONAL LABOR COALITIONS AND NETWORKS

1. Protection contracts (*contratos de protección*) refer to collective bargaining agreements that are frequently registered without the knowledge of employees and in which the employer retains significant discretion in the management of labor relations.

2. For example, for the Mexican government, signing the UN International Convention on the Protection of the Rights of All Migrant Workers and Members of Their Families has not been an impediment to denying basic protections to Central American migrants traversing its southern border while trying to reach the United States (Feldmann Pietsch, Bada, and Durand Arp-Niesse 2020). To complicate matters, the United States has not ratified this convention, and in 2017 it ended its participation in the UN Global Compact of Migration, arguing sovereignty concerns.

3. Interview, Global Workers Justice Alliance, Mexico City, August 3, 2015.

4. The concept of portable rights for migrant workers encompasses a demand for justice prior to, during, and even after migrants return to their country of origin, regardless of their immigration status (Piper and Grugel 2015).

5. Interview, Labor Council for Latin American Advancement, New York, May 26, 2015.

6. Interview, Border Network for Human Rights, El Paso, TX, October 28, 2019.

7. Interview, Border Network for Human Rights, El Paso, TX, October 28, 2019.

8. For a partial list of donors, see IMUMI (n.d.).

9. In an estimate calculated by Martha Rojas Wiesner, between 2000 and 2006, 1,050,287 migrants were deported by Mexico, and 95.1 percent were sent back to Central America (Rojas Wiesner 2022).

10. Interview, Comité Fronterizo de Obrer@s, Piedras Negras, Coahuila, June 9, 2018.

11. Interview, Frente Auténtico del Trabajo (FAT), Mexico City, June 26, 2018.

12. Interview, Red Mexicana de Acción Frente al Libre Comercio, Mexico City, July 3, 2018.

13. Interview, Comité Fronterizo de Obrer@s, Piedras Negras, Coahuila, June 9, 2018.

14. Interview, AFL-CIO, Mexico City, May 7, 2018.

15. Interview, Asociación Nacional de Empresas Comercializadoras de Productores del Campo, Mexico City, August 24, 2018.

16. Interview, Sin Fronteras, Mexico City, June 26, 2018.

17. Interview, Prevención, Capacitación y Defensa del Migrante, Mexico City, March 6, 2018.

18. By November of 2018, multiple migrant caravans from Central America were attempting to cross the Mexico-US border en masse and were met with Mexican and US police forces trying to disperse them with violent force and tear gas, thus shattering any aspirational goals toward government accountability and a more humane management of migrants along the southern and northern borders (París-Pombo and Varela-Huerta 2022).

19. Interview, Jornaleros SAFE, Mexico City, June 26, 2018.

20. Interview, FAT, Mexico City, June 26, 2018.

21. Interview, Centro de los Derechos del Migrante (CDM), Oaxaca, June 15, 2018.

22. Interview, United Food and Commercial Workers (UFCW), Mexico City, June 22, 2018.

23. Interview, Prevención, Capacitación y Defensa del Migrante, Mexico City, March 6, 2018.

24. The current administration of López Obrador (2018–23) has followed a populist strategy that includes drastic cuts to public funds that have been used to subsidize private social service organizations and civil society groups. In 2022, in order to privilege direct subsidies delivered to citizens and discourage the strengthening of independent civil society groups, the president supported a new fiscal initiative to restrict tax-deductible donations to civil society organizations from both private citizens and corporations (Camarena 2021; Olvera 2020).

25. Interview, Proyecto de Derechos Económicos, Sociales y Culturales, Mexico City, June 13, 2018.

26. Interview, AFL-CIO, Mexico City, May 7, 2018.

27. Interview, FAT, Mexico City, June 26, 2018.

28. Interview, UFCW, Mexico City, June 22, 2018.

29. Interview, Global Workers Justice Alliance, Mexico City, August 3, 2015.

30. Interview, CDM, Oaxaca, June 15, 2018.

31. Interview, Global Workers Justice Alliance, Mexico City, August 3, 2015.

32. Interview, CDM, Oaxaca, June 15, 2018.

6. CONCLUSION

1. For a comprehensive overview of post-1990s migrant civil society advocacy to gain political rights for Mexican migrants in the United States, see Badillo Moreno (2004).

2. Since the mid-1990s, the Mexican government has tried to privilege trade and economic cooperation as the most salient issues in the bilateral agenda as a public relations and media strategy. To do so, the Mexican government aims to hide from public view the most delicate issues, such as bilateral cooperation in Mexico's drug trafficking enforcement, immigration policy along Mexico's northern and southern borders, and US comprehensive immigration reform.

3. The 1952 Refugee Convention asserts the right to leave as a universal right but remains silent on the right to entry; therefore, the universal right to leave does not have a corresponding right to asylum (Sassen 1998).

4. Though this is surely an incomplete list, online archives revealed resources at each of the following offices: Albuquerque, Atlanta, Chicago, Houston, Las Vegas, Los Angeles, Miami, Milwaukee, New Orleans, New York, Orlando, Philadelphia, Phoenix, Portland, Saint Paul, Salt Lake City, San Antonio, San Bernardino, San Diego, San Francisco, San Jose, Seattle, and Tucson.

Key Institutions, Instruments, and Actors in Transnational Labor Regulation and Consular Affairs

TABLE 5 Key institutions, instruments, and actors in transnational labor regulation and consular affairs

Spanish	English Translation
Acuerdo de Cooperación Laboral de América del Norte (ACLAN)	North American Agreement on Labor Cooperation (NAALC)
Arreglos de entendimiento	Arrangements establishing understanding (AEUs)
Asuntos Comunitarios	Department of Community Affairs
Carpeta Informativa Básica Consular (CIBAC)	Basic Consular Information Binder*
Cartas de acuerdo a.k.a. memoranda de entendimiento	Letters of agreement (LOAs) a.k.a. memoranda of understanding (MOUs)
Centro de Información y Asistencia a Mexicanos (CIAM)	Center for Assistance and Information to Mexicans*
Confederación de Trabajadores de México (CTM)	Confederation of Mexican Workers
Consejo Consultivo del Instituto de los Mexicanos en el Exterior (CCIME)	Advisory Board of the Institute of Mexicans Abroad
Consulado móvil	Mobile consulate
Consulado sobre ruedas	Consulate on wheels*
Consultoría Jurídica	Legal Consulting*
Coordinación General del Servicio Nacional de Empleo	General Coordination for the National Employment Service*
Departamento de Protección y Asistencia Consular	Department of Legal Protection and Consular Assistance

(Contd.)

Spanish	English Translation
Dirección de Protección para Estados Unidos de América (DPEUA)	General Directorate of Protection for the United States[*]
Dirección General de Comunicación Social	General Directorate of Communications[*]
Dirección General de Delegaciones	General Directorate of Delegations (Field Offices)[*]
Dirección General de Protección a Mexicanos en el Exterior (DGPME)	General Directorate for the Protection of Mexicans Abroad[*]
Instituto de los Mexicanos en el Exterior (IME)	Institute of Mexicans Abroad
Instituto Nacional de Transparencia, Acceso a la Información y Protección de Datos Personales (INAI)	National Institute of Transparency, Information Access and Private Data Protection
Jornadas Informativas del IME	IME Informative Meetings[*]
Oficina Administrativa Nacional (OAN)	National Administrative Office (NAO)
Oficina Internacional de Asuntos Laborales	Bureau of International Labor Affairs (ILAB)
Organización Internacional del Trabajo (OIT)	International Labour Organization (ILO)
Procuraduría Federal de la Defensa del Trabajo	Federal Attorney's Office for Labor Protection[*]
Programa de Asistencia Jurídica a Personas Mexicanas a través de Asesorías Legales Externas en los Estados Unidos de América (PALE)	Legal Assistance Program to Mexicans by Attorneys in the United States[*]
Programa de Asistencia Jurídica Telefónica Gratuita (JURIMEX)	Free Legal Assistance Program Hotline[*]
Programa de Trabajadores Agrícolas Temporales México-Canadá (PTAT)	Mexico-Canada Seasonal Agricultural Workers Program (SAWP)
Programa Paisano	Paisano Program
Programa para las Comunidades Mexicanas en el Extranjero (PCME)	Program for the Mexican Communities Abroad
Secretaría de Desarrollo Social (SEDESOL 1992–2018)	Ministry of Social Development
Secretaría de Gobernación (SEGOB)	Ministry of the Interior
Secretaría de Hacienda y Crédito Público (SHCP)	Finance Ministry
Secretaría de la Función Publica	Ministry of the Civil Service
Secretaría de Relaciones Exteriores (SRE)	Ministry of Foreign Affairs
Secretaría del Trabajo y Previsión Social (STPS)	Ministry of Labor and Social Welfare
Seguro Popular	Public Health Insurance (with an annual sliding fee scale)
Semana de Derechos Laborales (SDL)	Labor Rights Week (LRW)
Servicio Exterior Mexicano (SEM)	Diplomatic Civil Service
Servicio Telefónico Gratuito para Citas (MEXITEL)	Free Consular Appointment Hotline[*]
Tratado de Libre Comercio de América del Norte (TLCAN)	North American Free Trade Agreement (NAFTA)
Ventanilla de Salud	Health Access Window Program[*]
Ventanilla Laboral	Labor Affairs Window Program[*]

[*] Translation by the authors

Adler, Lee H., Maite Tapia, and Lowell Turner, eds. 2014. *Mobilizing against Inequality: Unions, Immigrant Workers, and the Crisis of Capitalism.* Frank W. Pierce Memorial Lectureship and Conference Series. Ithaca, NY: Cornell University Press.

AFL-CIO. 2020. "In Solidarity with Workers on Strike against Asarco, and Condemning Grupo México's Violations of Labor, Human and Environmental Rights." Executive Council Statement, April 17. https://aflcio.org/about/leadership/statements/solidarity -workers-strike-against-asarco-and-condemning-grupo-mexicos.

Albiston, Catherine, Su Li, and Laura Beth Nielsen. 2017. "Public Interest Law Organizations and the Two-Tier System of Access to Justice in the United States." *Law and Social Inquiry* 42 (4): 990–1022.

Alexander, Charlotte S., and Arthi Prasad. 2014. "Bottom-Up Workplace Law Enforcement: An Empirical Analysis." *Indiana Law Journal* 89: 1069–1131.

Álvarez, Luis Fernando. 1995. *Vicente Lombardo Toledano y los sindicatos de México y Estados Unidos.* Ciudad Universitaria: Universidad Nacional Autónoma de México.

Amengual, Matthew, and Janice Fine. 2017. "Co-enforcing Labor Standards: The Unique Contributions of State and Worker Organizations in Argentina and the United States." *Regulation and Governance* 11 (2): 129–42.

American Immigration Council. 2017. "U.S. Citizen Children Impacted by Immigration Enforcement." American Immigration Council, fact sheet, March 28. https://asistahelp .org/wp-content/uploads/2019/08/AIC-Factsheet-US-Citizen-Children-Impacted-by -IE.pdf.

American University Washington College of Law, Immigrant Justice Clinic; and CDM (Centro de los Derechos del Migrante). 2013. *Taken for a Ride: Migrant Workers in the U.S. Fair and Carnival Industry.* Washington, DC: American University Washington College of Law; Baltimore: Centro de los Derechos del Migrante. https://cdmigrante .org/wp-content/uploads/2018/02/Taken_Ride.pdf.

American University Washington College of Law, Immigrant Justice Clinic; CDM (Centro de los Derechos del Migrante); and Georgetown University Law Center, Federal Legislation Clinic. 2020. *Breaking the Shell: How Maryland's Migrant Crab Pickers Continue to Be "Picked Apart."* Washington, DC: American University Washington College of Law; Baltimore: Centro de los Derechos del Migrante. https://cdmigrante.org/wp-content /uploads/2020/09/Breaking-The-Shell.pdf.

Andreas, Peter, and Thomas J. Biersteker. 2003. *The Rebordering of North America.* New York: Routledge.

Anner, Mark, and Peter Evans. 2004. "Building Bridges across a Double Divide: Alliances Between." *Development in Practice* 14 (1): 34–47.

Apostolidis, Paul. 2010. *Breaks in the Chain: What Immigrant Workers Can Teach America about Democracy.* Minneapolis: University of Minnesota Press.

A.R.E. Editorial Collective. 2015. "Resisting the Neoliberal Privatization of Education: Reclaiming Education, Organizing, and Epistemologies." *Regeneración: The Association of Raza Educators Journal* 6 (1).

Ashar, Sameer, and Annie Lai. 2019. "Access to Power." *Daedalus* 148 (1): 82–87.

Associated Press. 2019. "EEUU: Gobierno federal impugna ley migratoria de Alabama." *El Faro*, September 20, sec. Internacionales/Migración. https://elfaro.net/es/201107/inter nacionales/5095/EEUU-Gobierno-federal-impugna-ley-migratoria-de-Alabama.htm.

———. 2022. "Remittances to Mexico Soar during Covid Pandemic." NBC News, January 26. www.nbcnews.com/news/latino/remittances-mexico-soar-covid-pandemic-rcna13638.

Asylum Access México, Center for Gender and Refugee Studies, Kids in Need of Defense, Latin American Working Group, Women's Refugee Commission, El Instituto para las Mujeres en la Migración, AC, and International Detention Coalition. 2021. *Implementación de las reformas mexicanas que prohíben la detención de niñas, niños y adolescentes migrantes acompañados y no acompañados.* April. https://imumi.org/wp-content /uploads/2021/04/Reformas-en-materia-de-ninez-y-familias-migrantes-en-Mexico.pdf.

Audley, John, Demetrios G. Papademitriou, Sandra Polaski, and Scott Vaughan. 2004. *NAFTA's Promise and Reality: Lessons from Mexico for the Hemisphere.* Washington, DC: Carnegie Endowment for International Peace. https://carnegieendowment.org/files /nafta1.pdf.

Avilés, Martín. 2020. "'Te tratan como a una basura': Mexicanos denuncian malos tratos en el Consulado de Raleigh." *La Noticia*, December 29. https://lanoticia.com/noticias /usa/nc/te-tratan-como-a-una-basura-mexicanos-denuncian-malos-tratos-en-el-con sulado-de-raleigh/.

Ayón, David. 2010. "Taming the Diaspora: Migrants and the State, 1986–2006." In *Mexico's Democratic Challenges: Politics, Government and Society*, edited by Andrew Selee and Jacqueline Peschard, 231–50. Washington, DC: Woodrow Wilson Center Press; Stanford, CA: Stanford University Press.

Ayres, Ian, and John Braithwaite. 1992. *Responsive Regulation: Transcending the Deregulation Debate.* Oxford: Oxford University Press.

Bacon, David. 2014. *The Right to Stay Home: How US Policy Drives Mexican Migration.* Boston: Beacon Press.

———. 2015. *"Your Liberation Is Linked to Ours": International Solidarity Campaigns.* ILRE Report. Institute for Research on Labor and Employment, UCLA. September 1. https:// escholarship.org/uc/item/2h373831#author.

———. 2019. "In Mexico, a New Dawn for Independent Unions?" *NACLA Report on the Americas* 51 (3): 268–75.

Bada, Xóchitl. 2010. "Mexican Hometown Associations in Chicago: The Newest Agents of Civic Participation." In *¡Marcha! Latino Chicago and the Immigrant Rights Movement*, edited by Amalia Pallares and Nilda Flores González, 146-62. Urbana: University of Illinois Press.

———. 2011. "Participatory Planning across Borders: Mexican Migrant Civic Engagement in Community Development." *The Latin Americanist* 55 (4): 9–33.

———. 2014. *Mexican Hometown Associations in Chicagoacán: From Local to Transnational Civic Engagement*. New Brunswick, NJ: Rutgers University Press.

———. 2016. "Collective Remittances and Development in Rural Mexico: A View from Chicago's Mexican Hometown Associations." *Population, Space and Place* 22 (4): 343–55.

Bada, Xóchitl, and Andreas E. Feldmann. 2017. "Mexico's Michoacán State: Mixed Migration Flows and Transnational Links." *Forced Migration Review* 56 (October): 12–14.

Bada, Xóchitl, and Jonathan Fox. 2021. "Persistent Rurality in Mexico and 'the Right to Stay Home.'" *Journal of Peasant Studies* 49 (1): 29–53.

Bada, Xóchitl, and Shannon Gleeson. 2019. "The North American Agreement on Labor Cooperation and the Challenges to Protecting Low-Wage Migrant Workers." In *Accountability across Borders: Migrant Rights in North America*, edited by Xóchitl Bada and Shannon Gleeson, 83–109. Austin: University of Texas Press.

———. 2020. "Transnational Networks for Portable Migrant Labor Rights in North America." In *Diaspora Organizations in International Affairs*, edited by Dennis Dijkzeul and Margit Fauser, 43–63. New York: Routledge.

Badillo Moreno, Gonzalo, ed. 2004. *La puerta que llama: El voto de los Mexicanos en el extranjero*. Mexico City: Senado de la República.

Balderrama, Francisco. 1982. *In Defense of La Raza: The Los Angeles Mexican Consulate and the Mexican Community*. Tucson: University of Arizona Press.

Ballotpedia. n.d. "Sanctuary Jurisdictions." Accessed April 4, 2022. https://ballotpedia.org /Sanctuary_jurisdictions.

Barger, W.K., and Ernesto M. Reza. 1994. *The Farm Labor Movement in the Midwest: Social Change and Adaptation among Migrant Farmworkers*. Austin: University of Texas Press.

Bartra, Armando. 2008. "The Right to Stay: Reactivate Agriculture, Retain the Population." In *The Right to Stay Home: Alternatives to Mass Displacement and Forced Migration in North America*, 18–25. San Francisco: Global Exchange.

Basok, Tanya. 1999. "Free to Be Unfree: Mexican Guest Workers in Canada." *Labour, Capital and Society / Travail, Capital et Société* 32 (2): 192–221.

———. 2000. "Migration of Mexican Seasonal Farm Workers to Canada and Development: Obstacles to Productive Investment." *International Migration Review* 34 (1): 79–97.

Bayes, Jane H., and Laura Gonzalez. 2011. "Globalization, Transnationalism, and Intersecting Geographies of Power: The Case of the Consejo Consultivo del Instituto de los Mexicanos en el Exterior (CC-IME): A Study in Progress." *Politics and Policy* 39 (1): 11–44.

BBVA Foundation and Ministry of the Interior. 2021. *Anuario de migración y remesas México / Yearbook of Migration and Remittances Mexico* 1 (1). Mexico City: BBVA Foundation. www.bbvaresearch.com/wp-content/uploads/2021/07/Anuario_Migracion_y _Remesas_2021.pdf.

Beltran, Briana. 2018. "134,368 Unnamed Workers: Client-Centered Representation on Behalf of H-2A Agricultural Guestworkers." SSRN Scholarly Paper ID 3135578. Rochester, NY: Social Science Research Network. https://papers.ssrn.com/abstract=3135578.

Bend the Arc: A Jewish Partnership for Justice, and UFCW (United Food and Commercial Workers) Local 5. *The Courage to Fight for Our Future: Justice for Mercado Workers Campaign*. Report, April 23, 2013. Working Partnerships USA. www.wpusa.org/4-23-13%20mercado_report.pdf.

Benford, Robert D., and David A. Snow. 2000. "Framing Processes and Social Movements: An Overview and Assessment." *Annual Review of Sociology* 26: 611–39.

Bensusán, Graciela. 2000. *El modelo mexicano de regulación laboral.* Mexico City: Universidad Autónoma Metropolitana.

Bensusán, Graciela, and María Lorena Cook. 2003. "Political Transition and Labor Revitalization in Mexico." In *Labor Revitalization: Global Perspectives and New Initiatives,* edited by Daniel B. Cornfield and Holly J. McCammon, 229–67. Research in the Sociology of Work, vol. 11. Bingley: Emerald Group.

Berg, Laurie. 2016. *Migrant Rights at Work: Law's Precariousness at the Intersection of Immigration and Labour.* Routledge Research in Asylum, Migration and Refugee Law. Abingdon, Oxon: Routledge.

Bernhardt, Annette, Heather Boushey, Laura Dresser, and Chris Tilly. 2008. *The Gloves-Off Economy: Workplace Standards at the Bottom of America's Labor Market.* Labor and Employment Relations Association Series. Ithaca, NY: ILR Press.

Bernhardt, Annette, Ruth Milkman, and Nik Theodore. 2009. "Broken Laws, Unprotected Workers: Violations of Employment and Labor Laws in America's Cities." National Employment Law Project, report, September 1. www.nelp.org/publication/broken-laws-unprotected-workers-violations-of-employment-and-labor-laws-in-americas-cities/.

Bernhardt, Annette, Michael Spiller, and Diana Polson. 2013. "All Work and No Pay: Violations of Employment and Labor Laws in Chicago, Los Angeles and New York City." *Social Forces* 91 (3): 725–46.

Bernhardt, Annette, Michael Spiller, and Nik Theodore. 2013. "Employers Gone Rogue: Explaining Industry Variation in Violations of Workplace Laws." *ILR Review* 66 (4): 808–32.

Betancur, John J, and Maricela Garcia. 2011. "The 2006–2007 Immigration Mobilizations and Community Capacity: The Experience of Chicago." *Latino Studies* 9 (1): 10–37.

Bloemraad, Irene. 2006a. *Becoming a Citizen: Incorporating Immigrants and Refugees in the United States and Canada.* Berkeley: University of California Press.

———. 2006b. "Becoming a Citizen in the United States and Canada: Structured Mobilization and Immigrant Political Incorporation." *Social Forces* 85: 667–95.

Bloemraad, Irene, Els de Graauw, and Shannon Gleeson. 2020. "Immigrant Organizations: Civic Voice, Civic (In)Equality, and Civic (In)Visibility." In *The Nonprofit Sector: A Research Handbook*, 3rd ed., edited by Walter W. Powell and Patricia Bromley, 292–313. Stanford, CA: Stanford University Press.

BLS-DOL (Bureau of Labor Statistics, Department of Labor). 2019. "National Census of Fatal Occupational Injuries in 2018." News release, December 17. www.bls.gov/news.release/archives/cfoi_12172019.pdf.

———. 2021. "Union Members—2020." US Department of Labor, news release USDL-21-0081, January 22. www.bls.gov/news.release/archives/union2_01222021.htm.

Bodnar, John E. 1985. *The Transplanted: A History of Immigrants in Urban America.* Interdisciplinary Studies in History. Bloomington: Indiana University Press.

Boruchoff, Judith A. 2019. "Mexico-U.S. Migration and the Nation-State: A Transnational Perspective on Transformations since 1990." *Annals of the American Academy of Political and Social Science* 684 (1): 43–59.

Bracho, Christian A. 2020. "Trained to Resist: Teachers Learning Lucha in Oaxaca, Mexico." *FIRE: Forum for International Research in Education* 5 (2). https://fire-ojs-ttu.tdl.org/fire/index.php/FIRE/article/view/175.

Bronckers, Marco, and Giovanni Gruni. 2019. "Improving the Enforcement of Labour Standards in the EU's Free Trade Agreements." In *Perspectives on the Soft Power of the EU Trade Policy*, edited by San Bilal and Bernard Hoekman, 183–92. London: Centre for Economic Policy Research Press.

Brooks, David, and Jonathan Fox, eds. 2002a. *Cross-border Dialogues: U.S.-Mexico Social Movement Networking.* U.S.-Mexico Contemporary Perspectives Series 20. La Jolla: Center for US-Mexican Studies, University of California, San Diego.

———. 2002b. "Movements across the Border: An Overview." In *Cross-Border Dialogues: U.S.- Mexico Social Movement Networking*, edited by David Brooks and Jonathan Fox. La Jolla: Center for US-Mexican Studies, University of California.

Budiman, Abby. 2020. "Key Findings about U.S. Immigrants." Pew Research Center, Fact Tank, August 20. www.pewresearch.org/fact-tank/2020/08/20/key-findings-about-u-s-immigrants/.

Budiman, Abby, Christine Tamir, Lauren Mora, and Luis Noe-Bustamante. 2020. "Facts on U.S. Immigrants, 2018: Statistical Portrait of the Foreign-Born Population in the United States." Pew Research Center, report, August 20. www.pewresearch.org/hispanic/2020/08/20/facts-on-u-s-immigrants/.

Byrnes, Dolores M. 2003. *Driving the State: Families and Public Policy in Central Mexico.* Ithaca, NY: Cornell University Press.

Calavita, Kitty. 1992. *Inside the State: The Bracero Program, Immigration, and the INS.* New York: Routledge.

Cámara de Diputados. 2018. "Ley del Servicio Exterior Mexicano." Última Reforma DOF 19-04-2018. Cámara de Diputados del H. Congreso de la Unión—Secretaría General, Secretaría de Servicios Parlamentarios. https://sre.gob.mx/component/phocadownload/category/2-marco-normativo?download=292:ley-del-servicio-exterior-mexicano.

Camarena, Salvador. 2021. "La sociedad civil en tiempos de AMLO." *El País*, October 23. https://elpais.com/opinion/2021-10-23/la-sociedad-civil-en-tiempos-de-amlo.html.

Canales Cerón, Alejandro I., and Martha Luz Rojas Wiesner. 2018. "Panorama de la migración internacional en México y Centroamérica." *Población y Desarrollo*, June, no. 124. United Nations Economic Commission for Latin America and the Caribbean. https://repositorio.cepal.org/bitstream/handle/11362/43697/1/S1800554_es.pdf.

Capps, Randy, Heather Koball, James D. Bachmeier, Ariel G. Ruiz Soto, Jie Zong, and Julia Gelatt. 2016. *Deferred Action for Unauthorized Immigrant Parents: Analysis of DAPA's Potential Effects on Families and Children.* Washington, DC: Urban Institute and Migration Policy Institute. www.migrationpolicy.org/sites/default/files/publications/DAPA-Profile-FINALWEB.pdf.

Cárdenas Solórzano, Cuauhtémoc. 1989. "Responsabilidad de México para con los Mexicanos en el Exterior." *La Voz del Trabajador Inmigrante* 7 (2): 5–9.

Cárdenas Suárez, Héctor, Gonzalo Celorio Morayta, and Bernardo Mabire. 2019. "La política consular en Estados Unidos—Consular Policy in the United States: Protección, documentación y vinculación con las comunidades mexicanas en el exterior." *Foro Internacional* 59 (3–4): 1077–1114.

Caron, Cathleen. 2005. "Global Workers Require Global Justice: The Portability of Justice Challenge for Migrants in the USA," Discussion paper, Committee on Migrant Workers, Day of General Discussion on Protecting the Rights of All Migrant Workers as a Tool to Enhance Development, Geneva, December 15. https://www2.ohchr.org/english/bodies/cmw/docs/global.pdf.

Caron, Cathleen, and Beth Lyon. Forthcoming. "Portable Justice." In *Migration and the Sustainable Development Goals*, edited by Kavita Datta and Nicola Piper. Northampton: Edward Elgar.

Casa ALBA Melanie. n.d. "Mobile Consulate." Accessed 2021. www.casaalba.org/mobile-consulate.html.

Castañeda, Heide, and James Arango. 2014. "Health Concerns for Mexican Migrants in Central Florida: Collaborations with the Sending State via Mobile Consulates and Hometown Associations." *Practicing Anthropology* 36 (3): 43–47.

CDM (Centro de los Derechos del Migrante). 2018. "Second Regional Meeting on Labor Recruitment." Centro de Los Derechos del Migrante, February 7. https://cdmigrante.org/second-regional-meeting-on-labor-recruitment/.

———. 2019a. *Coerced under NAFTA: Abuses of Migrant Workers in the TN Visa Program and Recommendations for Reform*. Baltimore: Centro de los Derechos del Migrante. https://cdmigrante.org/wp-content/uploads/2018/01/Coerced-under-NAFTA_-Abuses-of-Migrant-Workers-in-TN-Visa-Program.pdf.

———. 2019b. *Fake Jobs for Sale: Analyzing Fraud and Advancing Transparency in U.S. Labor Recruitment*. Baltimore: Centro de los Derechos del Migrante. https://cdmigrante.org/wp-content/uploads/2019/04/Fake-Jobs-for-Sale-Report.pdf.

———. 2019c. *Trabajos falsos a la venta*. Mexico City: Centro de los Derechos del Migrante, April. https://cdmigrante.org/trabajos-falsos-a-la-venta/.

———. 2020. *Ripe for Reform: Abuses of Agricultural Workers in the H-2A Visa Program*. Baltimore: Centro de los Derechos del Migrante. https://cdmigrante.org/wp-content/uploads/2020/04/Ripe-for-Reform.pdf.

———. 2021. "Year One of the USMCA: Migrant Workers' Rights Become a Priority." Centro de los Derechos del Migrante, July 1. https://cdmigrante.org/year-one-of-the-usmca-migrant-workers-rights-become-a-priority/.

CEJIL (Centro por la Justicia y el Derecho Internacional). 2020. *El impacto del COVID-19 sobre los derechos humanos de los migrantes*. www.ohchr.org/Documents/Issues/Migration/CFI-COVID/SubmissionsCOVID/CSO/CEJIL.pdf.

CEMEFI (Centro Mexicano para la Filantropía). 2019. *Compendio estadístico del sector no lucrativo 2019*. Mexico City: CEMEFI. www.cemefi.org/images/stories/cifresbiblioteca/p30.pdf.

Cervantes, Rodrigo. 2021. "Mexico Will Offer COVID-19 Vaccine Regardless of Immigration Status." Fronteras Desk, February 25. https://fronterasdesk.org/content/1662215/mexico-will-offer-covid-19-vaccine-regardless-immigration-status.

Chávez Becker, Carlos, Pablo González Ulloa, and Gustavo Adolfo Venegas Maldonado. 2016. *Retos, perspectivas y horizontes de las organizaciones de la sociedad civil en México: Los caminos hacia una reforma de la LFFAROSC*. Mexico City: Instituto Belisario

Domínguez. Senado de la República. http://ibd.senado.gob.mx/sites/default/files/Estudio_Final_Retos_y_Perspectivas_de_las_OSC.pdf.

Chishti, Muzaffar, Julia Gelatt, and Doris Meissner. 2021. *Rethinking the US Legal Immigration System*. Washington, DC: Migration Policy Institute. www.migrationpolicy.org/sites/default/files/publications/Rethinking-LegalImmigration-Roadmap_FINAL.pdf.

Cholewinski, Ryszard. 2008. "The Human and Labor Rights of Migrants: Visions of Equality." *Georgetown Immigration Law Journal* 22 (2): 177–220.

Cleary, Matthew R., and Susan C. Stokes. 2006. *Democracy and the Culture of Skepticism: Political Trust in Argentina and Mexico*. Russell Sage Foundation Series on Trust. New York: Russell Sage Foundation.

CLINIC (Catholic Legal Immigration Network, Inc.). 2022. "FAQ: Advising DACA Clients in 2022." Last updated March 7. https://cliniclegal.org/resources/humanitarian-relief/deferred-action-childhood-arrivals/faq-advising-daca-clients-2022.

CMS (Center for Migration Studies of New York). 2021. "What You Should Know about the US Undocumented and Eligible-to-Naturalize Populations." News release, August 4. https://cmsny.org/undocumented-eligible-to-naturalize-population-democratizing-data-release-080421/.

———. n.d. "Constitutional Reform in Mexico Guarantees the Right to Free and Universal Birth Registration." Accessed August 18, 2014. https://cmsny.org/constitutional-reform-in-mexico-guarantees-the-right-to-free-and-universal-birth-registration/.

CNN Español. 2017. "Peña Nieto anuncia más recursos para los consulados en EEUU y destaca la solidaridad con México." CNN, January 31. https://cnnespanol.cnn.com/2017/01/31/pena-nieto-anuncia-mas-recursos-para-los-consulados-en-ee-uu-y-destaca-la-solidaridad-con-mexico/.

Collyer, Michael, ed. 2013. *Emigration Nations: Policies and Ideologies of Emigrant Engagement*. New York: Palgrave Macmillan.

Comisión de Relaciones Exteriores. 2021. "Opinión de la Comisión de Relaciones Exteriores respecto al proyecto de presupuesto de egresos de la Federación para el ejercicio fiscal 2021." Cámara de Diputados, LXIV Legislatura. http://archivos.diputados.gob.mx/Comisiones_LXIV/relaciones-exteriores/OpinionPPEF2021.docx.

Compa, Lance. 2001. "NAFTA's Labor Side Agreement and International Labor Solidarity." *Antipode* 33 (3): 451–67.

———. 2017. "Migrant Workers in The United States: Connecting Domestic Law with International Labor Standards: The Piper Lecture." *Chicago-Kent Law Review* 92 (1): 211–45.

Conexión Migrante. 2021. "Consulados de México en Estados Unidos: Maltrato y servicios deficientes." Poblanerías en Línea, January 11. www.poblanerias.com/2021/01/maltrato-consulados-de-mexico-en-usa/.

Conlan, Timothy J. 1998. *From New Federalism to Devolution: Twenty-Five Years of Intergovernmental Reform*. Washington, DC: Brookings Institution. www.brookings.edu/book/from-new-federalism-to-devolution/.

Constante, Agnes. 2015. "New Alliance: One-Stop Hotline for Filipinos with Workplace Woes." Inquirer.net, September 16. https://globalnation.inquirer.net/128401/new-alliance-one-stop-hotline-for-filipinos-with-workplace-woes.

———. 2018. "Bill Aimed at Protecting Immigrant Workers Reporting Violations Introduced in Congress." NBC News, June 1. www.nbcnews.com/news/asian-america/bill-aimed-protecting-immigrant-workers-reporting-violations-introduced-congress-n878991.

Consulado General de México en Chicago. 2009. "Semana de Derechos Laborales: Del 31 de agosto al 4 septiembre, 2009—Agenda." Personal files of Shannon Gleeson.

———. 2011. "¡Conozca sus derechos laborales y proteja su empleo!" Flyer. Personal files of Shannon Gleeson.

———. 2022. "COVID-19 guía de recursos y servicios para Illinois, Indiana, and Beneficiarios DACA." Last revised February 9. https://consulmex.sre.gob.mx/chicago/index.php/consulado/ubicacion-y-horarios?id=268.6Consulado General de México en Miami. 2021. *Guía de recursos COVID-19.* https://consulmex.sre.gob.mx/miami/images/PDF/Guia_de_recursos.pdf.

Consulado General de México en Salt Lake City. 2021. *Guía de recursos para personas mexicanas en el estado de Utah y el oeste de Wyoming ante COVID-19.* August. https://disabilitylawcenter.org/wp-content/uploads2/2021/08/Guia-de-Recursos-para-personas-mexicanas_SOCIAL-MEDIA.pdf.

Consulado General de México en San José. 2020. "Necesitas ayuda de alimentos para tu familia o personas de la tercera edad." Emailed weekly newsletter, May 7.

Cornfield, Dan. 2006. "Immigration, Economic Restructuring, and Labor Ruptures: From the Amalgamated to Change to Win." *WorkingUSA: The Journal of Labor and Society* 9 (2): 215–23.

Corporate Campaign, Inc. n.d. "FLOC vs. the Campbell Soup Company: 1985–86." Accessed May 22, 2021. www.corporatecampaign.org/history_floc_campbell_1985.php.

Correa-Cabrera, Guadalupe. 2020. "Chronicles of a War Foretold: Reversing Mexico's Current Course toward Redoubled Militarization Requires a Shift in US Policy Away from the Disastrous 'War on Drugs' and toward a Respect for Mexican Sovereignty." *NACLA Report on the Americas* 52 (1): 41–46.

Costa, Daniel. 2017. "Modern-Day Braceros: The United States Has 450,000 Guestworkers in Low-Wage Jobs and Doesn't Need More." *Working Economics Blog*, March 31. Economic Policy Institute. www.epi.org/blog/modern-day-braceros-the-united-states-has-450000-guestworkers-in-low-wage-jobs/.

———. 2018. *California Leads the Way: A Look at California Laws That Help Protect Labor Standards for Unauthorized Immigrant Workers.* Economic Policy Institute report, March 22. www.epi.org/publication/california-immigrant-labor-laws/.

———. 2020. "Temporary Migrant Workers or Immigrants? The Question for U.S. Labor Migration." *RSF: The Russell Sage Foundation Journal of the Social Sciences* 6 (3): 18–44.

Costa, Daniel, and Philip Martin. 2018. *Temporary Labor Migration Programs: Governance, Migrant Worker Rights, and Recommendations for the U.N. Global Compact for Migration.* Economic Policy Institute, report, August 1. www.epi.org/publication/temporary-labor-migration-programs-governance-migrant-worker-rights-and-recommendations-for-the-u-n-global-compact-for-migration/.

Cruz Guevarra, Ericka, Adhiti Bandlamudi, and Alan Montecillo. 2021. "The Immigrant Renters the Eviction Moratorium Didn't Protect." KQED, *The Bay* podcast, September 29. www.kqed.org/news/11890298/the-unofficial-evictions-affecting-latino-immigrants.

de Graauw, Els. 2016. *Making Immigrant Rights Real: Nonprofits and the Politics of Integration in San Francisco.* Ithaca, NY: Cornell University Press.

de Graauw, Els, and Shannon Gleeson. 2020. "Metropolitan Context and Immigrant Rights Experiences: DACA Awareness and Support in Houston." *Urban Geography* 42 (8): 1119–46.

de Graauw, Els, Shannon Gleeson, and Xóchitl Bada. 2019. "Local Context and Labour-Community Immigrant Rights Coalitions: A Comparison of San Francisco, Chicago, and Houston." *Journal of Ethnic and Migration Studies* 20 (4): 728–46.

de Graauw, Els, Shannon Gleeson, and Irene Bloemraad. 2013. "Funding Immigrant Organizations: Suburban Free Riding and Local Civic Presence." *American Journal of Sociology* 119 (1): 75–130.

De la Garza Toledo, Enrique. 2021. "Reflections on Mexico's Labor Reforms of 2012 and 2019." Paper presented at the IV ISA Forum of Sociology Annual Meeting: Labor Reforms in Latin America in the New Century, February, Porto Alegre, Brazil.

Délano, Alexandra. 2009. "From Limited to Active Engagement: Mexico's Emigration Policies from a Foreign Policy Perspective (2000–2006)." *International Migration Review* 43 (4): 764–814.

———. 2011. *Mexico and Its Diaspora in the United States: Policies of Emigration since 1848.* Cambridge: Cambridge University Press.

———. 2014. "The Diffusion of Diaspora Engagement Policies: A Latin American Agenda." *Political Geography* 41: 90–100.

Délano Alonso, Alexandra. 2018. *From Here and There: Diaspora Policies, Integration, and Social Rights beyond Borders.* New York: Oxford University Press.

Délano Alonso, Alexandra, and Harris Mylonas. 2019. "The Microfoundations of Diaspora Politics: Unpacking the State and Disaggregating the Diaspora." *Journal of Ethnic and Migration Studies* 45 (4): 473–91.

Delgadillo, Ana Lorena, Alma García, and Rodolfo Córdova Alcaraz. 2019. "Rebuilding Justice We Can All Trust: The Plight of Migrant Victims." In *Accountability across Borders: Migrant Rights in North America*, edited by Xóchitl Bada and Shannon Gleeson, 141–65. Austin: University of Texas Press.

Delgado, Héctor L. 1993. *New Immigrants, Old Unions: Organizing Undocumented Workers in Los Angeles.* Philadelphia: Temple University Press.

Delgado Wise, Raul. 2018. "Is There a Space for Counterhegemonic Participation? Civil Society in the Global Governance of Migration." *Globalizations* 15 (6): 746–61.

Dewan, Sabina, and Lucas Ronconi. 2018. "U.S. Free Trade Agreements and Enforcement of Labor Law in Latin America." *Industrial Relations. A Journal of Economy and Society* 57 (1): 35–56.

Dias-Abey, Manoj. 2016. "Sandcastles of Hope? Civil Society Organizations and the Working Conditions of Migrant Farmworkers in North America." PhD diss., Queen's University, Ontario.

———. 2018. "Justice on Our Fields: Can 'Alt-Labor' Organizations Improve Migrant Farm Workers' Conditions?" *Harvard Civil Rights-Civil Liberties Law Review* 53 (1): 168–211.

Díaz Prieto, Gabriela, and Gretchen Kuhner. 2009. "Mexico's Role in Promoting and Implementing the ICRMW." In *Migration and Human Rights: The United Nations Convention on Migrant Workers' Rights*, edited by Paul de Guchteneire, Antoine Pecoud, and Ryszard Cholewinski, 219–46. Cambridge: Cambridge University Press.

Dudley, Mary Jo. 2014. "Development of Spanish Language Educational Materials to Manage Pests in Immigrant Farmworker Housing." College of Agriculture and Life Sciences, Cornell Cooperative Extension, New York State Integrated Pest Management Program, Project Reports. eCommons—Open scholarship at Cornell. https://hdl.handle.net/1813/42547.

Duncan, Larry. 2008. "Crossborder Mural Project." Documentary film. Labor Beat #292. Chicago: Chicago Access Network TV, Labor Beat, and Committee for Labor Access.

Duncan, Whitney L., and Sarah B. Horton. 2020. "Serious Challenges and Potential Solutions for Immigrant Health during COVID-19." *Health Affairs Blog*, April 18. www.healthaffairs.org/do/10.1377/hblog20200416.887086/full/.

Duquette-Rury, Lauren. 2019. *Exit and Voice: The Paradox of Cross-border Politics in Mexico.* Berkeley: University of California Press.

Durand, Jorge. 2007. "The Bracero Program (1942–1964): A Critical Appraisal." *Migración y Desarrollo* 5 (9): 25–40. http://rimd.reduaz.mx/revista/rev9ing/e2.pdf.

———. 2013. "La 'desmigratización' de la relación bilateral: Balance del sexenio de Felipe Calderón." *Foro Internacional* 53 (3/4): 750–70.

Economic Policy Institute. n.d. "Minimum Wage Tracker." Accessed 2019. www.epi.org/minimum-wage-tracker/.

El Sol de México. 2021. "INM deporta a migrantes haitianos desde Tapachula, Chiapas." *El Sol de México,* October 6. www.elsoldemexico.com.mx/republica/sociedad/inm-deporta-a-migrantes-haitianos-desde-tapachula-chiapas-7305587.html.

Esquivel Hernandez, Gerardo. 2015. *Extreme Inequality in Mexico: Concentration of Economic and Political Power.* Mexico City: Oxfam.

EstanciaGyM. 2014. "Invitación rueda de prensa caso #Chambamex #Zacatecas." Twitter. September 7. https://twitter.com/EstanciaGyM/status/506954683609395202.

Farfán Mares, Gabriel, and Rafael Velázquez Flores. 2012. "Presupuesto y política exterior en México: Planeación estratégica, incrementalismo y discrecionalidad." *Revista Legislativa de Estudios Sociales y de Opinión Pública* 5 (9): 39–101.

Feldmann Pietsch, Andreas E., Xóchitl Bada, and Jorge Durand Arp-Niesse. 2020. *Informe de investigación: Centroamérica en el contexto de los flujos internacionales de migración: Principales tendencias.* ERCA Estado de la Región. Sexto Informe Estado de la Región. San José: CONARE-PEN.

Félix, Adrián. 2011. "Posthumous Transnationalism: Postmortem Repatriation from the United States to Mexico." *Latin American Research Review* 46 (3): 157–79.

———. 2019. *Specters of Belonging: The Political Life Cycle of Mexican Migrants.* Studies in Subaltern Latina/o Politics. Oxford: Oxford University Press.

Felstiner, William L.F., Richard L. Abel, and Austin Sarat. 1980. "The Emergence and Transformation of Disputes: Naming, Blaming, Claiming." *Law and Society Review* 15 (3–4): 631–54.

Fennema, Meindert. 2004. "The Concept and Measurement of Ethnic Community." *Journal of Ethnic and Migration Studies* 30 (3): 429–47.

Fernandez, Bina. 2013. "Traffickers, Brokers, Employment Agents, and Social Networks: The Regulation of Intermediaries in the Migration of Ethiopian Domestic Workers to the Middle East." *International Migration Review* 47 (4): 814–43.

Fine, Janice. 2006. *Worker Centers: Organizing Communities at the Edge of the Dream.* Ithaca, NY: ILR Press.

———. 2011. "Worker Centers: Entering a New Stage of Growth and Development." *New Labor Forum* 20 (3): 44–53.

Fine, Janice, and Tim Bartley. 2019. "Raising the Floor: New Directions in Public and Private Enforcement of Labor Standards in the United States." *Journal of Industrial Relations* 61 (2): 252–76.

Fine, Janice, Linda Burnham, Kati Griffith, Minsun Ji, Victor Narro, and Steven C. Pitts. 2018. *No One Size Fits All: Worker Organization, Policy, and Movement in a New Economic Age.* Champaign: Labor and Employment Relations Association, University of Illinois at Urbana-Champaign.

Fine, Janice, Daniel J. Galvin, Jenn Round, and Hana Shepherd. 2020. "Maintaining Effective U.S. Labor Standards Enforcement through the Coronavirus Recession." Washington Center for Equitable Growth, September 3. https://equitablegrowth.org/research-paper/maintaining-effective-u-s-labor-standards-enforcement-through-the-coronavirus-recession/.

Fine, Janice, and Jennifer Gordon. 2010. "Strengthening Labor Standards Enforcement through Partnerships with Workers' Organizations." *Politics and Society* 38 (4): 552–85.

Fine, Janice, and Jenn Round. 2021. "Strengthening Labor Standards Enforcement." Rutgers School of Management and Labor Relations. https://smlr.rutgers.edu/faculty-research-engagement/education-employment-research-center-eerc/eerc-programs/strengthening.

FitzGerald, David. 2008. *A Nation of Emigrants: How Mexico Manages Its Migration.* Berkeley: University of California Press.

FitzGerald, David, and Rawan Arar. 2018. "The Sociology of Refugee Migration." *Annual Review of Sociology* 44 (1): 387–406.

Fox, Jonathan. 1994. "The Politics of Mexico's New Peasant Economy." In *The Politics of Economic Restructuring: State-Society Relations and Regime Change in Mexico*, edited by Maria Lorena Cook, Kevin J. Middlebrook, and Juan Molinar Horcasitas, 243–76. La Jolla: Center for US- Mexican Studies, University of California, San Diego. https://escholarship.org/uc/item/84t497rz.

———. 1998. "Comparative Reflections on the African Dilemma: The Interdependent Democratization of States and Civil Societies." *Political Power and Social Theory* 12 (December): 235–42.

———. 2001. "Evaluación de las coaliciones binacionales de la sociedad civil a partir de la experiencia México-Estados Unidos." *Revista Mexicana de Sociología* 63 (3): 211–68.

———. 2007. *Accountability Politics: Power and Voice in Rural Mexico.* Oxford: Oxford University Press.

Fox, Jonathan, and Gaspar Rivera-Salgado. 2004. *Indigenous Mexican Migrants in the United States.* La Jolla: Center for US-Mexican Studies and Center for Comparative Immigration Studies. University of California, San Diego.

Freire, Paulo. 2000. *Pedagogy of the Oppressed.* 30th anniversary ed. New York: Continuum.

Fuller, Sylvia, and Leah F. Vosko. 2008. "Temporary Employment and Social Inequality in Canada: Exploring Intersections of Gender, Race and Immigration Status." *Social Indicators Research* 88 (1): 31–50.

Fundación para la Justicia y el Estado Democrático de Derecho. 2018. "Comunicado: México está obligado a brindar protección a personas desplazadas centroamericanas." Press release, October 22. www.fundacionjusticia.org/mexico-esta-obligado-a-brindar-proteccion-a-personas-desplazadas-centroamericanas/.

Fung, Archon. 2004. *Empowered Participation: Reinventing Urban Democracy.* Princeton, NJ: Princeton University Press.

Gacek, Stanley. 2019. "Mexico's Ratification of ILO Convention Number 98 and the Future of Protection Contracts." *Mexican Law Review* 12 (1): 157–67.

Galvez, Andrea, Pablo Godoy, and Paul Meneima. 2019. "Chapter 7: Transnational Labor Solidarity versus State-Managed Coercion: UFCW Canada, Mexico, and the Seasonal Agricultural Workers Program." In *Accountability across Borders: Migrant Rights in North America*, edited by Xóchitl Bada and Shannon Gleeson, 189–213. Austin: University of Texas Press.

Galvin, Daniel J. 2016. "Deterring Wage Theft: Alt-Labor, State Politics, and the Policy Determinants of Minimum Wage Compliance." *Perspectives on Politics* 14 (2): 324–50.

Gamlen, Alan. 2014. "Diaspora Institutions and Diaspora Governance." *International Migration Review* 48 (s1): 180–217.

Garcia, Ruben J. 2012. *Marginal Workers: How Legal Fault Lines Divide Workers and Leave Them without Protection*. New York: NYU Press.

García Agustín, Óscar, and Martin Bak Jørgensen, eds. 2016. *Solidarity without Borders: Gramscian Perspectives on Migration and Civil Society Alliances*. Reading Gramsci. London: Pluto Press.

García y Griego, Manuel. 1988. "The Bracero Policy Experiment: U.S.-Mexican Responses to Mexican Labor Migration, 1942–1955." PhD diss., University of California, Los Angeles.

Garrapa, Anna Mary. 2019. "Jornaleros agrícolas y corporaciones transnacionales en el Valle de San Quintín." *Frontera Norte* 31 (1): 1–22.

Gest, Justin, Ian M. Kysel, and Tom K. Wong. 2019. "Protecting and Benchmarking Migrants' Rights: An Analysis of the Global Compact for Safe, Orderly and Regular Migration." *International Migration* 57 (6): 60–79.

Gleeson, Shannon. 2009. "From Rights to Claims: The Role of Civil Society in Making Rights Real for Vulnerable Workers." *Law and Society Review* 43 (3): 669–700.

———. 2012. *Conflicting Commitments: The Politics of Enforcing Immigrant Worker Rights in San Jose and Houston*. Ithaca, NY: Cornell University Press.

———. 2014. "Means to an End: An Assessment of the Status-Blind Approach to Protecting Undocumented Worker Rights." *Sociological Perspectives* 57 (3): 301–20.

———. 2016. *Precarious Claims: The Promise and Failure of Workplace Protections in the United States*. Oakland: University of California Press.

Gleeson, Shannon, and Xóchitl Bada. 2019. "Institutionalizing a Binational Enforcement Strategy for Migrant Worker Rights." *International Journal of Comparative Labour Law and Industrial Relations* 35 (2): 255–77.

Global Preparedness Monitoring Board. 2019. *A World at Risk: Annual Report on Global Preparedness for Health Emergencies*. Geneva: World Health Organization.

Glynn, Sarah Jane. 2021. "Breadwinning Mothers Are Critical to Families' Economic Security." Center for American Progress, March 29. www.americanprogress.org/issues /women/news/2021/03/29/497658/breadwinning-mothers-critical-familys-economic -security/.

Godoy Padilla, Eva. 2018. *Consejeros titulares (2003-2005)*. https://silo.tips/download /consejeros-titulares-olga-beatriz-aguilar-houston-texas-5.

Golash-Boza, Tanya. 2015. *Deported: Policing Immigrants, Disposable Labor and Global Capitalism*. New York: NYU Press.

Goldman, Tanya L. 2018. *The Labor Standards Enforcement Toolbox—Tool 4: Introduction to Strategic Enforcement*. New Brunswick, NJ: Rutgers Center for Innovation in Worker Organization (CIWO) and Center for Law and Social Policy (CLASP). https://smlr

.rutgers.edu/sites/default/files/Documents/Centers/CIWO/2018_introductiontostrate
gicenforcement.pdf.

Goldring, Luin. 2002. "The Mexican State and Transmigrant Organizations: Negotiating the
Boundaries of Membership and Participation." *Latin American Research Review* 37 (3):
55–99.

———. 2003. "Re-thinking Remittances: Social and Political Dimensions of Individual
and Collective Remittances." CERLAC Working Paper Series, Centre for Research on
Latin America and the Caribbean, York. www.semanticscholar.org/paper/Re-thinking
-Remittances%3A-Social-and-Political-of-Goldring/dc8c9b9b784fdf113ad3cf534
23632fa3d40228a.

———. 2017. "Resituating Temporariness as the Precarity and Conditionality of Non-Citi-
zenship." In *Liberating Temporariness? Migration, Work, and Citizenship in an Age of Insecurity*, edited by Leah F. Vosko, Valerie Preston, and Robert Latham, 218–54. Montreal:
McGill-Queen's University Press.

Gómez Arnaud, Remedios. 1990. *México y la protección de sus nacionales en Estados Unidos.*
Mexico City: Universidad Nacional Autónoma de México.

González, Gilbert G. 1999. *Mexican Consuls and Labor Organizing: Imperial Politics in the
American Southwest.* Austin: University of Texas Press.

González Araiza, Luis Enrique. 2018. *De la legalidad a la trata laboral: El caso de trabajadores temporales mexicanos en Estados Unidos.* Guadalajara, Jalisco: Universidad de
Guadalajara, Centro Universitario de Ciencias Sociales y Humanidades.

Gonzalez-Barrera, Ana, and Jens Manuel Krogstad. 2019. "What We Know about Illegal
Immigration from Mexico." Pew Research Center, Fact Tank, June 28. www.pewresearch
.org/fact-tank/2019/06/28/what-we-know-about-illegal-immigration-from-mexico/.

González Gutiérrez, Carlos. 2019. "A Conversation with Mexico consul general Carlos
González Gutiérrez." *San Diego Union-Tribune*, August 1, sec. Opinion. www.sandi
egouniontribune.com/opinion/story/2019-08-01/mexico-consul-general-carlos-gonza
lez-gutierrez-interview.

Goodman, Adam. 2020. *Deportation Machine: America's Long History of Expelling Immigrants.* Politics and Society in Modern America. Princeton, NJ: Princeton University Press.

Gordon, Jennifer. 2005. *Suburban Sweatshops: The Fight for Immigrant Rights.* Cambridge,
MA: Harvard University Press.

———. 2006. "Transnational Labor Citizenship." *Southern California Law Review* 503 (80):
503–88.

Graubart, Jonathan. 2010. *Legalizing Transnational Activism: The Struggle to Gain Social
Change from NAFTA's Citizen Petitions.* University Park: Penn State University Press.

Greer, Ian, Zinovijus Ciupijus, and Nathan Lillie. 2013. "The European Migrant Workers
Union and the Barriers to Transnational Industrial Citizenship." *European Journal of
Industrial Relations* 19 (1): 5–20.

Griffith, Kati L. 2011. "Discovering 'Immployment' Law: The Constitutionality of Subfederal
Immigration Regulation at Work." *Yale Law and Policy Review* 29:389–451.

———. 2012. "Undocumented Workers: Crossing the Borders of Immigration and Workplace Law." *Cornell Journal of Law and Public Policy* 21: 611–97.

Griffith, Kati L., and Shannon Gleeson. 2019. "Immigration Enforcement and the Employment Sphere: Unpacking Trump-Era 'Immployment' Law." *Southwestern Law Review* 48
(3): 475–501.

Guevarra, Anna Romina. 2009. *Marketing Dreams, Manufacturing Heroes: The Transnational Labor Brokering of Filipino Workers*. New Brunswick, NJ: Rutgers University Press.

Guild, Alexis, and Iris Figueroa. 2018. "The Neighbors Who Feed Us: Farmworkers and Government Policy—Challenges and Solutions." *Harvard Law and Policy Review* 13 (1): 157–86.

Gunningham, Neil A., Dorothy Thornton, and Robert A. Kagan. 2005. "Motivating Management: Corporate Compliance in Environmental Protection." *Law and Policy* 27 (2): 289–316.

Gutelius, Beth, and Nik Theodore. 2019. *The Future of Warehouse Work: Technological Change in the U.S. Logistics Industry*. With Working Partnerships USA. Berkeley: UC Berkeley Labor Center. https://laborcenter.berkeley.edu/future-of-warehouse-work/.

Guthrie, Doug. 2010. "Corporate Philanthropy in the United States: What Causes Do Corporations Back?" In *Politics + Partnerships: The Role of Voluntary Associations in America's Political Past and Present*, edited by Elisabeth S. Clemens and Doug Guthrie, 183–204. Chicago: University of Chicago Press.

Hall, Matthew, and Emily Greenman. 2014. "The Occupational Cost of Being Illegal in the United States: Legal Status, Job Hazards, and Compensating Differentials." *International Migration Review* 49 (2): 406–42.

Hamlin, Rebecca. 2021. *Crossing: How We Label and React to People on the Move*. Redwood City, CA: Stanford University Press.

Hathaway, Dale A. 2000. *Allies across the Border: Mexico's "Authentic Labor Front" and Global Solidarity*. Cambridge, MA: South End Press.

Héctor, J.G.F. 2017. "Letter from Mexico: Zapatistas Support U.S. Migrants." News and Letters Committees, May 2. https://newsandletters.org/letter-mexico-zapatistas-support-u-s-migrants/.

Helton, Arthur. 1991. "The New Convention from the Perspective of a Country of Employment: The US Case." *International Migration Review* 25 (4): 851–57.

Hennessy, Rosemary, and Martha Ojeda. 2005. "Coalition for Justice in the Maquiladoras." In *The Oxford Encyclopedia of Latinos and Latinas in the United States*, edited by Suzanne Oboler and Deena J. González. New York: Oxford University Press.

Hertel, Shareen. 2006. *Unexpected Power: Conflict and Change among Transnational Activists*. Ithaca, NY: Cornell University Press.

Hillman, Anne. 2015. "Anchorage's Mexican Consulate Will Close in November." Alaska Public Media, September 25. www.alaskapublic.org/2015/09/24/anchorages-mexican-consulate-will-close-in-november/.

Hirsch, Barry T., and David A. Macpherson. 2020. "Union Membership and Coverage Database." Database, accessed for 2020. www.unionstats.com/.

Hirschman, Albert O. 1970. *Exit, Voice, and Loyalty. Responses to Decline in Firms, Organizations, and States*. Cambridge, MA: Harvard University Press.

Hoogesteger, Jaime, and Federico Rivara. 2021. "The End of the Rural/Urban Divide? Migration, Proletarianization, Differentiation and Peasant Production in an *Ejido*, Central Mexico." *Journal of Agrarian Change* 21 (2): 332–55.

Houston Interfaith Worker Justice Center. 2012. *Houston, We Have a Wage Theft Problem: The Impact of Wage Theft on Our City and the Local Solutions Necessary to Stop It*. May. Houston, TX: Houston Interfaith Worker Justice Center. http://stopwagetheft.files.wordpress.com/2012/05/2012-houston-wage-theft-report.pdf.

Human Rights Watch. 2022. "'Remain in Mexico': Overview and Resources." News release, February 7. www.hrw.org/news/2022/02/07/remain-mexico-overview-and-resources.

ILAB (Bureau of International Labor Affairs). 2005. *North American Agreement on Labor Cooperation: A Guide*. Washington, DC: US National Administrative Office, Bureau of International Labor Affairs, US Department of Labor. www.dol.gov/agencies/ilab/trade /agreements/naalcgd.

———. 2014a. "Consular Partnership News: News from the U.S. Department of Labor and Consular Partners." Issue 1. Bureau of International Labor Affairs, Department of Labor. Emailed newsletter, received August 22, 2014.

———. 2014b. "Consular Partnership News: News from the U.S. Department of Labor and Consular Partners." Issue 2. Bureau of International Labor Affairs, Department of Labor. Emailed newsletter, received August 22, 2014.

———. 2014c. "Consular Partnership News: News from the U.S. Department of Labor and Consular Partners." Issue 3. Bureau of International Labor Affairs, Department of Labor. Emailed newsletter, received September 24, 2014.

———. 2014d. "Consular Partnership News: News from the U.S. Department of Labor and Consular Partners." Issue 4. Bureau of International Labor Affairs, Department of Labor. Emailed newsletter, received November 20, 2014.

———. 2021. "U.S. Response to Mexico's Request for Migrant Worker Outreach." Bureau of International Labor Affairs, US. Department of Labor. www.dol.gov/agencies/ilab /trade/preference-programs/US-Mexico.

ILO (International Labour Organization). 2014. "World Congress on Safety and Health at Work: ILO Director-General: 'Work Claims More Victims Than War.'" News release, August 26. www.ilo.org/global/about-the-ilo/newsroom/news/WCMS_302517/lang—en /index.htm.

ILRWG (International Labor Recruitment Working Group). 2013. *The American Dream Up for Sale: A Blueprint for Ending International Labor Recruitment Abuse*. RESPECT. International Labor Recruitment Working Group, report, February. https://respect.inter national/the-american-dream-up-for-sale-a-blueprint-for-ending-international-labor -recruitment-abuse-2/.

———. 2018. *Shortchanged: The Big Business behind the Low Wage J-1 Au Pair Program*. International Labor Recruitment Working Group, report. https://cdmigrante.org /wp-content/uploads/2018/08/Shortchanged.pdf.

———. 2019. *Shining a Light on Summer Work: A First Look at the Employers Using the J-1 Summer Work Travel Visa*. International Labor Recruitment Working Group, report. https://cdmigrante.org/wp-content/uploads/2019/07/Report-Shining-A-Light-on -Summer-Work.pdf.

IMUMI (Instituto para las Mujeres en la Migración). n.d. "IMUMI—Instituto para las Mujeres en la Migración, AC." Accessed 2021. https://imumi.org/transparencia/.

INEGI. 2018. "Tasa de Sindicalización. Derechos Sindicales. Recepción del Derecho." https://datos.gob.mx/busca/dataset/tasa-de-sindicalizacion-derechos-sindicales-recepcion -del-derecho.

———. 2020. "Resultados de La Encuesta Telefónica de Ocupación y Empleo: Cifras oportunas de Abril de 2020." Press release, June 1, no. 264/20. www.inegi.org.mx/contenidos /saladeprensa/boletines/2020/enoe_ie/ETOE.pdf.

———. 2021. "Resultados de La Encuesta Nacional de Ocupación y Empleo Nueva Edición."

www.inegi.org.mx/contenidos/saladeprensa/boletines/2021/enoe_ie/enoe_ie2021_05.pdf.

IOM (International Organization for Migration) Research. n.d. "COVID-19 Analytical Snapshot #4: Consular and Other Assistance for Stranded Migrants and Travelers." Migration Data Portal. Accessed 2021.www.migrationdataportal.org/resource/covid-19-analytical-snapshot-4-consular-and-other-assistance-stranded-migrants-and.

IPUMS (Integrated Public Use Microdata Series) USA. n.d.-a. Database, accessed for 2021. "IPUMS USA: Descr: BPL." https://usa.ipums.org/usa-action/variables/BPL#description_section.

———. n.d.-b. "IPUMS USA: Descr: CITIZEN." Database, accessed for 2021. https://usa.ipums.org/usa-action/variables/CITIZEN#universe_section.

———. n.d.-c. "IPUMS USA: Descr: HISPAN." Database, accessed for 2021. https://usa.ipums.org/usa-action/variables/HISPAN#description_section.

Iskander, Natasha. 2010. *Creative State: Forty Years of Migration and Development Policy in Morocco and Mexico.* Ithaca, NY: Cornell University Press.

Israel, Emma, and Jeanne Batalova. 2020. "Mexican Immigrants in the United States." *Migration Information Source*, November 5. Migration Policy Institute. www.migrationpolicy.org/article/mexican-immigrants-united-states-2019.

Kader, Adam. 2020. "Worker Centers and the Future of the Labor Movement." *LERA for Libraries* 24 (4). http://lerachapters.org/OJS/ojs-2.4.4-1/index.php/PFL/article/view/3386.

Kaiser Family Foundation. 2021. "Health Coverage of Immigrants." Fact sheet, July. www.kff.org/racial-equity-and-health-policy/fact-sheet/health-coverage-of-immigrants/.

Kanno-Youngs, Zolan. 2020. "'He Turned Purple': U.S. Overlooks Ill Asylum Seekers." *New York Times*, February 20. www.nytimes.com/2020/02/22/us/politics/trump-asylum-remain-in-mexico.html.

Kay, Tamara. 2011. *NAFTA and the Politics of Labor Transnationalism.* Cambridge: Cambridge University Press.

Kay, Tamara, and R.L. Evans. 2018. *Trade Battles: Activism and the Politicization of International Trade Policy.* New York: Oxford University Press.

Keck, Margaret E., and Kathryn Sikkink. 1998. *Activists beyond Borders: Advocacy Networks in International Politics.* Ithaca, NY: Cornell University Press.

Kip, Markus. 2017. *The Ends of Union Solidarity: Undocumented Labor and German Trade Unions.* Labor and Globalization, vol. 10. Augsburg: Rainer Hampp.

La Botz, Dan. 1992. *Mask of Democracy: Labor Suppression in Mexico Today.* Boston: South End Press.

Lafleur, Jean-Michel. 2012. *Transnational Politics and the State: The External Voting Rights of Diasporas.* New York: Routledge.

Lafleur, Jean-Michel, and Daniela Vintila, eds. 2020. *Migration and Social Protection in Europe and Beyond.* Vol. 2, *Comparing Consular Services and Diaspora Policies.* IMISCOE Research Series. Cham: Springer International.

Landon, Simone. 2008. "Immigration Raid Breaks Up Organizing Drive at Iowa Meatpacking Plant: Employers Are Using Immigration Enforcement by ICE to Hurt Workers, Both Natives and Migrants." *Labor Notes*, August 25. https://labornotes.org/2008/08/immigration-raid-breaks-organizing-drive-iowa-meatpacking-plant.

Lara, Jovana. 2017. "Mexican Consulate General in LA Says Country Won't Pay for Border Wall." ABC7 Los Angeles, January 25. https://abc7.com/1721099/.

Layton, Michael D. 2011. "Focos rojos en las cifras sobre sociedad civil organizada." *Este País*, January 11.

Layton, Michael D., and Alejandro Moreno. 2010. *Filantropía y sociedad civil en México*. Mexico City: Miguel Ángel Porrúa-Instituto Tecnológico Autónomo de México.

Leal, David L., Byung-Jae Lee, and James A. McCann. 2012. "Transnational Absentee Voting in the 2006 Mexican Presidential Election: The Roots of Participation." In "Special Symposium: Economic Crisis and Elections: The European Periphery," edited by Michael S. Lewis-Beck, Marina Costa Lobo, and Paolo Bellucci, special issue, *Electoral Studies* 31 (3): 540–49.

Leco Tomás, Casimiro. 2009. *Migración indígena a Estados Unidos: Purhépechas en Burnsville, Norte Carolina*. Morelia: Universidad Michoacana de San Nicolás de Hidalgo.

Lederer, Shannon. 2019. "Working Families Must Be Together, and Free." *AFL-CIO Blog*, July 12. https://aflcio.org/2019/7/12/working-families-must-be-together-and-free.

Lee, Min Sook. 2003. *El contrato*. Documentary film. National Film Board of Canada. www.nfb.ca/film/el_contrato/.

Lee, Tamara L., and Maite Tapia. 2021. "Confronting Race and Other Social Identity Erasures: The Case for Critical Industrial Relations Theory." *ILR Review* 74 (3): 637–62.

Legal Aid at Work. 2012. "New Employment Law Clinic for Low-Wage Workers to Open in Fresno." Press release, April 16. https://legalaidatwork.org/releases/new-employment-law-clinic-for-low-wage-workers-to-open-in-fresno/.

Legal Services Corporation. 2020. "Can LSC Grantees Represent Undocumented Immigrants?" Report. www.lsc.gov/our-impact/publications/other-publications-and-reports/can-lsc-grantees-represent-undocumented.

Lesniewski, Jacob, and Shannon Gleeson. 2022. "Mobilizing Worker Rights: The Challenges of Claims-Driven Processes for Re-regulating the Labor Market." *Labor Studies Journal*, January 11. https://doi.org/10.1177/0160449X211072565.

Lichtenstein, Nelson. 2002. *State of the Union: A Century of American Labor*. Princeton, NJ: Princeton University Press.

Linares, Juan C. 2006. "Hired Hands Needed: The Impact of Globalization and Human Rights Law on Migrant Workers in the United States." *Denver Journal of International Law and Policy* 34:321–52.

Li Ng, Juan José. 2022. "México. Remesas crecieron 27.1% en 2021, llegan a nuevo máximo histórico." BBVA Research, report, February. www.bbvaresearch.com/publicaciones/mexico-remesas-crecieron-271-en-2021-llegan-a-nuevo-maximo-historico/.

Lipsky, Michael. 1980. *Street Level Bureaucracy: Dilemmas of the Individual in Public Services*. New York: Russell Sage Foundation.

Litrownik, Michael, and Daniel Kessler. 2020. "Legal Protections for Workers with Different Immigration Statuses." Outten & Golden, *Employment Law Blog*, January 9. https://outtengolden.com/blog/2020/01/legal-protections-for-workers-with-different-immigration-statuses/.

Loh, Katherine, and Scott Richardson. 2004. "Foreign-Born Workers: Trends in Fatal Occupational Injuries, 1996–2001." *Monthly Labor Review*, June, 42–53.

Lomnitz, Claudio. 2001. *Deep Mexico, Silent Mexico: An Anthropology of Nationalism*. Public Worlds, vol. 9. Minneapolis: University of Minnesota Press.

López, Gustavo, and Jens Manuel Krogstad. 2017. "Key Facts about Unauthorized Immigrants Enrolled in DACA." Pew Research Center, Fact Tank, September 25, 2017. www.pewresearch.org/fact-tank/2017/09/25/key-facts-about-unauthorized-immigrants-enrolled-in-daca/.

López Obrador, Andrés Manuel. 2020. "Versión estenográfica de la conferencia de prensa matutina del presidente Andrés Manuel López Obrador." News release, December 17. https://lopezobrador.org.mx/2020/12/17/version-estenografica-de-la-conferencia-de-prensa-matutina-del-presidente-andres-manuel-lopez-obrador-440/.

Luce, Stephanie. 2004. *Fighting for a Living Wage.* Ithaca, NY: Cornell University Press.

Macías-Rojas, Patrisia. 2016. *From Deportation to Prison: The Politics of Immigration Enforcement in Post-Civil Rights America.* Latina/o Sociology Series. New York: New York University Press.

———. 2018. "Immigration and the War on Crime: Law and Order Politics and the Illegal Immigration Reform and Immigrant Responsibility Act of 1996." *Journal on Migration and Human Security* 6 (1): 1–25.

Mangaliman, Jessie. 2007. "Labor Groups Seek Relief from What They Call Sweatshop Work." *East Bay Times*, April 21. www.eastbaytimes.com/2007/04/21/labor-groups-seek-relief-from-what-they-call-sweatshop-work/.

Margheritis, Ana. 2016. *Migration Governance across Regions: State-Diaspora Relations in the Latin America-Southern Europe Corridor.* New York: Routledge.

Marsden, Sarah, Eric Tucker, and Leah F. Vosko. 2021. "Flawed by Design? A Case Study of Federal Enforcement of Migrant Workers' Labour Rights in Canada." *Canadian Labour and Employment Law Journal (CLELJ)* 23 (1): 71–102.

Martin, Philip L. 2003. *Promise Unfulfilled: Unions, Immigration, and the Farm Workers.* Ithaca, NY: Cornell University Press.

———. 2017. *Merchants of Labor: Recruiters and International Labor Migration.* Oxford: Oxford University Press.

Martín, Rubén. 2017. "La lacra del 'charrismo sindical.'" *El Informador*, May 3. www.informador.mx/Ideas/La-lacra-del-charrismo-sindical-20170503-0190.html.

Martínez, Fernando. 2021. "Pandemic Delays for Consular Services Upend Immigrants' Lives." *CityLimits*, March 23. https://citylimits.org/2021/03/23/pandemic-delays-for-consular-services-upend-immigrants-lives/. Originally published in *El Diario*, March 20, 2021.

Martínez, Oscar Enrique. 2013. *The Beast: Riding the Rails and Dodging Narcos on the Migrant Trail.* London: Verso Books.

Martínez-Schuldt, Ricardo D. 2020. "Mexican Consular Protection Services across the United States: How Local Social, Economic, and Political Conditions Structure the Sociolegal Support of Emigrants." *International Migration Review* 54 (4): 1016–44.

Martínez-Schuldt, Ricardo D., Jacqueline Maria Hagan, and Deborah M. Weissman. 2021. "The Role of the Mexican Consulate Network in Assisting Migrant Labor Claims across the U.S.-Mexico Migratory System." *Labor Studies Journal* 46 (4): 345–68.

Marwell, Nicole P. 2010. "Privatizing the Welfare State: Non-profit Community Based Organizations as Political Actors." In *Politics + Partnerships: The Role of Voluntary Associations in America's Political Past and Present*, edited by Elisabeth S. Clemens and Doug Guthrie, 209–30. Chicago: University of Chicago Press.

Masferrer, Claudia, and Luicy Pedroza. 2021. *La intersección de la política exterior con la política migratoria en el México de hoy.* Mexico City: El Colegio de México. https://migdep.colmex.mx/publicaciones/politica-exterior-migratoria-reporte.pdf.

Massa, Felipe G., and Siobhan O'Mahony. 2021. "Order from Chaos: How Networked Activists Self-Organize by Creating a Participation Architecture." *Administrative Science Quarterly* 66 (4): 1037–83.

Massey, Douglas S., Jorge Durand, and Nolan J. Malone. 2002. *Beyond Smoke and Mirrors: Mexican Immigration in an Era of Economic Integration.* New York: Russell Sage Foundation.

McCartin, Joseph A. 2009. "Building the Interfaith Worker Justice Movement: Kim Bobo's Story." *Labor: Studies in Working-Class History* 6 (1): 87–105.

McCubbins, Mathew D., and Thomas Schwartz. 1984. "Congressional Oversight Overlooked: Police Patrols versus Fire Alarms." *American Journal of Political Science* 28 (1): 165–79.

McNeill, Jim. 2007. "Work in Progress: The State of the Unions Two Years after the AFL-CIO Split." *Dissent* 54 (2): 71–76.

Medina Vidal, Xavier. 2018. "Latino Immigrant Home-Country Media Use and Participation in U.S. Politics." *Hispanic Journal of Behavioral Sciences* 40 (1): 37–56.

Mendoza, Alexandra. 2021. "Constitutional Amendment Guarantees Nationality to Descendants of Mexicans Born Abroad." *San Diego Union-Tribune*, July 15. www.sandie gouniontribune.com/latest/story/2021-07-15/constitutional-amendment-guarantees -nationality-to-offspring-of-mexicans-born-abroad.

Mendoza González, Miguel Ángel, and Marcos Valdivia López. 2016. "Remesas, crecimiento y convergencia regional en México: Aproximación con un modelo panel-espacial." *Estudios Económicos de El Colegio de México* 31 (June): 125–67.

Middlebrook, Kevin J. 1995. *The Paradox of Revolution: Labor, the State, and Authoritarianism in Mexico.* Baltimore: Johns Hopkins University Press.

Milkman, Ruth. 2020. *Immigrant Labor and the New Precariat.* Cambridge: Polity Press.

Milkman, Ruth, Joshua Bloom, and Victor Narro. 2010. *Working for Justice: The L.A. Model of Organizing and Advocacy.* Ithaca, NY: ILR/Cornell Press.

Milkman, Ruth, and Stephanie Luce. 2020. *The State of the Unions 2020.* New York: Joseph S. Murphy Institute for Worker Education and Labor Studies, Center for Urban Research, and NYC Labor Market Information Service, CUNY. https://slu.cuny.edu/wp-content /uploads/2020/09/CUNY-SLU-Union_Density-Report-2020pdf.pdf.

Miroff, Nick. 2020. "'Kids in Cages': It's True That Obama Built the Cages at the Border. But Trump's 'Zero Tolerance' Immigration Policy Had No Precedent." *Washington Post*, October 23. www.washingtonpost.com/immigration/kids-in-cages-debate-trump-obama /2020/10/23/8ff96f3c-1532-11eb-82af-864652063d61_story.html.

Moloney, Anastasia. 2017. "Mexico's Indigenous Migrant Workers Risk Enslavement on Farms: Rights Commission." Reuters, December 4, sec. americas-test-2. www.reuters.com /article/us-mexico-slavery-idUSKBN1DY2IV.

Moody, Kim. 1995. "NAFTA and the Corporate Redesign of North America." *Latin American Perspectives* 22 (1): 95–116.

Murray, Stephanie. 2018. "Mexican Foreign Minister Calls U.S. Family Separations 'Cruel and Inhumane.'" *Politico*, June 19. https://politi.co/2yq4Z7v.

National Employment Law Project. 2016. "Immigration and Labor Enforcement in the Workplace: The Revised Labor Agency-DHS Memorandum of Understanding." Fact sheet, May 23. www.nelp.org/publication/immigration-and-labor-enforcement-in-the-workplace/.

National Low Income Housing Coalition. n.d. "Frequently Asked Questions: Eligibility for Assistance Based on Immigration Status." Accessed 2021. https://nlihc.org/sites/default /files/FAQs_Eligibility-for-Assistance-Based-on-Immigration-Status.pdf.

Navarro, Carlos. 2017. "Debate over Capital Punishment Resurfaces after Texas Executes Mexican National." Latin America Data Base, Article ID: 80461, November.

NEO Philanthropy. 2017. "Philanthropy Needs to Lean in on Anti-trafficking." August 3. https://neophilanthropy.org/philanthropy-needs-lean-anti-trafficking/.

Nevins, Joseph. 2002. *Operation Gatekeeper: The Rise of the "Illegal Alien" and the Making of the US-Mexico Boundary.* New York: Routledge.

———. 2007. "Dying for a Cup of Coffee? Migrant Deaths in the US-Mexico Border Region in a Neoliberal Age." *Geopolitics* 12 (2): 228–47.

Newland, Kathleen, Marie McAuliff, and Céline Bauloz. 2020. "Recent Developments in the Global Governance of Migration: An Update to World Migration Report 2018." In *World Migration Report 2020*, 291–312. Geneva: International Organization for Migration.

Nicholls, Walter J. 2019. *The Immigrant Rights Movement: The Battle over National Citizenship.* Stanford, CA: Stanford University Press.

NILC (National Immigration Law Center). 2015. "Frequently Asked Questions: The Obama Administration's DAPA and Expanded DACA Programs." Last updated March 2. www.nilc.org/issues/immigration-reform-and-executive-actions/dapa-and-expanded-daca-programs/.

Noe-Bustamante, Luis, and Antonio Flores. 2019. "Facts on Latinos in the U.S." Pew Research Center, fact sheet, September 16. www.pewresearch.org/hispanic/fact-sheet/latinos-in-the-u-s-fact-sheet/.

Nolan García, Kimberly A. 2011. "Transnational Advocates and Labor Rights Enforcement in the North American Free Trade Agreement." *Latin American Politics and Society* 53 (2): 29–60.

Noriega, Brianda Elena Peraza, and Arturo Santamaría Gómez. 2017. "Turistas o inmigrantes estadounidenses? Identidad y economías étnicas en Mazatlán, Sinaloa (México)." *Revista Latino-Americana de Turismología* 3 (2): 24–37.

Ocampo, Arantza, and César Reveles. 2021. "De empleados de SRE a inmigrantes: Más de 300 trabajadores serían despedidos." *Animal Político*, January 17. www.animalpolitico.com/2021/01/empleados-sre-a-inmigrantes-consulados-seran-despedidos/.

Okano-Heijmans, Maaike, and Caspar Price. 2019. "Providing Consular Services to Low-Skilled Migrant Workers: Partnerships That Care." *Global Affairs* 5 (4–5): 427–43.

Olvera, Alberto J. 2020. "De la elección plebiscitaria al populismo nostálgico: López Obrador y la 'Cuarta Transformación' en México." In *Populismo, democracia y resistencias en América Latina*, edited by Ysuke Murakami and Enrique Perzzotti, 1–22. Lima: Instituto de Estudios Peruanos.

Ornelas, Izaac, Wenson Fung, Susan Gabbard, and Daniel Carroll. 2021. *Findings from the National Agricultural Workers Survey (NAWS), 2017–2018: A Demographic and Employment Profile of United States Farmworkers.* JBS International, Research Report No. 14. https://wdr.doleta.gov/research/FullText_Documents/ETAOP2021-22%20NAWS%20Research%20Report%2014%20(2017-2018)_508%20Compliant.pdf.

OSHA (Occupational Safety and Health Administration). 2021. *Annual Report on the Alliance Program, October 1, 2019, to September 30, 2020.* www.osha.gov/alliances/alliance-successes.

———. n.d. "OSHA Alliance Program." Accessed 2021. www.osha.gov/alliances.

Osorio, Liliana, Hilda Dávila, and Xóchitl Castañeda. 2019. "Binational Health Week: A Social Mobilization Program to Improve Latino Migrant Health." In *Accountability across*

Borders: Migrant Rights in North America., edited by Xóchitl Bada and Shannon Gleeson, 260–80. Austin: University of Texas Press.

Oswalt, Michael M., and César F. Rosado Marzán. 2018. "Organizing the State: The 'New Labor Law' Seen from the Bottom-Up." *Berkeley Journal of Employment and Labor Law* 39 (2): 415–80.

Pallares, Amalia, and Nilda Flores-González. 2010. *¡Marcha! Latino Chicago and the Immigrant Rights Movement.* Urbana: University of Illinois Press.

———. 2011. "Regarding Family: New Actors in the Chicago Protests." In *Rallying for Immigrant Rights: The Fight for Inclusion in 21st Century America,* edited by Irene Bloemraad and Kim Voss, 161–79. Berkeley: University of California Press.

París-Pombo, Dolores. 2017. "The Infrastructure of Mexico's Migrant Civil Society. Presentation to the Panel Enforcing Rights across Borders: The Case of Mexican Migrants. June 21st." Paper presented at the Law and Society Association Annual Meeting, Mexico City.

París-Pombo, Dolores, and Amarela Varela-Huerta. 2022. "Caravans Adrift: Central American Migrants Stranded along the Northern Border of Mexico." In *The Routledge History of Modern Latin American Migration,* edited by Andreas E Feldmann, Jorge Durand, Stephanie Schütze, and Xóchitl Bada, chap. 31. New York: Routledge.

Parker, Christine. 2013. "Twenty Years of Responsive Regulation: An Appreciation and Appraisal." SSRN Scholarly Paper ID 2315368, Social Science Research Network. https://papers.ssrn.com/abstract=2315368.

Parks, Virginia. 2014. "Enclaves of Rights: Workplace Enforcement, Union Contracts, and the Uneven Regulatory Geography of Immigration Policy." *Annals of the Association of American Geographers* 104 (2): 329–37.

Partnership for Working Families. n.d. "About the Partnership for Working Families." Accessed April 13, 2012. www.forworkingfamilies.org/about/partners/wpusa-working-partnerships-usa.

Passel, Jeffrey S., and D'Vera Cohn. 2016. *Size of U.S. Unauthorized Immigrant Workforce Stable after the Great Recession.* Pew Research Center, report, November 3. www.pewresearch.org/hispanic/2016/11/03/size-of-u-s-unauthorized-immigrant-workforce-stable-after-the-great-recession/.

———. 2018. *Unauthorized Immigrant Workforce Is Smaller.* Pew Research Center, report, November 27. www.pewhispanic.org/2018/11/27/unauthorized-immigrant-workforce-is-smaller-but-with-more-women/.

———. 2019. "Mexicans Decline to Less Than Half the U.S. Unauthorized Immigrant Population for the First Time." Pew Research Center, Fact Tank, June 12. www.pewresearch.org/fact-tank/2019/06/12/us-unauthorized-immigrant-population-2017/.

Pedroza, Luicy, Pau Palop García, Bert Hoffmann, and Pau Palop. 2016. *Emigrant Policies in Latin America and the Caribbean.* Santiago de Chile: FLACSO-Chile Editions.

Peña, Evy. 2021. "Migrantes al Consejo Laboral." *Reforma*, June 29. www.reforma.com/migrantes-al-consejo-laboral-2021-06-29/0p207455.

Perez-Lopez, Jorge F. 1996. "Conflict and Cooperation in U.S.-Mexican Labor Relations: The North American Agreement on Labor Cooperation." *Journal of Borderlands Studies* 11 (1): 43–58.

Pham, Huyen, and Pham Hoang Van. 2014. "Measuring the Climate for Immigrants: A State-by-State Analysis." In *Strange Neighbors: The Role of States in Immigration Policy,* edited by Carissa Byrne Hessick and Gabriel J. Chin, 21–39. New York: New York University Press.

Piore, Michael J., and Andrew Schrank. 2018. *Root-Cause Regulation: Protecting Work and Workers in the Twenty-First Century.* Cambridge, MA: Harvard University Press.

Piper, Nicola. 2005. "Rights of Foreign Domestic Workers—Emergence of Transnational and Transregional Solidarity?" *Asian and Pacific Migration Journal* 14 (1–2): 97–119.

Piper, Nicola, and Jean Grugel. 2015. "Global Migration Governance, Social Movements, and the Difficulties of Promoting Migrant Rights." In *Migration, Precarity, and Global Governance: Challenges and Opportunities for Labour,* edited by Carl-Ulrik Schierup, Ronaldo Munck, Branka Likic-Brboric, and Anders Neergaard, 261–78. Oxford: Oxford University Press.

Pintor-Sandoval, Renato. 2021. "El programa 3X1 en México. Nuevos escenarios en la re-estructuración de la agenda pública migrante." *FORUM: Revista Departamento Ciencia Política* 19:211-41. https://doi.org/10.15446/frdcp.n19.78792.

Politico. 2016. "2016 Election Results: President Live Map by State, Real-Time Voting Updates." December 13. www.politico.com/mapdata-2016/2016-election/results/map/president.

Polletta, Francesca. 2012. *Freedom Is an Endless Meeting: Democracy in American Social Movements.* Chicago: University of Chicago Press.

Preibisch, Kerry L., and Evelyn Encalada Grez. 2010. "The Other Side of el Otro Lado: Mexican Migrant Women and Labor Flexibility in Canadian Agriculture." *Signs* 35 (2): 289–316.

ProDESC (Proyecto de Derechos Económicos, Sociales y Culturales). n.d. "The RADAR Program." Accessed 2021. https://prodesc.org.mx/en/the-radar-program/.

ProDESC (Proyecto de Derechos Económicos, Sociales y Culturales) and CDM (Centro de los Derechos del Migrante). 2010. *Manual for Binational Justice: A Regulatory Framework for the Defense of Migrant Workers in the United States and Mexico.* Mexico City: Proyecto de Derechos Económicos, Sociales y Culturales and Centro de los Derechos del Migrante.

Pycior, Julie Leininger. 2014. *Democratic Renewal and the Mutual Aid Legacy of US Mexicans.* College Station: Texas A&M University Press.

Ramírez García, Telésforo, and Manuel Ángel Castillo, eds. 2012. *México ante los recientes desafíos de la migración internacional.* Mexico City: Consejo Nacional de Población.

Ramos Pacheco, María, and Alfredo Corchado. 2021. "'Abrazos, no muros': Familias separadas por leyes migratorias se reúnen en la frontera, al menos por tres minutos." *Dallas News,* June 19. www.dallasnews.com/espanol/al-dia/inmigracion/2021/06/19/abrazos-no-muros-familias-separadas-por-leyes-migratorias-se-reunen-en-la-frontera-por-tres-minutos/.

Raphael, Ricardo. 2021. "El ejército mexicano está bajo sospecha en el caso Ayotzinapa." *Washington Post,* October 5, sec. Opinión. www.washingtonpost.com/es/post-opinion/2021/10/05/ayotzinapa-ejercito-investigacion-encinas-filtraciones/.

Redacción Animal Político. 2020. "Suman 959 mexicanos muertos por COVID-19 en Estados Unidos." *Animal Político,* May. www.animalpolitico.com/2020/05/mexicanos-muertos-contagiados-eu-covid-19/.

Rhode, Deborah L. 2004. *Access to Justice.* New York: Oxford University Press.

Roberts, Ken. 2014. *Changing Course in Latin America: Party Systems in the Neoliberal Era.* Cambridge: Cambridge University Press.

Rocha Romero, David, Ramón Medina Sánchez, and Pedro Paulo Orraca Romano. 2022. "Los salarios y riesgos laborales de los inmigrantes mexicanos en Estados Unidos." *Estudios Demográficos y Urbanos* 37 (1): 9–41.

Rodriguez, Robyn M. 2008. "(Dis)Unity and Diversity in Post-9/11 America." *Sociological Forum* 23 (2): 379–89.

———. 2010. *Migrants for Export: How the Philippine State Brokers Labor to the World.* Minneapolis: University of Minnesota Press.

Rojas Wiesner, Martha Luz. 2022. "More Than a Northward Migratory Corridor: Changes in Transit Migration and Migration Policy in Mexico." In *The Routledge History of Modern Latin American Migration,* edited by Andreas E. Feldmann, Jorge Durand, Stephanie Schütze, and Xóchitl Bada, chap. 25. New York: Routledge.

Rosenberg, Mica, and Kristina Cooke. 2019. "Allegations of Labor Abuses Dogged Mississippi Plant Years before Immigration Raids." Reuters, August 10. www.reuters.com /article/us-usa-immigration-koch-foods-idUSKCN1UZ1OV.

Ross Pineda, Raúl, and Juan Andrés Mora. 2003. *Instituto de los Mexicanos en el exterior (notas para una discusión).* Chicago: Ediciones MX Sin Fronteras.

Rubio, Blanca. 2004. "¡El Campo No Aguanta Más! A un año de distancia." *El Cotidiano* 19 (124): 33–40.

Rubio Campos, Jesús. 2017. "Proposal for a Model for Analyzing Strategies for Cross-border Trade Union Collaboration." *Estudios Fronterizos* 18 (37): 103–30.

Ruhs, Martin. 2013. *The Price of Rights: Regulating International Labor Migration.* Princeton, NJ: Princeton University Press.

Russo, Robert. 2011. "A Cooperative Conundrum? The NAALC and Mexican Migrant Workers in the United States." *Law and Business Review of the Americas* 17 (1): 27–38.

Santamaría Gómez, Arturo. 2001. *Mexicanos en Estados Unidos: La nación, la política y el voto sin fronteras.* Mexico City: Universidad Autónoma de Sinaloa/PRD.

Sassen, Saskia. 1998. *Globalization and Its Discontents: Essays on the New Mobility of People and Money.* New York: New Press.

———. 2014. *Expulsions: Brutality and Complexity in the Global Economy.* Cambridge, MA: Harvard University Press.

SCOTUS (Supreme Court of the United States). 2012. "In the Supreme Court of the United States State of Arizona and Janice K. Brewer, Governor of the State of Arizona, in Her Official Capacity, Petitioners, v. United States of America, Respondent. On Writ of Certiorari to the United States Court of Appeals for the Ninth Circuit, Amicus Curiae Brief of the United Mexican States in Support of Respondent." No. 11-182. Supreme Court of the United States.

Secretaría de Gobernación. 2014. "Programa Especial de Migración 2014–2018." Diario Oficial de la Federación, April 30. www.dof.gob.mx/nota_detalle.php?codigo=5343074&fecha=30/04/2014.

SEIU (Service Employees International Union). n.d. "Raising America with Good Jobs— Justice for Janitors." Accessed 2021. www.seiu.org/justice-for-janitors.

Serna de la Garza, José Ma. 2019. "Global Governance and the Protection of Migrant Workers' Rights in North America: In Search for a Theoretical Framework." In *Accountability across Borders: Migrant Rights in North America,* edited by Xóchitl Bada and Shannon Gleeson, 55–82. Austin: University of Texas Press.

Shafer, Margie. 2011. "Labor Activists Protest at Mexican Consulate in San Francisco." KCBS, February 4. https://sanfrancisco.cbslocal.com/2011/02/04/labor-activists-protest-at-mexican-consulate-in-san-francisco/.

SHCP (Secretaría de Hacienda y Crédito Público). 2021. "Analíticos del presupuesto de egresos de la Federación 2021." www.pef.hacienda.gob.mx/en/PEF2021/analiticos_presupuestarios.

Sherman, Rachel. 1999. "From State Introversion to State Extension in Mexico: Modes of Emigrant Incorporation, 1900–1997." *Theory and Society* 28 (6): 835–78.

Simsek-Caglar, Ayse, and Nina Glick Schiller. 2018. *Migrants and City-Making: Dispossession, Displacement, and Urban Regeneration.* Durham, NC: Duke University Press.

Singer, Audrey. 2015. "Metropolitan Immigrant Gateways Revisited, 2014." Brookings, December 1. www.brookings.edu/research/metropolitan-immigrant-gateways-revisited-2014/.

Smith, Ben. 2021. "How Mexico Helped the *Times* Get Its Journalists Out of Afghanistan." *New York Times,* August 25, sec. Business. www.nytimes.com/2021/08/25/business/media/new-york-times-mexico-afghanistan.html.

Smith, Michael Peter, and Luis Eduardo Guarnizo. 2009. "Global Mobility, Shifting Borders and Urban Citizenship." *Tijdschrift voor Economische en Sociale Geografie* 100 (5): 610–22.

Smith, Robert Courtney, Don J. Waisanen, and Guillermo Yrizar Barbosa. 2019. *Immigration and Strategic Public Health Communication: Lessons from the Transnational Seguro Popular Project.* New York: Routledge.

Spener, David. 2011. "Coyotaje as a Cultural Practice Applied to Migration." In *Clandestine Crossings: Migrants and Coyotes on the Texas-Mexico Border,* 87–120. Ithaca, NY: Cornell University Press.

SPLC (Southern Poverty Law Center). 2006. "New Project Aims for Harassment-Free Workplace." March 14. www.splcenter.org/news/2006/03/14/new-project-aims-harassment-free-workplace.

———. 2013. "Close to Slavery: Guestworker Programs in the United States." February 19. www.splcenter.org/20130218/close-slavery-guestworker-programs-united-states.

SRE (Secretaría de Relaciones Exteriores). 2008. "55a. Jornada Informativa del IME: Líderes Sindicales." Agenda for event held by the Instituto de los Mexicanos en el Exterior, May, Mexico City. Attachment to email in author's personal files.

———. 2011a. *Manual de organización de la Dirección General de Protección a Mexicanos en el Exterior.* Mexico City: Subsecretaría para América del Norte, Dirección General de Programación, Organización y Presupuesto. https://sre.gob.mx/images/stories/docnormateca/manadmin/2012/12modgpme.pdf.

———. 2011b. "Mexico reconoce la demanda contra la ley HB 56 en Alabama." July 8. https://embamex.sre.gob.mx/suecia/index.php/en/comunicados/15-comunicados2011/516-mexico-reconoce-la-demanda-contra-la-ley-hb-56-en-alabama.

———. 2011c. *Normas para la ejecución de los programas de protección a Mexicanos en el exterior.* Versión 2. Mexico City: SRE. https://sre.gob.mx/images/stories/docnormateca/dgpme/normas/norm.pdf.

———. 2013. *Guía de procedimientos de protección consular.* Mexico City: SRE. www.gob
.mx/cms/uploads/attachment/file/472919/Gu_a_de_Procedimientos_de_Protecci_n
_Consular.pdf.

———. 2015. *3er informe de labores (2014–2015).* Mexico City: SRE. https://sre.gob.mx/sre-docs
/infolab/3erinfolab_a.pdf.

———. 2016. "Notificación consular." January 20. www.gob.mx/sre/documentos/notificacion
-consular?state=published.

———. 2018. *Cuenta pública 2018—Análisis del ejercicio del presupuesto de egresos relaciones exteriores.* Mexico City: SRE. www.cuentapublica.hacienda.gob.mx/work/models
/CP/2018/tomo/III/Print.R05.03.AEPE.pdf.

———. 2019. "Derechos laborales de mexicanos en el extranjero: Semana de Derechos Laborales en Estados Unidos." https://transparencia.sre.gob.mx/transparencia-categorias
/category/2047-estadisticas-dgpme-primer-semestre-2019?download=101066:9
-semana-de-derechos-laborales-en-estados-unidos.

———. 2020. "Casos de protección y/o asistencia consular atendidos en la RDCM en
Estados Unidos—Ámbito laboral." https://transparencia.sre.gob.mx/transparencia-
categorias/category/2042-estadisticas-dgpme-actualizadas-al-31-de-diciembre-2019?
download=100531:17-casos-de-proteccion-consular-del-ambito-laboral-atendidos
-por-la-rdcmx.

———. 2021a. "Acción diferida." April. https://consulmex.sre.gob.mx/seattle/index.php/es
/proteccion/daca.

———. 2021b. "Mexico's Consulates in North America to Open for a Third Saturday on
September 11." Press release #403, September 5. www.gob.mx/sre/prensa/mexico-s-con
sulates-in-north-america-to-open-for-a-third-saturday-on-september-11?idiom=en.

———. 2021c. "Precios." Last updated January. https://consulmex.sre.gob.mx/denver/index
.php/documenta/tarifas.

———. 2021d. "Programa de Asistencia Jurídica a Personas Mexicanas a Través de
Asesorías Legales Externas en los Estados Unidos de América (PALE)—Listado Prov-
eedores Ejercicio PALE, 2018–2021." https://transparencia.sre.gob.mx/transparencia
-categorias/category/2043-estadisticas-dgpme-actualizadas-al-30-de-junio-de
-2020?download=100556:14-listado-de-proveedores-del-programa-pale.

———. 2021e. "Tercer informe de labores 2020–2021 de la SRE." August 27. www.gob.mx
/sre/documentos/tercer-informe-de-labores-2020-2021-de-la-sre.

———. n.d.-a. "Centro de Información y Asistencia a Mexicanos." www.gob.mx/ciam. Accessed 2021. www.gob.mx/ciam.

———. n.d.-b. "Consulados de México." Accessed 2021. https://directorio.sre.gob.mx/index
.php/consulados-de-mexico-en-el-exterior.

———. n.d.-c. *Criterios técnicos para la distribución de los recursos asignados al programa de-
nominado fortalecimiento para la atención a Mexicanos en Estados Unidos.* Accessed 2021.
https://transparenciaproteccion.sre.gob.mx/pdfs/presupuestos/400_1502474505.pdf.

———. n.d.-d. "Delegaciones." Accessed 2021. https://directorio.sre.gob.mx/index.php
/delegaciones.

SRE (Secretaría de Relaciones Exteriores) and Consulado General de México en Chicago.
2020. *Guía de derechos laborales.* https://consulmex.sre.gob.mx/chicago/images/stories
/2020/PDF/guia-derechos-laborales-310820.pdf.

Stone, Syd. 2019. "This Hidden Mural on South Ashland Avenue Tells the Story of One of the Most Radical Labor Unions." *Chicago Sun-Times*, August 30. https://chicago.suntimes.com/murals-mosaics/2019/8/30/20826871/united-electrical-workers-union-mural-john-pitman-weber-jose-guerrero-ashland-avenue-near-west-side#:~:text=Anyone%20driving%20on%20Ashland,celebrates%20international%20unity%20among%20workers.

Storrs, K.L. 2006. *Mexico's Importance and Multiple Relationships with the United States.* Library of Congress, Congressional Research Service, report. www.everycrsreport.com/reports/RL33244.html.

STPS (Secretaría de Trabajo y Previsión Social-Servicio Nacional de Empleo). 2019. *Lineamientos generales del Programa de Trabajadores Agrícolas Temporales México-Canadá (PTAT).* March 3. Mexico City: STPS. www.gob.mx/cms/uploads/attachment/file/450096/DML_1.2.2_Lineamientos_PTAT_19_03_29.pdf.

———. 2022. "En 2022, 26 mil jornaleros agrícolas viajarán con trabajo temporal a Canadá." News release, January 25. www.gob.mx/stps/prensa/222604.

Straulino-Rodriguez, Pietro, and Ana Paula Delsol Espada. 2019. "Mexico's Labor Law Amendments in Effect." *National Law Review* 9 (124). www.natlawreview.com/article/amendment-mexican-labor-law-finally-effective.

Suárez, Ximena, Andrés Díaz, José Knippen, and Maureen Meyer. 2017. *El acceso a la justicia para personas migrantes en México: Un derecho que existe sólo en el papel.* Washington, DC: Washington Office for Latin America (WOLA). www.wola.org/wp-content/uploads/2017/07/Accesoalajusticia_Versionweb_Julio20172.pdf.

teleSUR. 2017. "Costureras del 85, una historia de lucha tras sismo en México." September 20. www.telesurtv.net/news/Costureras-del-85-una-historia-de-lucha-tras-el-terremoto-en-Mexico-20170920-0064.html.

———. 2021. "México dará refugio a 13 mil migrantes haitianos." September 29. www.telesurtv.net/news/mexico-haiti-asilo-migrantes--20210929-0007.html.

Theodore, Nik. 2020. "Regulating Informality: Worker Centers and Collective Action in Day-Labor Markets." *Growth and Change* 51 (1): 144–60.

Thomas, Suja A. 2020. "The Wild, Wild West for Low Wage Workers with Wage and Hour Claims Courts Law." *Jotwell: The Journal of Things We Like (Lots)*, April 9: 1–2.

Thomason, Sarah, and Annette Bernhardt. 2018. "The Union Effect in California #2: Gains for Women, Workers of Color, and Immigrants." UC Berkeley Labor Center, report, June 7. https://laborcenter.berkeley.edu/union-effect-in-california-2/.

Thomsen, Jacqueline. 2018. "Montana State Employee Goes Viral for Quitting over Work on ICE Subpoena." *The Hill*, February 9. http://thehill.com/blogs/blog-briefing-room/news/373152-montana-state-employee-goes-viral-for-quitting-over-working-on.

Torres-Mazuera, Gabriela. 2013. "Geopolitical Transformation in Rural Mexico: Toward New Social and Territorial Boundaries in an Indigenous Municipality of Central Mexico." *Journal of Peasant Studies* 40 (2): 397–422.

Turner, Lowell, and Dan B. Cornfield. 2007. *Labor in the New Urban Battlegrounds: Local Solidarity in a Global Economy.* Ithaca, NY: ILR Press/Cornell University Press.

UFCW (United Food and Commercial Workers International Union). n.d. "UFCW: Packing and Processing Union." Accessed 2021. www.ufcw.org/who-we-represent/packing-and-processing/.

UFCW (United Food and Commercial Workers International Union) Canadá and Alianza de Trabajadores Agrícolas. 2020. *La situación de los trabajadores agrícolas migrantes en Canadá, informe especial: Tres décadas de lucha en defensa de los trabajadores más vulnerables de Canadá.* Report, January 25. www.oaxaca.gob.mx/ioam/wp-content/up loads/sites/25/2021/01/UFCW-Canada-Migrant-Workers-Report_SP_2020_email.pdf.

UNHCR (United Nations High Commissioner for Refugees). 2014. "Declaración y plan de acción de Brasil: Un marco de cooperación y solidaridad regional para fortalecer la protección internacional de las personas refugiadas, desplazadas y apátridas en América Latina y el Caribe." December 3. www.acnur.org/prot/instr/5b5100c04/declaracion-y -plan-de-accion-de-brasil.html.

———. 2021. "¿Qué es la apatridia?" www.unhcr.org/ibelong/es/que-es-la-apatridia/.

United Nations. 1967. Vienna Convention on Consular Relations (VCCR) of 1963. https:// legal.un.org/ilc/texts/instruments/english/conventions/9_2_1963.pdf.

UNITE-HERE! 2006. "Hotel Workers Rising Campaign Gathering Heat." UNITE HERE!, January 26. https://unitehere.org/unite-here-hotel-workers-rising-campaign-gathering-heat/.

US Census Bureau. 2019. "American Community Survey 2014–2018 5-Year Estimates Now Available." Press release, December 19. www.census.gov/newsroom/press-releases/2019 /acs-5-year.html.

US Centers for Medicare and Medicaid Services. n.d. "Health Coverage for Immigrants." Accessed 2021. www.healthcare.gov/immigrants/coverage/.

US Department of State. 2018. "Consular Notification and Access." Revised September. https://travel.state.gov/content/dam/travel/CNAtrainingresources/CNA%20Manual %205th%20Edition_September%202018.pdf.

———. 2021. *2021 Trafficking in Persons Report.* Office to Monitor and Combat Trafficking in Persons June. www.state.gov/reports/2021-trafficking-in-persons-report/.

US DOL (Department of Labor). 2004. "U.S. Labor Secretary Elaine L. Chao and Mexican Foreign Secretary Luis Ernesto Derbez Sign Joint Declaration to Improve Working Conditions for Mexican Workers." Press release, July 21. www.dol.gov/opa/media/press /osha/archive/OSHA20041371.htm#.

———. 2011. "Revised Memorandum of Understanding between the Departments of Homeland Security and Labor Concerning Enforcement Activities at Worksites." www.dol.gov /asp/media/reports/DHS-DOL-MOU.pdf.

USTR (Office of the United States Trade Representative). 2020. "Chapter 23. Labor. United States Canada Mexico Agreement USMCA." https://ustr.gov/sites/default/files/files /agreements/FTA/USMCA/Text/23-Labor.pdf.

Valdés, Dionicio Nodín. 2000. *Barrios Norteños: St. Paul and Midwesterner Communities in the Twentieth Century.* Austin: University of Texas Press.

Varsanyi, Monica W. 2010. *Taking Local Control: Immigration Policy Activism in U.S. Cities and States.* Stanford, CA: Stanford University Press.

Varsanyi, Monica W., Paul G. Lewis, Doris Marie Provine, and Scott Decker. 2012. "A Multilayered Jurisdictional Patchwork: Immigration Federalism in the United States." *Law and Policy* 34 (2): 138–58.

Vega, Griselda. 2000. "Maquiladora's Lost Women: The Killing Fields of Mexico—Are NAFTA and NAALC Providing the Needed Protection?" *Journal of Gender, Race and Justice* 4 (1): 137–58.

Verel, Patrick. 2017. "Mexican Ambassador: DACA Reversal Is a Loss for U.S." Fordham Newsroom, October 9. https://news.fordham.edu/politics-and-society/mexican-am bassador-declares-daca-loss-u-s/.

von Bülow, Marisa. 2010. *Building Transnational Networks: Civil Society and the Politics of Trade in the Americas.* New York: Cambridge University Press.

Vosko, Leah F. 2016. "Blacklisting as a Modality of Deportability: Mexico's Response to Circular Migrant Agricultural Workers' Pursuit of Collective Bargaining Rights in British Columbia, Canada." *Journal of Ethnic and Migration Studies* 42 (8): 1371–87.

———. 2018. "Legal but Deportable: Institutionalized Deportability and the Limits of Collective Bargaining among Participants in Canada's Seasonal Agricultural Workers Program." *ILR Review* 71 (4): 882–907.

———. 2019. *Disrupting Deportability: Transnational Workers Organize.* Ithaca, NY: ILR Press.

———. 2020. "7 Strengthening Participatory Approaches to Enforcement." In *Closing the Enforcement Gap: Improving Employment Standards Protections for People in Precarious Jobs,* 177–98. Toronto: University of Toronto Press.

Voss, Kim, and Irene Bloemraad. 2011. *Rallying for Immigrant Rights.* Berkeley: University of California Press.

Wage and Hour Division. 2021. "WHD Community Outreach Staff Contact Information (CORPS)." US Department of Labor. Last updated April. www.dol.gov/whd/corpsFlyer .pdf.

Wagner, Ines. 2018. *Workers without Borders: Posted Work and Precarity in the EU.* Ithaca, NY: ILR Press.

Weil, David. 2014. *The Fissured Workplace: Why Work Became So Bad for So Many and What Can Be Done to Improve It.* Cambridge, MA: Harvard University Press.

———. 2016. "Strategic Enforcement in the Fissured Workplace." In *Who Is an Employee and Who Is the Employer? Proceedings of the New York University 68th Annual Conference on Labor,* edited by Kati L. Griffith and Samuel Estreicher. New York: LexisNexis.

Weise, Julie M. 2015. *Corazón de Dixie: Mexicanos in the US South since 1910.* Chapel Hill: University of North Carolina Press.

Whyte, William Foote, and Kathleen King Whyte. 1991. *Making Mondragón: The Growth and Dynamics of the Worker Cooperative Complex.* Ithaca, NY: Cornell University Press.

Williams, Heather. 2002. "Lessons from the Labor Front: The Coalition for Justice in the Maquiladoras." In *Cross-border Dialogues: U.S.-Mexico Social Movement Networking,* edited by David Brooks and Jonathan Fox, 87–112. La Jolla: Center for U.S. Mexican Studies, University of California, San Diego.

WOLA (Washington Office on Latin America). 2020. "A Decade after San Fernando Massacre, Migrants Still Face Violence, Impunity for Abuses in Mexico." August 20. www.wola .org/2020/08/justice-massacre-san-fernando-mexico-migrants/.

Wong, Tom K. 2012. "287 (g) and the Politics of Interior Immigration Control in the United States: Explaining Local Cooperation with Federal Immigration Authorities." *Journal of Ethnic and Migration Studies* 38 (5): 737–56.

———. 2017. *The Politics of Immigration: Partisanship, Demographic Change, and American National Identity.* Oxford: Oxford University Press.

Yankelevich, Pablo. 2019. *Los otros: Raza, normas y corrupción en la gestión de la extranjería en México, 1900–1950*. Mexico City: El Colegio de México.

Zapata, Gisela P., and Victoria Prieto Rosas. 2020. "Structural and Contingent Inequalities: The Impact of COVID-19 on Migrant and Refugee Populations in South America." *Bulletin of Latin American Research* 39 (S1): 16–22.

Zepeda, Juan. 2020. "Proposición con punto de acuerdo por el que la Comisión Permanente del Congreso de La Unión exhorta a la Secretaría de Relaciones Exteriores a que, a través de su red consular, garantice el pago de los gastos funerarios y la repatriación de restos de los mexicanos que han fallecido en el extranjero a causa de COVID-19, a cargo del Senador Juan Zepeda." Senado de la República, Consulta de Información, May 27. https://infosen.senado.gob.mx/sgsp/gaceta/64/2/2020-05-27-1/assets/documentos/PA_MC_Sen_Jaun_Zepeda_gastos_funerarios_personas_fallecidas.pdf.

ZonaDocs—Periodismo en Resistencia. 2021. "Personas migrantes mayores de 18 años en Jalisco podrán vacunarse contra COVID-19." ZonaDocs, August 5. www.zonadocs.mx/2021/08/05/personas-migrantes-mayores-de-18-anos-en-jalisco-podran-vacunarse-contra-covid-19/.